PROFESSIONAL PORTFOLIOS FOR TEACHERS:

A Guide for Learners, Experts, and Scholars

M.A. Roth

PROFESSIONAL PORTFOLIOS FOR TEACHERS:

A Guide for Learners, Experts, and Scholars

Bonita L. Wilcox
Lawrence A. Tomei

Duquesne University, School of Education

Christopher-Gordon Publishers, Inc.
Norwood, Massachusetts

Credits

Every effort has been made to contact copyright holders for permission to reproduce borrowed material where necessary. We apologize for any oversights and would be happy to rectify them in future printings.

Apple and the Apple Logo are trademarks of Apple Computer, Inc., registered in the United States and other countries and used with permission. The use of company trademarks and icons will be restricted to the "Professional Portfolios for Teachers" book.

Portions Copyright Netscape Communications Corporation, 1998, All Rights Reserved. Netscape, Netscape Navigator and the Netscape N Logo are registered trademarks of Netscape in the United States and other countries, used with permission.

Copyright © 1999 Lotus Development Corporation. Used with permission of Lotus Development Corporation. Lotus and 1-2-3 are registered trademarks of Lotus Development Corporation.

The use of IBM company trademarks and icons are used with permission and are restricted to the "Professional Portfolios for Teachers" book.

Copyright ©1999 by Christopher-Gordon Publishers, Inc.

All rights reserved. Except for review purposes, no part of this material protected by this copyright notice may be reproduced or utilized in any form or by any means, electronic or mechanical, including photocopying, recording, or any information and retrieval system, without the express written permission of the publisher or copyright owner.

Christopher-Gordon Publishers, Inc.
1502 Providence Highway, Suite #12
Norwood, MA 02062
(800) 934-8322

Printed in the United States of America

10 9 8 7 6 5 4 3 2 1   03 02 01 00 99

Library of Congress Catalogue Number: 98-74794
ISBN: 0-926842-92-7

We dedicate this book to our families—

Joan, Melissa, and Laura Tomei

and

Jim, Tamara, Benjamin, and Jascha Wilcox

Contents

Preface xi

How to Use This Book xiii

PART I   The Evolution of the Portfolio in Teacher Education 1

CHAPTER 1
Portfolios: Past to Present 3

    Influence of National Organizations 3
    Influence of Higher Education 3
    Influence of Classroom Teachers 4
    Influence of Teacher Educators 4
    Professional Portfolios in Teacher Education 5
    Conclusion 5
    References 7

PART II   The Emergence of a Professional Portfolio Model 9

CHAPTER 2
Smart Portfolios for Teachers 11

    Background 11
    The Five Foundations of the Smart Portfolio 11
    Artifacts of the Smart Portfolio 13
    Organizing Artifacts of the Smart Portfolio 14
    Building a Smart Portfolio 14
    Conclusion 14
    References 15

CHAPTER 3
Intelligent Portfolios for Teachers 17

    Background 17
    The Intelligent Portfolio Platform 17
    Foundations of the Intelligent Portfolio 17
    The Artifacts of the Intelligent Portfolio 19
    Conclusion 24
    Transition 24

CHAPTER 4
Portfolio Exercise for Learners, Experts, and Scholars 25

    Background 25
    The Portfolio Exercise 25

How to Access the CD-ROM Exercises 26
Frequently Asked Questions 27
Conclusion 28

PART III   Portfolios for the Teacher as Learner 29

CHAPTER 5
The Smart Portfolio for the Teacher as Learner 31

Introduction 31
Where Do I Begin? 31
How Do I Organize My Portfolio? 32
What Do I Collect? 35
Who Will Assess My Portfolio? 37
The Portfolio Poster 37
Conclusion 39
Foley Tips 40
References 40

CHAPTER 6
The Intelligent Portfolio for the Teacher as Learner 41

Introduction 41
Step One: Creating Portfolio Folders 41
Step Two: Populating Portfolio Folders 42
Step Three: Organizing Folders and Collection Points 52
Conclusion 56
Foley Tips 56

CHAPTER 7
Portfolios in Transition: The Teacher as Learner Perspective 59

The Results of James's Efforts 60
The Results of Jason's Efforts 62
Summative Results of the Study 65
Concluding Remarks 66

PART IV   Portfolios for the Teacher as Expert 67

CHAPTER 8
The Smart Portfolio for the Teacher as Expert 69

Introduction 69
Where Do I Begin? 69
How Do I Organize the Portfolio? 71
What Do I Collect? 73
Who Will Assess My Work? 77

The Portfolio Poster 77
Conclusion 78
Foley Tips 80

CHAPTER 9
The Intelligent Portfolio for the Teacher as Expert 81

Introduction 81
Step One: Creating Portfolio Folders 81
Step Two: Populating Portfolio Folders 82
Step Three: Organizing Folders and Collection Points 91
Conclusion 97
Foley Tips 97

CHAPTER 10
Portfolios in Transition: The Teacher as Expert Perspective 99

Introduction 99
A Teacher-Expert 100
Jennifer's Smart Portfolio 100
Jennifer's Intelligent Portfolio 104
Results of the Study 108
Conclusion 109

PART V Portfolios for the Teacher as Scholar 111

CHAPTER 11
The Smart Portfolio for the Teacher as Scholar 113

Introduction 113
Where Do I Begin? 113
How Do I Organize the Portfolio? 115
What Do I Collect? 117
Who Will Assess My Work? 119
The Portfolio Poster 120
Conclusion 121
Foley Tips 121

CHAPTER 12
The Intelligent Portfolio for the Teacher as Scholar 123

Introduction 123
Step One: Creating Portfolio Folders 123
Step Two: Populating Portfolio Folders 125
Step Three: Organizing Folder and Collection Points 138
Conclusion 142
Foley Tips 142

CHAPTER 13
Portfolios in Transition: The Teacher as Scholar Perspective 143

    Introduction 143
    Introducing the Portfolio 143
    The Questions 144
    And Now, Some Answers… 144
    Conclusion 147

PART VI   Assessing Teacher Portfolios 149

CHAPTER 14
Assessing the Professional Portfolio 151

    Introduction 151
    The Portfolio Assessment Tool 152
    A Look At the Portfolio Assessment Tool In Action 161
    The Portfolio Exhibition 182
    Conclusion 184
    References 184

Postscript 185

Appendix 187

Index 259

About the Authors 267

PREFACE

In the beginning we intended to write a book about electronic portfolios. An article on the "Smart Portfolio" concept had already been published, and by integrating the latest technology, we believed an "Intelligent" (electronic) portfolio would be an exciting innovation.

To our surprise, technology became the means rather than the end, as the professional development portfolio surfaced as a transitional tool, connecting the teaching-learning endeavors of the Teacher as Learner, Teacher as Expert, and Teacher as Scholar. We also realized that monitoring and managing one's own professional development is not only challenging, but also has the potential to change the culture of schools and make them a place for teachers to be lifelong learners.

Having worked with teachers in various stages of their careers, we had the advantage of seeing the "big picture." We had introduced portfolios to undergraduates, to master's level initial certification students, to classroom teachers taking refresher courses, and to doctoral level students in instructional leadership. The relationship between learning and assessment through portfolios dramatically changed as undergraduate teachers in training moved to classrooms and classroom teachers moved into doctoral level courses of study. Constructing a portfolio from the bottom up made sense. If one had a knowledge base in place, building and continuing a portfolio on that foundation would be easy. The difficulty began when students came with diverse backgrounds and levels of knowledge, with different goals and philosophies, and with individual ways of knowing and habits of mind.

So, we actually began writing this book with Part III, Teacher as Learner, and this is a good place to begin reading if one already has knowledge and experience in portfolio assessment. Chapter 5 is a step-by-step guide useful in constructing a Smart Portfolio. Chapter 6 guides the reader in constructing an Intelligent (electronic) Portfolio. Chapter 7 contains a narrative of our early attempts to work through the portfolio process for Teachers as Learners.

Part IV has three parallel chapters for Teachers as Experts. Chapter 8 guides the construction of a Smart Portfolio, and Chapter 9 guides the construction of the Intelligent (electronic) Portfolio. Chapter 10 reviews early attempts to work through the portfolio process with Teachers as Experts.

Part V continues with three parallel chapters for Teachers as Scholars—Chapter 11 for constructing a Smart Portfolio, Chapter 12 for constructing an Intelligent Portfolio, and Chapter 13 for reviewing our work with Teachers as Scholars.

After working through these three parts, we could see a need to share our theoretical framework and explain how our portfolio model had evolved. After a short overview on portfolios in education in Chapter 1, Chapter 2 offers an introduction to our professional portfolio model, "Smart Portfolios for Teachers." Chapter 3, "Intelligent Portfolios for Teachers," describes the electronic version of the Smart Portfolio.

Chapter 4 is an exercise on CD-ROM intended to assist readers in deciding exactly how this book could help them and where they should focus their attention. Most readers will begin with the introductory chapters and choose Part III, IV, or V, depending on whether they are a teacher in training (learner), a seasoned teacher (expert), or a teacher leader (scholar).

Finally, one of the most important features of this book appears in Part VI, Assessing Teacher Portfolios. Chapter 14 explains our Professional Portfolio Assessment Tool offering examples for Teachers as Learners, Experts, and Scholars. To conclude a comprehensive assessment process, we suggest and explain the Portfolio Exhibition in this chapter..

In the end, we wanted a portfolio process well-suited to all teachers as they transitioned through a career, whether the emphasis was on gathering information to build a knowledge base, honing skills to gain expertise, or doing research and writing to make a contribution to the discipline. Second, we wanted a portfolio process that balanced assessment and learning through emphasis on self-reflection and metacognitive approaches to teaching and learning. Thus, by encouraging deeper understanding of assessment and its relationship to learning, we ensured better understanding of the balance between assessment and learning for students. And finally, we wanted a portfolio process that was reliable and valid, promising a more authentic assessment of teachers.

We think *Professional Portfolios for Teachers* will spark a change in attitudes toward the process of assessment as teachers begin to record their own histories of teaching and learning.

HOW TO USE THIS BOOK

Part I

The Evolution of the Portfolio in Teacher Education

Chapter 1—Portfolios: Past to Present

Part I offers an overview of the portfolio in education as it has evolved from a writing folder to a professional development tool for teachers.

Part II introduces a Professional Development Portfolio Model. Beginning in Chapter 2 with a "Smart Portfolio," following with an "Intelligent Portfolio" in Chapter 3, and ending in Chapter 4 with an exercise for readers, our professional development portfolio concept is described.

Part II

The Emergence of a Professional Development Portfolio Model

Chapter 2—Smart Portfolios for Teachers

Chapter 3—Intelligent Portfolios for Teachers

Chapter 4—Portfolio Exercise for Learners, Experts, and Scholars

Part III

Portfolios for the Teacher as Learner

Chapter 5—Constructing the Smart Portfolio

Chapter 6—Constructing the Intelligent Portfolio

Chapter 7—A Teacher as Learner's Perspective

Part III is written specifically for the **Teacher as Learner** and contains Chapters 5, 6, and 7. Chapter 5 provides detailed information about the design, construction, and use of the Smart Portfolio. Chapter 6 describes the Intelligent Portfolio and suggests a series of hardware and software components that support the Teacher as Learner. Chapter 7 relates the results of a prototype study conducted with pre-service teachers to determine the benefits of the Smart and Intelligent Portfolios for the Teacher as Learner.

Part IV
Portfolios for the Teacher as Expert

Chapter 8—Constructing the Smart Portfolio

Chapter 9—Constructing the Intelligent Portfolio

Chapter 10—A Teacher as Expert's Perspective

Part IV addresses the needs of the **Teacher as Expert**. Chapter 8 presents the construction of the Smart Portfolio, and Chapter 9 presents the construction of the Intelligent Portfolio. Chapter 10 relates a second prototype study of a teacher-practitioner who used the portfolio for personal and professional development.

Part V is for the **Teacher as Scholar**. Noticeable changes in both formats characterize the final version of the portfolio. For the Teacher as Scholar, Chapters 11 and 12 provide the structure of the Smart and Intelligent Portfolios. Chapter 13 presents the results of using these portfolios in a doctoral program.

Part V
Portfolios for the Teacher as Scholar

Chapter 11—Constructing the Smart Portfolio

Chapter 12—Constructing the Intelligent Portfolio

Chapter 13—A Teacher as Scholar's Perspective

Part VI
Assessing Teacher Portfolios

Chapter 14—Assessing the Professional Portfolio

Part VI is focused on an assessment tool for evaluating a teacher's professional portfolio. This tool can be used for teacher portfolios with or without the capstone experience—the Portfolio Exhibition.

PART I
The Evolution of the Portfolio in Teacher Education

Chapter 1

Portfolios:
Past to Present

Chapter 1 contains a short overview of the evolution of the professional portfolio in teacher education.

CHAPTER 1

Portfolios:
Past to Present

Ten years ago, little had been published on portfolios in education. Early studies in writing assessment at the university level indicated a need for better ways to assess student learning (Burnham, 1986; Camp, 1985; Elbow, 1987). Yet even at the elementary level, teachers were questioning the negative effects of assessment on beginning writers (Graves, 1983; Hansen, Newkirk, & Graves, 1985). In the secondary schools, teachers were exploring the notion of "writing to learn" (Atwell, 1987; Bechtel, 1985; Fulwiler, 1987) and the value of teaching writing as a process. Between 1985 and 1990, with the movement toward whole language and the tremendous influence of the National Writing Project on how we teach and learn, the use of portfolios as an assessment tool gained momentum.

By the early 1990s, portfolio assessment had become widely accepted as an authentic assessment alternative—especially in the primary grades. Portfolios could be found in classrooms throughout educational institutions. Teachers at all levels were experimenting with portfolios in many different situations—not just in writing, not just with students, and not just as an assessment tool. Portfolio publications throughout the nineties provided further evidence of this growing trend (Black, Daiker, Sommers, & Stygall, 1994; Glazer & Brown, 1993; Graves & Sunstein, 1992; Yancey & Weiser, 1997).

Influence of National Organizations

When the National Board for Professional Teaching Standards (NBPTS) began to examine "what teachers should know and be able to do," portfolios offered a methodology for gathering evidence (NBPTS, 1994). The existing literature on portfolio assessment for practicing teachers was finally getting the attention it deserved (Barton & Collins, 1993; Denus & St. Hilaire, 1992; Teacher Assessment Project, 1988; Wolf, 1991; Zubizarreta, 1994), and a variety of innovative approaches were initiated (Danielson, 1996; Wolf, Whinery, & Hagerty, 1995). By 1997, the National Council of Accreditation of Teacher Education (NCATE) assigned a special task force to create a performance assessment package for teacher preparation programs (Elliott, 1997). Many wondered how the individual performance of a teacher-candidate could relate to quality assessment of a university program. NCATE's New Professional Teacher Standards Development Project continues to investigate a portfolio model of performance assessment (NCATE, 1998).

Influence of Higher Education

While language and writing scholars were looking for better ways to assess their students, other researchers directed their efforts toward the issue of university promotion and tenure qualifications. They, too, were looking at portfolio assessment (Bird, 1990; Edgerton, Hitchings, & Quinlan, 1991; Seldin, 1993; Wolf, 1991). In 1995, a major study suggested that by evaluating a professor's performance using a portfolio, universities could push their faculty toward improved teaching and learning (1995 Report Eight ASHE-ERIC Higher Education Reports). In a 1997 publication depicting the results of this study, Murray wrote, "One of the greatest advantages of teaching portfolios is that they place control of one's professional life in one's own hands. In other words, they empower faculty to become professional educators and to define it in their own terms. Setting goals and measuring success in attaining them through use of a teaching portfolio enables one to take charge of his or her life" (Murray, 1997).

Influence of Classroom Teachers

By far, classroom teachers deserve the lion's share of credit for their role in the spread of portfolios for assessment. With little time to conduct empirical studies, classroom teachers continue to redefine the portfolio process with their students at all levels and across every subject matter area. They share "action research" in faculty rooms, at conventions, and in their journals. Teachers have changed the way we think about portfolio assessment, expanding the process as well as the product (Porter & Cleland, 1994). They have extended the possibilities for lifelong teaching and learning using the portfolio. Many teachers are convinced that the portfolio greatly improves their teaching techniques and personal learning skills. The influence of the classroom teacher on the "portfolio revolution" has been extensive. For this reason, it is important to look closely at the kinds of portfolios teachers use.

Influence of Teacher-Educators

Recent publications illustrate considerable interest in how teachers are using portfolios and what can be learned from their "best practices." Many of these publications were written by teacher educators conducting action research with classroom teachers and teachers in training. This combination of scholars and practitioners changed forever the concept of portfolios and their potential for gathering evidence, promoting new thinking, and assessing performance at all levels of educational pursuit.

Portfolios in Teacher Education (McLaughlin & Vogt, 1996) describes a portfolio process for both graduate and undergraduate students in a teacher education program with a focus on design, implementation, and evaluation. While the book provides some theoretical foundations, it is mostly concerned with practice, particularly the way two teachers successfully used portfolios with elementary and secondary teachers. The portfolio process described is goal-oriented and content-specific. The authors present the story of how teacher-educators and classroom teachers developed reflective habits and self-assessing attitudes in their students, clearly establishing the connection between assessment and learning with portfolios. In a more recent publication, McLaughlin & Vogt (1998) extended their portfolio concept to classroom teachers, focusing on reflection and interaction.

How to Develop a Professional Portfolio: A Manual for Teachers (Campbell, Cignetti, Melenyzer, Nettles, & Wyman, 1997) focuses its attention on the use of portfolios to assess the inexperienced pre-service teacher. In one of the first such examples of applied portfolio research, the authors introduce the use of portfolios to demonstrate the competence of pre-service teachers in accordance with national standards. In this case, the Interstate New Teacher Assessment and Support Consortium (INTASC) standards were examined. A concentration on artifacts was proposed as evidence of knowledge, skills, and dispositions. The portfolio was recommended for beginning teachers searching for their first teaching position. The text offers a comprehensive overview of teacher training experiences and serves as a helpful manual for assessing the tangible and intangible evidence addressing competencies as they compare to national standards.

Teacher Portfolios: Literacy Artifacts and Themes (Rogers & Danielson, 1996) emphasizes the idea of learning rather than the "assessment only" role of the portfolio. With a change in focus to artifacts as evidence of learning, the authors present a variety of models for pre-service and in-service teachers in their roles as a reader, writer, and collector. Portfolio requirements are specifically stated, and an assessment rubric is suggested. The book clearly shows how to create this type of portfolio and explains in detail how it is beneficial to both teachers and learners. The book's major contribution is its focus on deep understanding through reflective and critical thinking over an extended period of time.

Finally, the *Teacher's Portfolio: Fostering and Documenting Professional Development* (Glatthorn, 1996) is an informative and helpful text for supervisors and administrators who are inclined to "tell" and "prescribe" what experienced classroom teachers ought to know and be able to do. It has overtones of "I know best" while advocating a path for a teacher's personal and professional development. Assessment wins out over learning in this text, but it certainly merits consideration when it comes to issues of individual accountability for professional development. Glatthorn describes in detail the process of documenting teaching and learning, and as a result, the book stands out as one of the first successful efforts to acquaint readers with this aspect of portfolios. In Glatthorn's opinion, portfolios represent a "systematic collection of materials selected and assembled by a professional to document professional accomplishments" (p. 122).

Professional Portfolios in Teacher Education

Contributions to the knowledge base continue to strengthen the arguments for alternatives to testing and grading. The multidimensional assessment encouraged by the portfolio process provides a much more accurate and complete picture than a letter grade, percentage score, or check mark. The movement of teachers toward emphasizing the learning aspects of the portfolio confirms what many suspected from the beginning—assessment should not prevail as the single, all-encompassing reason for implementing portfolios.

With research on cognition came interest in reflective self-assessment as teacher-educators began to see the impact of journals on learning and performance. Of course, we never lost sight of accountability and what better way to showcase teaching and learning than with a portfolio.

Building a knowledge base, implementing classroom applications, and generating contributions through presentations and publications are facilitated by a portfolio designed to encourage lifelong learning and professional growth.

Conclusion

This introductory chapter provides an overview of the major influences on portfolios for professional development. University professors and scholars strengthened the notion of performance assessment through research on writing and through studies on faculty accountability. Classroom teachers focused on more authentic, alternative assessments of student learning. Teacher educators initiated the idea of reflective self-assessments for teachers as lifelong learners (see Figure 1-1). *Professional Portfolios for Teachers* extends the possibilities for portfolios in education by going beyond assessment, learning, and professional development to the use of the portfolio as a living history of a teaching-learning life.

Figure 1-1. The Portfolio Evolution

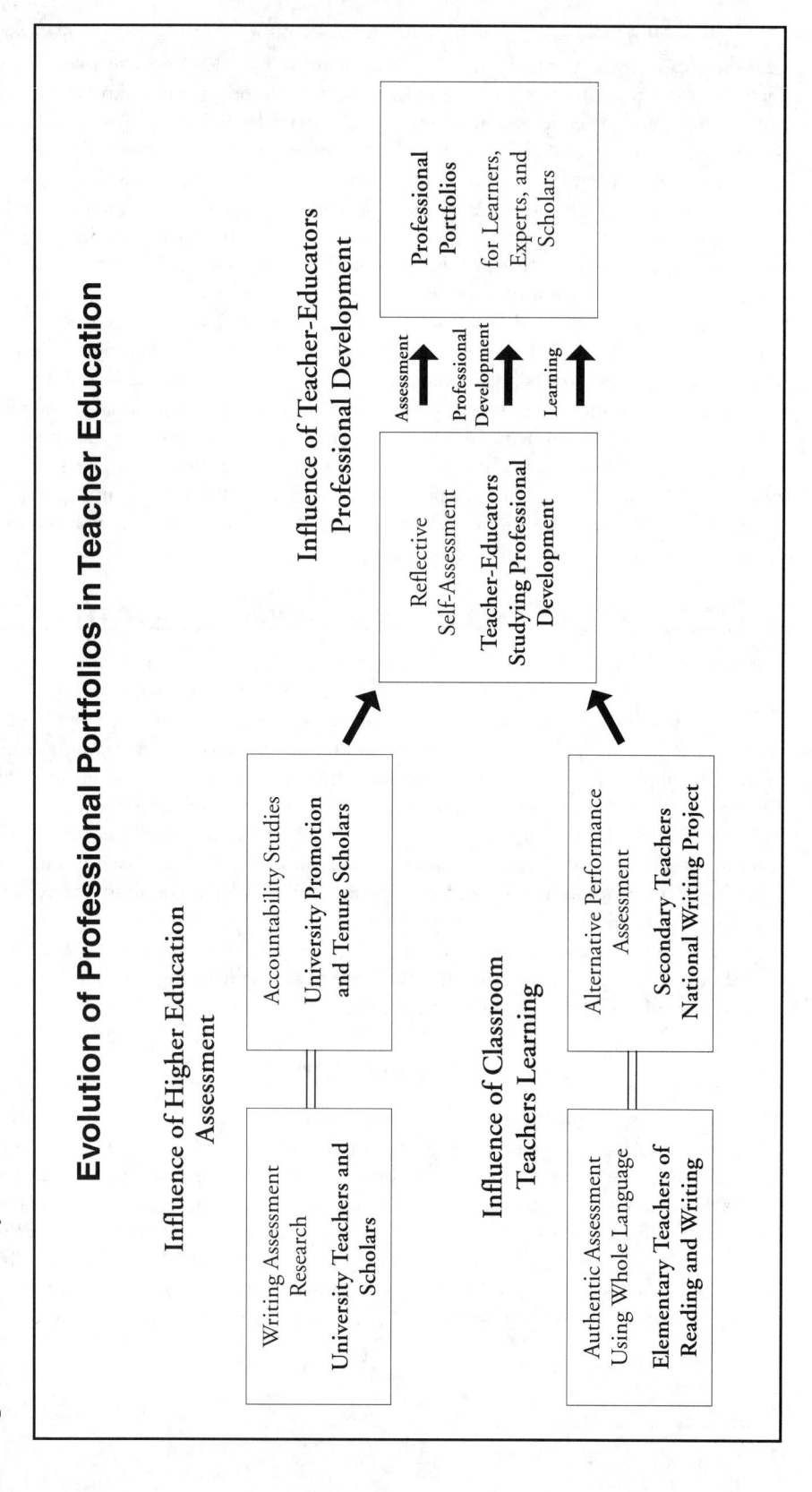

Evolution of Professional Portfolios in Teacher Education

Influence of Higher Education Assessment

- Writing Assessment Research
- University Teachers and Scholars

- Accountability Studies
- University Promotion and Tenure Scholars

Influence of Classroom Teachers Learning

- Authentic Assessment Using Whole Language
- Elementary Teachers of Reading and Writing

- Alternative Performance Assessment
- Secondary Teachers National Writing Project

Influence of Teacher-Educators Professional Development

- Reflective Self-Assessment
- Teacher-Educators Studying Professional Development

↑ Assessment
↑ Professional Development
↑ Learning

Professional Portfolios for Learners, Experts, and Scholars

References

Atwell, N. (1987). *In the middle: Writing, reading and learning with adolescents.* Upper Montclair, NJ: Boynton/Cook.

Barton, J. & Collins, A. (1993). Portfolios in teacher education. *Journal of Teacher Education, 44,* 200–210.

Bechtel, J. (1985). *Improving writing and learning: A handbook for teachers in every class.* Boston: Allyn and Bacon.

Bird, T. (1990). The schoolteacher's portfolio: An essay on possibilities. In J. Millman & L. Darling-Hammond (Eds.), *The new handbook of teacher evaluation* (pp. 241–256). Newbury Park, CA: Corwin Press.

Black, L., Daiker, D., Sommers, J., & Stygall, G. (1994). *New directions in portfolio assessment: Reflective practice, critical theory, and large-scale scoring.* Portsmouth, NH: Heinemann.

Burnham, C. (1986). Portfolio evaluation: Room to breathe and grow. In C. Bridges (Ed.), *Training the new teacher of college composition* (pp. 125–138). Urbana, IL: NCTE.

Camp, R. (1985). "The writing folder in postsecondary assessment." In P. Evans (Ed.), *Directions and misdirections in English evaluations.* Urbana, IL: NCTE.

Campbell, D., Cignetti, P., Melenyzer, B., Nettles, D., & Wyman, R. (1997). *How to develop a professional portfolio: A manual for teachers.* Needham, MA: Allyn & Bacon.

Danielson, C. (1996). *Enhancing professional practice: A framework for teaching.* Alexandria, VA: Association of Supervision and Curriculum Development.

Denus, J. & St. Hilaire, B. (1992). *Portfolios with real value: Teacher portfolios.* Available from Seven Oaks School Division, 830 Powers Street, Winnipeg, Manitoba, R2V 4E7, Canada.

Edgerton, R., Hitchings, P., & Quinlan, K. (1991). *The teaching portfolio: Capturing the scholarship in teaching.* Washington, DC: American Association of Higher Education.

Elbow, P. (1987). Using portfolios to judge writing proficiency at SUNY Stony Brook. In P. Connolly & T. Vilardi (Eds.), *New methods in college writing programs: Theory and practice* (pp. 95–105). New York: Modern Language Association.

Elliott, E. (1997). Performance: A new look at program quality evaluation in accreditation. *Action in Teacher Education, 19,* 38–45.

Fulwiler, T. (1988). *Teaching with writing.* Portsmouth, NH: Heinemann.

Glatthorn, A. (1996). *The teacher's portfolio: Fostering and documenting professional development.* Rockport, MA: Pro>Active Publications.

Glazer, S. & Brown, C. (1993). *Portfolios and beyond: Collaborative assessment in reading and writing.* Norwood, MA: Christopher-Gordon.

Graves, D. (1983). *Writing: Teachers and children at work.* Portsmouth, NH: Heinemann.

Graves, D. & Sunstein, B. (1992). *Portfolio portraits.* Portsmouth, NH: Heinemann.

Hansen, J., Newkirk, T., & Graves, D. (1985). *Breaking ground: Teachers relate reading and writing in the elementary school.* Portsmouth, NH: Heinemann.

McLaughlin, M. & Vogt, M. E. (1996). *Portfolios in teacher education.* Newark, DE: International Reading Association.

McLaughlin, M., Vogt, M. E., Anderson, J., DuMez, J., Peter, M., Hunter, A. (1998). *Professional portfolio models.* Norwood, MA: Christopher-Gordon.

Murray, J. (1997). *Successful faculty development and evaluation.* Washington, DC: The George Washington University Press.

National Board for Professional Teaching Standards (1994). "What Teachers Should Know and Be Able to Do." Detroit, MI: NBPTS.

National Council for Accreditation of Teacher Education (NCATE) (November, 1998). NCATE: Making a difference [on-line]. Available: http://www.ncate.org/.

Porter, C. & Cleland, J. (1994). *The portfolio as a learning strategy.* Portsmouth, NH: Boynton/Cook.

Rogers, S. & Danielson, K. (1996). *Teacher portfolios: Literary artifacts and themes.* Portsmouth, NH: Heinemann.

Seldin, P. (1993). *Successful use of teaching portfolios.* Bolton, MA: Anker Publishing Company.

Teacher Assessment Project (1988). The school teacher's portfolio: Practical issues in design, implementation and evaluation. Available from Stanford University, School of Education. CERAS 507 Stanford, CA 94395.

Wolf, K. (1991). *Teaching portfolios: Synthesis of research and annotated bibliography.* Available from Far West Laboratory for Educational Research and Development, 730 Harrison Street, San Francisco, CA 94107.

Wolf, K., Whinery, B., & Hagerty, P. (1995). Teaching portfolios and portfolio conversations for teacher educators and teachers. *Action in Teacher Education.* Spring, pp. 30–39.

Yancey, K. & Weiser, I. (1997). *Situating portfolios: Four perspectives.* Logan, UT: Utah State University.

Zubizaretta, J. (December, 1994). Teaching portfolios and the beginning teacher. *Phi Delta Kappan*, 323–326.

PART II

The Emergence of a Professional Portfolio Model

Chapter 2	Chapter 3	Chapter 4
Smart Portfolios for Teachers	*Intelligent Portfolios for Teachers*	*Portfolio Exercise for Learners, Experts, and Scholars*
Chapter 2 describes the essential parts of the Smart Portfolio and shows how to organize artifacts.	Chapter 3 describes the Collection Points of the Intelligent Portfolio and gives examples for the placement of electronic artifacts.	Chapter 4 introduces an online exercise to facilitate the selection of a portfolio format best-suited for you.

CHAPTER 2
Smart Portfolios for Teachers

Background

In *Outsmarting IQ, The Emerging Science of Learnable Intelligence*, Perkins writes, "Hardly anything in conventional educational practice promotes, in a direct and straight forward way, thoughtfulness and the use of strategies to guide thinking" (1995, p. 117). A portfolio that encourages teachers to practice thinking strategies will help them become less dependent on the school environment which is not always conducive to the professional development of its faculty. Schools, in fact, seem to expect their novice teachers to perform on par with their more experienced teachers. Further, some schools seem to believe that a college education prepares the teacher for a lifetime career in the classroom.

For the teacher-in-training, a four year pre-service program, more often than not, results in an impressive collection of content area reserves, classroom resources, and library materials. The requisite thinking skills needed to transform these materials from artifacts into applications is left to the devices of the individual.

For the classroom teacher, few schools provide periodicals containing recent research or books on methodology and professional knowledge. Rarely do they encourage teachers to attend professional conferences which might prove expensive or disruptive to the school's routine. Time to share thoughts and ideas and time to read, write, and reflect are not built into a teacher's schedule. It seems that teachers are expected to produce lifelong learners without becoming lifelong learners themselves.

Creating Smart Portfolios requires systematic self-assessment and allows teachers to experience the power of their own reflective thinking—thinking which can, and often does, result in new and better ways of teaching. Research shows that responding to reading in writing, sharing ideas, and reflecting on the various "ways of knowing" are processes that indeed enhance learning and improve thinking. Practicing reflective thinking strategies, as easy as "thinking about your thinking processes," enables a good thinker to become a better thinker.

In Chapter One, the portfolio earned its well-deserved reputation as an assessment tool; however, a more focused portfolio generates ideas and offers new ways of thinking marked by unlimited possibilities for teaching and learning. Educators who know about assessment as learning will never be satisfied with a portfolio only for assessment. Soon, you will see that the Smart Portfolio is a powerful tool for professional development. It will become your single repository for the collection, working, and showcasing of artifacts that will evidence your participation in, and mastery of, lifelong learning.

The Five Foundations of the Smart Portfolio

The Smart Portfolio begins with five essential Foundations: Reading, Writing, Thinking, Interacting, and Demonstrating. Let's take a closer look at each of the components.

Reading ↔ Writing ↔ Thinking ↔ Interacting ↔ Demonstrating

Reading

Reading is primary; it is the first of the Foundations. Reading is concerned with gathering new knowledge and developing new perspectives. Whether you read a compendium of basic skills and teaching strategies, individual texts on innovative approaches, or handouts from professional journals—new information and new ideas are critical to the successful implementation of the Smart Portfolio and the continued lifelong development of the teacher.

> **READING**
> Gathering evidence of new knowledge and information from texts, articles, and other resources.

Writing

Teachers first learn to recognize the benefits of writing by writing, but continuous practice in both formal and informal writing is necessary for growth. Reflective journal writing and "writing to learn" exercises help to transfer that personal knowledge into practical classroom applications. The formal paper is the capstone experience in which Reading, Thinking, Interacting, and Demonstrating come together. New thinking is presented, defended, and extended. Course assignments, classroom materials, and publications are the most common artifacts produced by teachers who use their writing to prove that prior knowledge has been assessed, new knowledge integrated, and current knowledge documented.

> **WRITING**
> Formal and informal writing demonstrating thoughtfulness and integrating of new knowledge.

Thinking

This Foundation of the Smart Portfolio is composed of a journal in which thinking becomes visible. The Thinking journal incorporates book notes along with reactions to readings and writings, recorded thoughts from class interactions, and personal reflections about new ideas and teaching strategies under investigation. Making thinking visible is necessary for developing an understanding of how we learn and how we can best teach others. Thoughtfulness in teaching and learning will be emphasized throughout all implementations of the Smart Portfolio.

> **THINKING**
> Making new meaning, connecting ideas, taking stock, constructing new perspectives.

Interacting

Artifacts from group activities and exercises illustrate the importance of group inquiry and problem-solving. Tasks focus on analyzing, discussing, and assessing. Interacting in small groups has impact when participants are engaged in strategic thinking. Also included in this Foundation are the explorations of common interest areas with peers and colleagues, so critical to a healthy Smart Portfolio.

> **INTERACTING**
> Sharing ideas, discussing and defending, actively constructing artifacts during group inquiry.

Demonstrating

Demonstrating implies the preparation of presentations and lessons. Teachers demonstrate their understanding of pedagogical theory through practical applications of specific content material. They are expected to design learning objectives deliver classroom instruction, and provide evidence of significant enhancements to traditional lessons by incorporating new teaching and learning strategies. The Smart Portfolio holds these artifacts as proof of experience and competence, illustrating personal and professional growth.

> **DEMONSTRATING**
> Presenting, critiquing, publishing, enhancing traditional lessons, applying thinking and learning.

Artifacts of the Smart Portfolio

Evidences of teaching and learning through reading, writing, thinking, interacting, and demonstrating are called *artifacts*. Artifacts are key to professional development. Through constant collecting, working, and showcasing our artifacts, the portfolio becomes an historical compendium of teaching and learning throughout a career. As a teacher's role changes from learner to expert to scholar, artifacts show evidence of the ways new knowledge is integrated, applied, and created.

We will discuss three types of artifacts: Collecting artifacts, Working Artifacts, and Showcase Artifacts. *Collecting Artifacts* accumulated from reading, observing, interpreting, listening, and investigating comprise the requisite knowledge base for Teachers as Learners. *Working Artifacts* evidence deeper thinking; they consist of practical applications used in the classroom to improve teaching and learning for the Teacher as Expert. *Showcase Artifacts* document competence, experience, and accomplishments for the Teacher-Scholar.

Collecting Artifacts

Many artifacts are simply collected. They represent resources that are important enough to be saved in the portfolio, where new information is stored. Evidence of Reading will most likely enter the Smart Portfolio as one of the categories of Collecting artifacts: Content Area Material, Classroom Resources, Library Resources, or World Wide Web (WWW) Sites. Remember, the Smart Portfolio is your tool for professional development. Artifacts move to other folders in the Smart Portfolio as they become resources for teaching or presentation. Where you place artifacts is your decision, based on personal preferences for organization and quick retrieval.

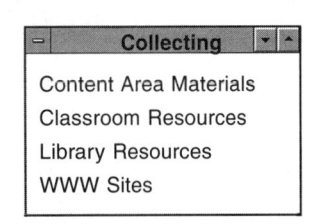

Collecting
Content Area Materials
Classroom Resources
Library Resources
WWW Sites

Working Artifacts

Some artifacts are the consequence of our own thinking—they are the products of collected artifacts applied to create new knowledge and skills. For example, many writing efforts become Learning Projects and Classroom Applications. Our interactions with peers and colleagues result in attempts at Making Connections through Reflection and Self-Assessment. And our best efforts at creating student handouts and study guides can become Working artifacts.

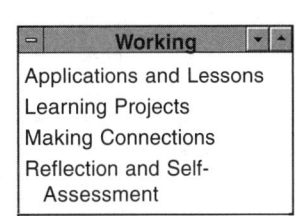

Working
Applications and Lessons
Learning Projects
Making Connections
Reflection and Self-Assessment

Showcase Artifacts

When the results of our thinking produce quality outcomes, Showcase artifacts are the result. Examples of Showcase artifacts include presentations, best papers, classroom-ready materials, and publications, as well as personal education-related documents such as teaching certificates and graduate transcripts. Showcase artifacts are often indicative of self-initiated contributions to the field as we share our new knowledge.

Showcase
Presentations & Best Papers
Professional Documents

Organizing Artifacts of the Smart Portfolio

Throughout a teaching career, collecting artifacts becomes both a challenge and commitment. The myriad artifacts gathered by the teacher is a direct product of the five Foundations—that is, all artifacts are obtained by Reading, Writing, Thinking, Interacting, and Demonstrating. By considering these five Foundations, a pattern emerges for easy storage and retrieval of artifacts in the Collecting, Working, and Showcase folders of the Smart Portfolio.

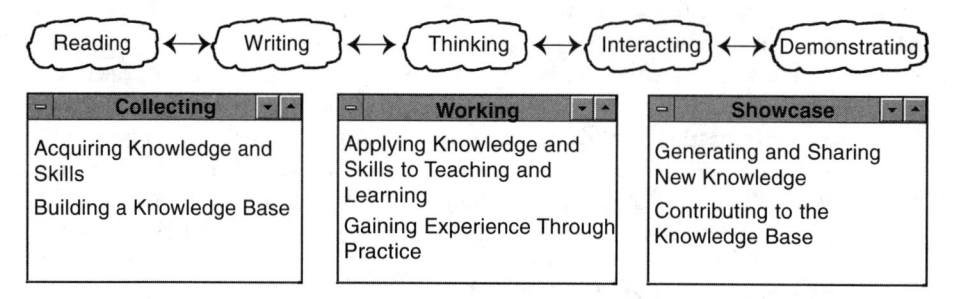

Reading ↔ Writing ↔ Thinking ↔ Interacting ↔ Demonstrating

Collecting	Working	Showcase
Acquiring Knowledge and Skills Building a Knowledge Base	Applying Knowledge and Skills to Teaching and Learning Gaining Experience Through Practice	Generating and Sharing New Knowledge Contributing to the Knowledge Base

Building a Smart Portfolio

The Smart Portfolio is built in a community of learners where the consensus is that "two heads are better than one." Thoughtfulness and inquiry are shared experiences. A closer look at some sample artifacts shows the natural integration of the five Foundations (see Figure 2-1).

Conclusion

The Smart Portfolio's unique organizational structure can be used as the teacher develops from learner to expert to scholar. The Smart Portfolio becomes a place where thinking becomes visible, where it can be finely tuned, where the thinker is engaged, and where making meaning is personalized. The portfolio tells the story of the writer—past and present—with a glimpse at what might come in the future.

Smart schools, Perkins tells us, have to be "an informed and energetic setting for teachers' thoughtful learning, too" (1992, p. 221). The Smart Portfolio empowers you as a teacher and as a learner. Gathering new information, developing new ideas for the classroom, considering whether these new ideas would be helpful to your students, and deciding which to keep and which to abandon makes you a more thoughtful teacher. You do not need a Smart Portfolio to be a thoughtful teacher, but your Smart Portfolio will contain the unequivocal evidence that you are.

Figure 2-1. Portfolio Artifacts

Representative Artifacts in a Portfolio

READING ARTIFACTS
- Book list
- Book notes
- Summaries
- Best Web Sites
- Diagrams
- Overviews
- Outlines

WRITING ARTIFACTS
- Formal papers
- Publication piece
- Philosophy of teaching and learning
- Evaluation of artifacts
- Descriptions of effective strategies
- Self-evaluations of teaching
- Goals
- Reports

THINKING ARTIFACTS
- Thinking about our thinking
- Responses to prompts
- Written dialogue with texts
- Mind wanderings and maps
- Charts and graphs
- Steps in problem-solving
- Process memos
- Reader responses

DEMONSTRATING ARTIFACTS
- Illustrations
- Teacher assessments
- Lesson plans
- Lesson critiques
- Feedback from others
- Videos
- Checklists
- Teacher-made materials
- Presentations
- Transcripts

INTERACTING ARTIFACTS
- Photographs
- Journal assessments
- Thinking exercises
- In-class entries
- Group brainstorming
- Group consensus products
- Peer assessments
- Problems/solutions
- Projects
- Charts

References

Perkins, D. (1992). *Smart schools, from training memories to educating minds.* New York: The Free Press.

Perkins, D. (1995). *Outsmarting IQ, the emerging science of learnable intelligence.* New York: The Free Press.

CHAPTER 3
Intelligent Portfolios for Teachers

Background

In Chapter Two, the Smart Portfolio introduced its unique characteristics that pushed the evolution of the portfolio beyond previous implementations. Reading, Writing, Thinking, Interacting, and Demonstrating were adopted as the Foundation of all portfolio artifacts. Collecting, Working, and Showcase folders hold artifacts that show evidence of continuous learning and professional growth. The structure of the Smart Portfolio encouraged the active integration of new information with prior knowledge and facilitated the organization and creation of artifacts.

The Intelligent Portfolio moves the concept of portfolios to the point of animation, speed, and motion—bringing each element to life. It begins with a core package of hardware and software and creates Collection Points to electronically house the artifacts.

The Intelligent Portfolio Platform

The laptop portable computer serves as the platform of choice for the Intelligent Portfolio. Minimally configured with either the Windows or Macintosh operating system and a 2 gigabyte hard drive, 24 megabytes of random access memory (RAM), CD-ROM, an external Zip drive for back-ups and mass storage, and a high-speed modem for communications. To this basic list of technical features will be added software applications including a word processor, spreadsheet, communications, and several other packages depending on your status as a learner, expert, or scholar.

Foundations of the Intelligent Portfolio

The sources for artifacts in the Smart Portfolio are identical for the Intelligent Portfolio: the foundations of Reading, Writing, Thinking, Interacting, and Demonstrating are used to locate artifacts. Everything you accumulate is the result of these five activities.

Reading

Reading is the most encompassing foundation of the portfolio, whether Smart or Intelligent. With the Intelligent Portfolio, however, on-line searches of automated card catalogs, electronic books, and digital library files are now possible. Virtual sojourns to tens of thousands of World Wide Web ("WWW" or "Web") sites is a reality. Electronic literature reviews demand that teachers employ the latest in automated search inquiries. The Intelligent Portfolio supports the typical computer account including multiple *email addresses, electronic mailing lists*, and subscriptions to the latest Web *sites*. Never before has

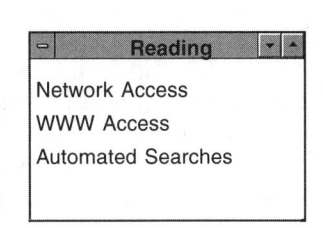

Reading
Network Access
WWW Access
Automated Searches

gathering information taken on such real-time impact, with journals and periodicals forming a part of the ever-growing domain of computing resources.

Writing

Writing
Word Processing
Desktop Publishing
Authoring Tools

Publications, formal papers, and classroom materials require two of the most common applications of personal computers: *word processing* and *desktop publishing*. With a growing number of automated PC tools including the *spelling checker, thesaurus, word counter, reading level gauge, hyphenator,* and *grammar checker*, the Intelligent Portfolio concentrates on the content and presentation of material as well as the quality of its syntax. Clip art, tables, and graphics add professionalism to the final product. Expert *authoring tools* provide graphics presentation capabilities which infuse course presentations with the images and sounds of the Internet in a multisensory package, making textbook-only assignments appear as antiquated as the word-of-mouth lectures must have appeared to the post-Gutenberg textbook-equipped library.

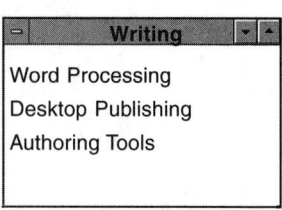

Thinking

Thinking
Databases
Spreadsheets
Project Management
Web Helper Applications
Multimedia Players

By reflecting on artifacts accumulated in other areas of the portfolio, professional educators gain a better understanding of their own learning style. Solving problems, formulating personal theories of learning, and developing lesson objectives based on sound principles of teaching are enhanced with the Intelligent Portfolio and its suite of technological tools.

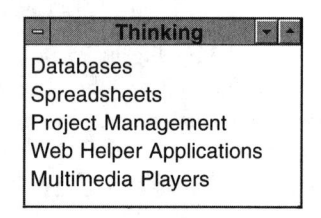

Web Helper Applications expand the exploration of the Internet and form robust skills supporting "thinking about thinking." *Image, sound, and video clip players* download files that add to a teacher's cache of classroom resource materials. Instructional materials prepared by professional educators are available for the taking. Lesson plans, news videos, even personalized audio greetings from key public officials are readily captured in the expansive storage media of the electronic Intelligent Portfolio. A *database software package* solves the problem of managing the enormous quantity of phone numbers, personal and professional contacts, bibliographic references, and potential WWW sites. An *electronic spreadsheet* tabularizes numeric information, allowing the portfolio to electronically project "what if" scenarios to existing research information. And by using professional *project management software* to schedule course work, literature reviews, journal and peer assessments, and other vital milestones of your personal development program, more time can be devoted to thinking.

Interacting

Interacting
Electronic Mail
Newsgroups
Distance Learning
List Servers
Chat Rooms

Perhaps the most successful application of computer technology is in the foundation of Interacting—exploring one's discipline with other experts sharing similar interests. Communication tools move the portfolio into the "Intelligent" range with the introduction of electronic mailing lists, newsgroups, and distance learning opportunities.

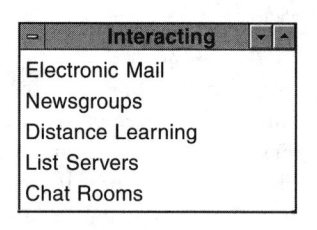

The Intelligent Portfolio contains the *electronic addresses* of colleagues who share ideas, brainstorm new concepts, and assess learning objectives while still in the design phase.

Newsgroups broaden communication channels further by providing a wide target of potential colleagues. For example, a newsgroup focusing on social studies brings together educators interested in the general aspects of lesson planning, classroom presentations, and assessments. It includes a broader scope of interested parties such as teachers, students, and renowned educators from national and international settings. For cohorts separated by distance and opportunity, the use of *Distance Learning* media brings otherwise disparate interest groups together for the first time in a virtual classroom.

Demonstrating

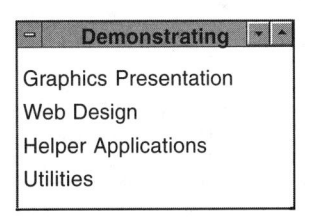

For the educator, Demonstrating houses some of the most important artifacts of the Intelligent Portfolio. With only a few capabilities added to the core system, technology can display the products of the Intelligent Portfolio. A *graphics presentation package,* common in integrated office productivity software packages, provides the ability to combine materials containing images, sounds, text, and video into a multisensory presentation. *Web design software* assists in the creation of Internet-based course material. Easy-to-use helper applications and utilities round out a comprehensive list of development tools.

Demonstrating
Graphics Presentation
Web Design
Helper Applications
Utilities

The Artifacts of the Intelligent Portfolio

The CD-ROM is the ultimate by-product of the Intelligent Portfolio, allowing it to remain a living document. A single CD-ROM holds nearly a gigabyte of images, sounds, videos, literature research, text, ideas, spreadsheets, databases, presentations, lesson plans, and assessments stored on a single medium. Artifacts are accompanied by a state-of-the-art search engine for quick recall, retrieval, and display of complex search requests. Captured initially to hard disk media, they are transferred to a Zip drive and pressed permanently to the CD-ROM.

Tracking artifacts obtained by Reading, Writing, Thinking, Interacting, and Demonstrating can be overwhelming. But, when organized electronically, the process is faster and more efficient. In the Intelligent Portfolio, the teacher sets up a system of "collection points" to hold specific artifacts. Collection Points reside in folders corresponding to the three types of artifacts: Collecting, Working, and Showcase. Let's take a few representative artifacts of a typical portfolio and examine into which Collection Point and into which folder they would be placed in the Intelligent Portfolio (see Figure 3-1).

Collecting Folder

By far the most versatile component of the Intelligent Portfolio will be the Collecting folder. Resources for teaching and learning are the source of many artifacts. See if you agree with the placement of the sample artifacts in the Collection Points of this folder.

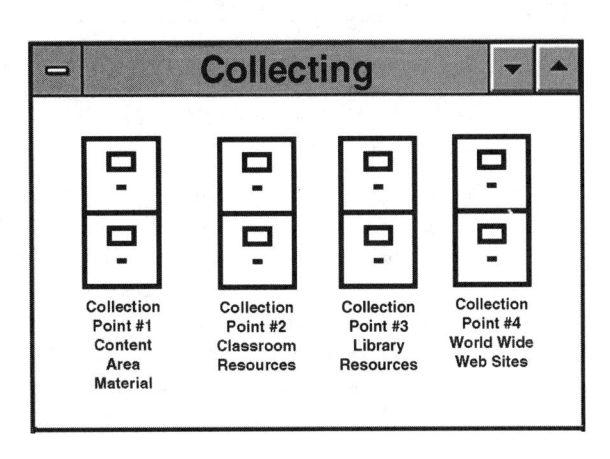

Collecting

- Collection Point #1 Content Area Material
- Collection Point #2 Classroom Resources
- Collection Point #3 Library Resources
- Collection Point #4 World Wide Web Sites

Figure 3-1. The Portfolio Evolution

Representative Artifacts in a Portfolio

Reading Artifacts
Book Lists
Historical Timelines
Book Notes
Textbook Summaries
Curriculum Overviews
Journal Articles
Best Web Sites

Writing Artifacts
Formal Class Papers
Publication Pieces
Philosophy of Teaching and Learning
Grant Applications
Self-Evaluations
Resumes
Subject Area URLs
Lesson Plans

Thinking Artifacts
Thinking Explorations
Mind Maps
Biology Charts/Graphs
Problem-Solving Steps
Reaction to Readings
Process Memos

Demonstrating Artifacts
Illustrations
Civil War Videos
Teacher-Made Materials
Classroom Presentations
Thematic Units
Awards
Transcripts
Letters of Recommendation
Lesson Critiques and Feedback
Lesson Plans

Interacting Artifacts
Photographs
Journal Assessments
Thinking Exercises
Group Brainstorming
Projects
In-Class Exercises

Collection Point #1: Content Area Material
- Reading Artifacts: Book Notes, Textbook Summaries, Historical Timelines, Curriculum Overviews

Educators tend to concentrate on particular disciplines. Language arts, math, social studies, and science are examples of specific content areas. Collection Point #1 offers a location to store artifacts that contribute to a body of personal knowledge. Handwritten notes, typed summaries, and photocopied class handouts were the purview of the Smart Portfolio. The Intelligent Portfolio stores their electronic equivalents: word processing documents and graphics files. Historical timelines provide visual aids for concrete learners, curriculum overviews help teachers select new course materials, and on-line textbook reviews help target the best hardbound resources for classroom instruction.

Collection Point #2: Classroom Resources
- Writing Artifacts: Lesson Plans
- Thinking Artifacts: Biology Charts and Graphs
- Demonstrating Artifacts: Civil War Videos, Grade Sheets

The Intelligent Portfolio requires a collection point to house classroom-ready artifacts such as a lesson plan developed for a social studies class, a biology visual aid depicting the respiratory system of mammals, a video purchased during a visit to the Gettysburg Civil War battlefield, or an electronic spreadsheet modified to hold student scores. These Writing, Thinking, and Demonstrating artifacts are stored in Collection Point #2.

Collection Point #3: Library Resources
- Reading Artifacts: Bibliographies, Journal Articles

Libraries provide endless artifacts for the portfolio. While many of these items retain their hardcopy format, more libraries are opting to provide electronic artifacts than ever before. Entire bibliographies are available on digitized media, while compact disks serve as the media of choice for nearly all of the most popular journals, magazines, and professional periodicals. One publisher alone provides over 350 publications on CD-ROM every month. Imagine how easy it is to locate digitized reference material when that information is stored in your Intelligent Portfolio.

Collection Point #4: World Wide Web Sites
- Reading Artifacts: Best World Wide Web Sites

Collecting electronic artifacts for the Intelligent Portfolio is no longer complete without a repository of World Wide Web sites. The teacher can use the "Bookmarks" of a web browser to store an on-line catalog of the best the Internet has to offer. As the educator "surfs" in search of available lesson plans, discovery-based learning exercises, and multimedia materials, the addresses (known as Uniform Resource Locators, or URLs) of the best of these sites should be "bookmarked" and included in Collection Point #4.

Working Folder

Artifacts created as the result of teaching and learning are placed in the Working folder. These Working artifacts represent your attempts to create, test, and hone new knowledge and skills. Current writing projects and nearly all thinking exercises are stored, at least temporarily, in these Collection Points: Making Connections, Reflection and Self-Assessment, Learning Projects, and Applications and Lessons. Take a look at where we placed some of the sample artifacts electronically.

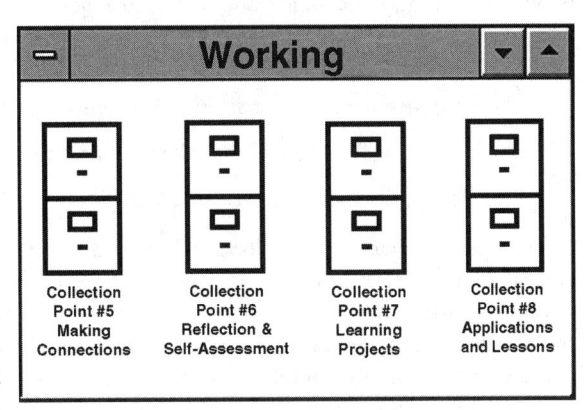

Working
- Collection Point #5 Making Connections
- Collection Point #6 Reflection & Self-Assessment
- Collection Point #7 Learning Projects
- Collection Point #8 Applications and Lessons

Collection Point #5: Making Connections

- Thinking Artifacts: Steps in Problem-Solving, Reactions to Readings
- Interacting Artifacts: Mindmaps, Thinking Explorations

Interactions with peers and colleagues become part of Working artifacts. Educators, perhaps more than members of other professional disciplines, appreciate and acknowledge the importance of personal contacts. The sample artifacts identified above are indicative of how connections improve thinking. Problem-solving and reactions to readings are true Thinking artifacts advanced in large measure by peer interaction. Mindmaps and explorations are typically advanced in the same way. Did you agree with the placement of these particular examples? Collection Points are the most versatile aspects of the portfolio. They are also the most flexible. Because assignments to collection points are subjective, it is perfectly acceptable to disagree with the placement of these sample artifacts—you should store these items where they make the most sense to you. Remember, the purpose of the collection points is to rapidly retrieve artifacts.

Collection Point #6: Reflection & Self-Assessment

- Writing Artifacts: Philosophy of Teaching and Learning, Evaluation of Artifacts, Self-Evaluation of Teaching
- Thinking Artifacts: Responses to Prompts, Written Dialog with Texts, Process Memos
- Interacting Artifacts: Problem/Solutions
- Demonstrating Artifacts: Feedback from Others

A major component of the Working folder is a repository for reflection and self-assessment. We recommend that you include a "Philosophy of Teaching and Learning" in this Collection Point of your portfolio—a theme paper that you write and revise as you mature as an educator. The Intelligent Portfolio provides the forum for this artifact. Most teachers have a collection of evaluations: self-evaluations, formal written evaluations, and student evaluations. These, too, should be maintained in Collection Point #6. Optical scanners provide digitized images of peer feedback, written critiques, and reflective memos. Once expressed electronically, these artifacts can be analyzed, sorted, and merged with other data to suggest possible personal improvements or to extend professional goals.

Collection Point #7: Learning Projects

- Demonstrating Artifacts: Thematic Units
- Interacting Artifacts: Group Discussions, Projects, Group Brainstorming Sessions
- Writing Artifacts: Subject Area Web Sites

Certain artifacts are developed for immediate use in the classroom. Thematic units are excellent examples of Learning Projects since most of these integrated lessons combine discovery learning with real-life projects. Bulletin boards, group processes, and subject-specific Web sites are further examples. Again, these artifacts address specific learning goals and are not necessarily complete lessons—those are found in the next Collection Point. The Intelligent Portfolio serves as a catalyst for creative learning projects believed impossible just a few years ago. Cut an excellent learning objective from one source and paste it into an exciting teaching example from another. The result is a new idea or strategy.

Collection Point #8: Applications and Lessons

- Demonstrating Artifacts: Lesson Plans, Teacher-Made Materials, Presentations
- Reading Artifacts: Subject-Specific Web Sites

Collection Point #8 houses instructional units. The sample artifacts include lesson plans, critiques, complete presentations, and nearly all teacher-made materials. Lessons are easily revised and updated or completely redesigned for individualized instruction. With the number of subject-matter-area Web sites growing exponentially, the opportunity to locate and download complete, integrated units is fast becoming the norm. By adding these electronic units to Collection Point #8, educators can streamline the material to the specific needs of their own classroom.

Showcase Folder

Your best works and professional accomplishments are stored as artifacts in the Showcase folder of the Intelligent Portfolio. Electronic presentations, word-processed materials, and desktop-published journal articles are examples. In addition, this is the place to store vocation-related documents such as teaching credentials, college transcripts, and letters of recommendation.

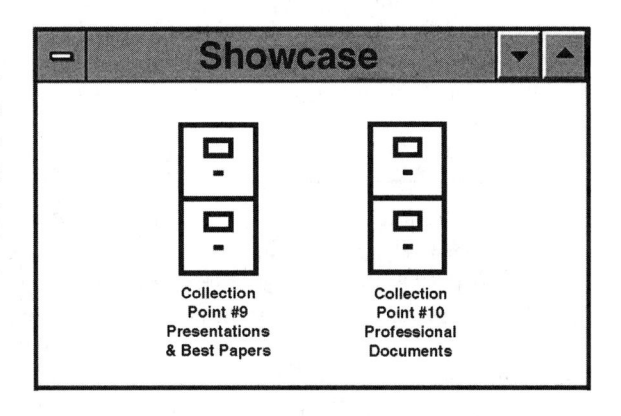

Collection Point #9: Presentations & Best Papers

- Writing Artifacts: Formal Papers, Publications, Grant Applications
- Interacting Artifacts: Photographs
- Demonstrating Artifacts: Classroom Presentations

This Collection Point is reserved for your best works: artifacts that have been shared, critiqued, and revised. While publications are the most obvious, Presentations and Best Papers also include a wider assortment of items created by educators at all levels: learner, expert, and scholar. Teacher-Learners create formal papers in response to in-class assignments. Teacher-Experts develop materials for immediate classroom application. Teacher-Scholars prepare articles for publication, exposing their thinking to the critical review of colleagues. Collection Point #9 takes the form and function of a professional electronic display portfolio with many practical uses throughout a career in education.

Collection Point #10: Professional Documents

- Writing Artifacts: Resumes and Curriculum Vitae
- Demonstrating Artifacts: Transcripts, Letters of Recommendation, Awards

Educators are compelled by law and tradition to seek excellence in their chosen profession. Oftentimes, that excellence is measured in professional certificates, college transcripts, letters of recommendation, and an up-to-date vita. These artifacts are stored in the final collection point of the Intelligent Portfolio. They require some manipulation to transfer from hard copy into electronic media. But once a teaching certificate is scanned, a vita is composed, or a photograph of an award presentation is captured, the artifacts provide an instantaneous resource for future retrievals.

Conclusion

The Smart and Intelligent Portfolios are interchangeable. With the addition of collection points, artifacts stored in one portfolio are placed in the exact same location in the other. Our research with portfolios indicates that there is a tendency to view the Intelligent Portfolio as the ultimate goal—as somehow *better* than the Smart Portfolio. Both have advantages and shortcomings. Either format is acceptable as a pattern for organizing your portfolio. If you find that the labels of the Collection Points (e.g., Classroom Resources, Reflection and Self-Assessment, Professional Documents) are not to your liking, change them to something you like better. Just be careful not to overlook important categories of artifacts.

Transition

Chapter Four introduces an on-line, CD-ROM-based exercise to help you select which portfolio format is best suited for you at a particular stage in your educational career. Are you a Teacher as Learner, Teacher as Expert, or Teacher as Scholar? Is the Smart or Intelligent Portfolio better suited to your needs? Chapter 4 will enable you to answer these questions and define, design, and implement the version of the portfolio that will be immediately useful for your personal development and professional growth. Feel free to skip the chapters that do not apply to your specific situation.

CHAPTER 4

Portfolio Exercise for Learners, Experts, and Scholars

Background

This chapter introduces a four-step exercise provided on the accompanying CD-ROM. Over two megabytes of hypertext files, graphics, images, and text provide a sequenced introduction to the remaining chapters of the book.

The Portfolio Exercise

Here's what you will see in the CD-ROM-based exercise...

We would like to introduce you to Foley, our cartoon character icon, who will serve as your guide through the four steps of the Portfolio Exercise.

Step One: Artifacts Exercise

Step One will familiarize you with the concepts and procedures for collecting artifacts. For the avid portfolio user, artifacts are the essence of portfolios. Each artifact represents an element of personal intellectual value, a document to be thoughtfully considered for its potential application in some future academic endeavor. To grasp the fundamental organizational aspects of the portfolio, carefully consider the examples presented and categorize each one as a Collecting, Working, or Showcase artifact. Place the artifact into one of several possible "containers," keeping in mind that you may need to find it again. So choose wisely.

Step Two: Learner, Expert, or Scholar?

Step Two involves a decision that is crucial to the selection of the portfolio format. What "flavor" of portfolio you adopt depends in large measure on where you are in your teaching-learning career. A checklist helps identify your own characteristics as a teacher and helps you determine how you will use this portfolio.

- The portfolio for the *Teacher as Learner* focuses on **Collecting** artifacts. Reading is a key foundation of the portfolio and new information is gathered from books, lectures, libraries, and Web sites. Classroom resources and content area materials are located and stored in the portfolio. The foundation of your entire academic career is based on your role as a Teacher-Learner. The portfolio becomes a lifelong tool for professional development, and the process begins by housing artifacts as the Teacher as Learner builds and extends a knowledge base.

- As a practicing teacher, the *Teacher as Expert* finds that most artifacts are clustered in the **Working** section of the portfolio. Application becomes the focus as artifacts are created around the presentation of materials in a classroom environment. Your role as a classroom teacher requires on-the-job training and continual testing of new teaching strategies. While the Teacher as Learner gathers new knowledge, the Teacher as Expert gleans experience through practice.

- The *Teacher as Scholar* has the most comprehensive portfolio. **Showcase** artifacts take precedence as the educator shares ideas which span a career in the field. A Teacher as Scholar carries on discussions with colleagues, demonstrates artifacts in professional forums, and pursues thinking and learning in shared works. If you are a Teacher-Scholar, you have a responsibility to contribute to the discipline by sharing your expertise, understanding, and dedication.

Step Three: Smart or Intelligent Portfolio

Step Three examines the question of whether to use the Smart or Intelligent Portfolio. This exercise aids in selecting and designing the portfolio most appropriate for your situation. Here are a few considerations:

- Both formats are based on the foundations of Reading, Writing, Thinking, Interacting, and Demonstrating.

- The emphasis on Collecting, Working, and Showcase artifacts depends on who is using the portfolio.

- Collection Points are flexible and designed to meet your needs. Your artifacts represent your progress on a journey through a teaching career.

- Not every portfolio must evolve into its electronic counterpart. The selection of format should be considered a matter of personal preference, convenience, and technological literacy.

- Both the Smart and Intelligent Portfolios are designed to serve the needs of the Teacher-Learner, Teacher-Expert, and Teacher-Scholar as they proceed through a career in education.

Step Four: Build Your Portfolio

Step Four completes the exercise by providing instructions for building the portfolio that best suits your needs. The CD-ROM contains separate instructions for the Teacher as Learner, Teacher as Expert, and Teacher as Scholar. Examine each of the three formats to gain a better overall understanding of portfolios before seeking out the most appropriate portfolio for your situation.

How to Access the CD-ROM Exercises

The CD-ROM-based exercise is accessed by either a Windows or Macintosh personal computer. Both sets of files are stored on each CD-ROM.

- For **Windows** systems. Load the CD-ROM and click on **Start** —> **Run** to view the Run Dialog Box. Use the Browse button to open the files on the CD-ROM drive (typically drive D:). Find the file named **Portfolio.htm**. Click on **OK** to begin the exercise.

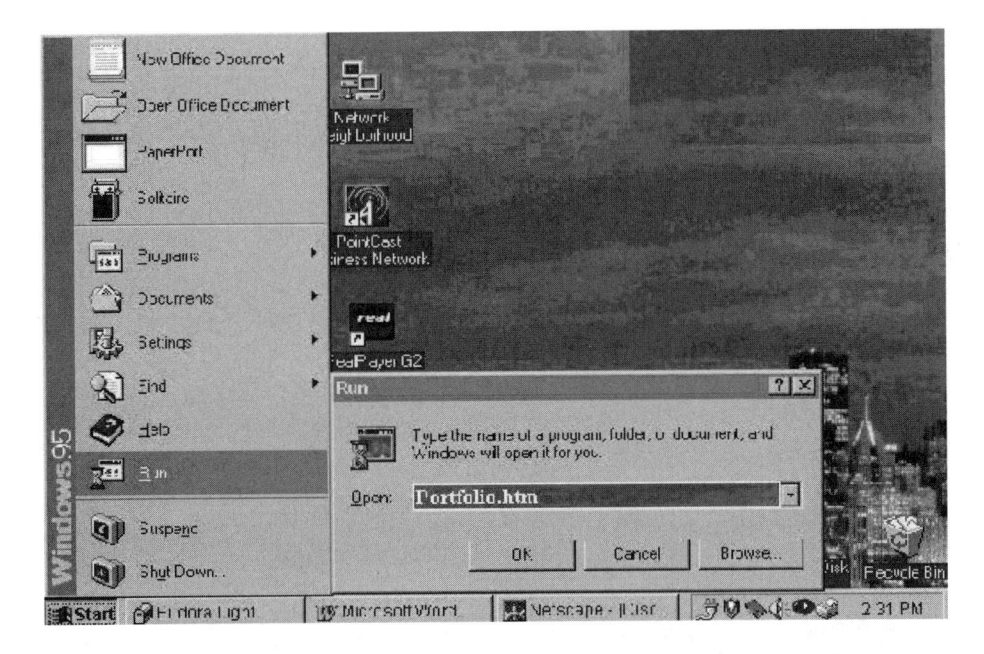

- For **Macintosh** systems. Load the **Portfolio** CD-ROM into the drive and wait for the CD icon to appear on your desktop. Open the folder named **Portfolio Exercise** and double click on the file named **Portfolio.htm** to begin the exercise.

- For **All** systems. The Portfolio Exercise runs entirely from within a Web browser such as Netscape (version 3.0 or higher) or Microsoft Explorer. One of these browsers **must** be available on your computer for you to use the CD.

Frequently Asked Questions

The exercise concludes with a review of the most commonly asked questions about portfolios, whether Smart or Intelligent. Included in the database of questions are the following:

- The Smart Portfolio or the Intelligent Portfolio . . . must I decide to go completely with one format or the other?

- Must the portfolio consist of all of the Collection Points described or can I develop a similar but more individualized format?

- What's in this for me? Why should I want a Smart or Intelligent Portfolio?
- How long will it take to create a portfolio?
- Who will evaluate my portfolio?

Conclusion

The remaining chapters of this book are structured for easy reference based on whether you are a Teacher-Learner, Teacher-Expert, or Teacher-Scholar. The pattern is very easy to follow.

> Novice portfolio users should begin with Part III of the Book, specifically written for the Teacher as Learner. Classroom teachers—Go directly to Part IV for the Teacher as Expert.
> If you have considerable portfolio experience—Part V was written with you in mind.

PART III
Portfolios for the Teacher as Learner

Are you enrolled in a teacher education program? Do you need some guidance in designing your first personal or professional portfolio?

Chapters 5, 6, and 7 will guide you through a closer examination of the Smart and Intelligent Portfolios for the Teacher as Learner.

Chapter 5	Chapter 6	Chapter 7
The Smart Portfolio for the Teacher as Learner	*The Intelligent Portfolio for the Teacher as Learner*	*Portfolios in Transition: The Teacher as Learner Perspective*
Chapter 5 explains the basics—all you will need to get started: Locate a 3-ring binder, some large manila folders with tabs, and a posterboard for the final presentation.	If computers are your forte, choose the Intelligent Portfolio described in this chapter. It tells you all about software, hardware, and specific collection points for your electronic artifacts.	Be sure to read Chapter 7 to discover how James and Jason designed their Teacher as Learner portfolios. They can help you avoid mistakes.

CHAPTER 5
The Smart Portfolio for the Teacher as Learner

Introduction

The portfolio often seems to generate more questions than it answers. This is especially true when the Teacher as Learner begins to create a Smart Portfolio. For this reason, we have made the Smart Portfolio easy to comprehend, easy to create, and even easier to use. For the Teacher as Learner, there are four basic questions that you must consider before constructing a Smart Portfolio:

(1)   Where Do I Begin?
(2)   How Do I Organize the Portfolio?
(3)   What Do I Collect? and
(4)   Who Will Assess My Work?

Foley is here to answer these four questions and guide you through the creation of your first Smart Portfolio.

Where Do I Begin?

Where do I begin? I'm here to help answer those questions. So if you are ready, let's begin...at the beginning.

Begin with the five essential foundations of the Smart Portfolio. In Chapter 2, the Smart Portfolio introduced the five foundations: Reading, Writing, Thinking, Interacting, and Demonstrating. Understanding that these elements are totally integrated when we teach and learn is essential to the proper construction of the Smart Portfolio. Consider the graphic at the top of page 32.

Reading starts the process of gathering evidence and information in the form of artifacts. Diagrams, booklists, booknotes, summaries, outlines, sketches, and drawings mix with previous learning, and patterns begin to form. With little conscious help it seems from us, the mind makes its own connections. This is how an individual's knowledge base is built, how new meaning is constructed, and how new levels of understanding are reached.

Writing goes hand-in-hand with reading when constructing new knowledge. Making meaning through writing involves formal papers, book reports, thematic units, poems and letters, publication-ready articles, and written classroom lesson plans. Writing efforts may be as short as a one-page outline of a publication or the accumulation of manuscripts for a course thesis. Informal writing, such as "free writing exercises" can stretch the imagination and extend thinking almost automatically.

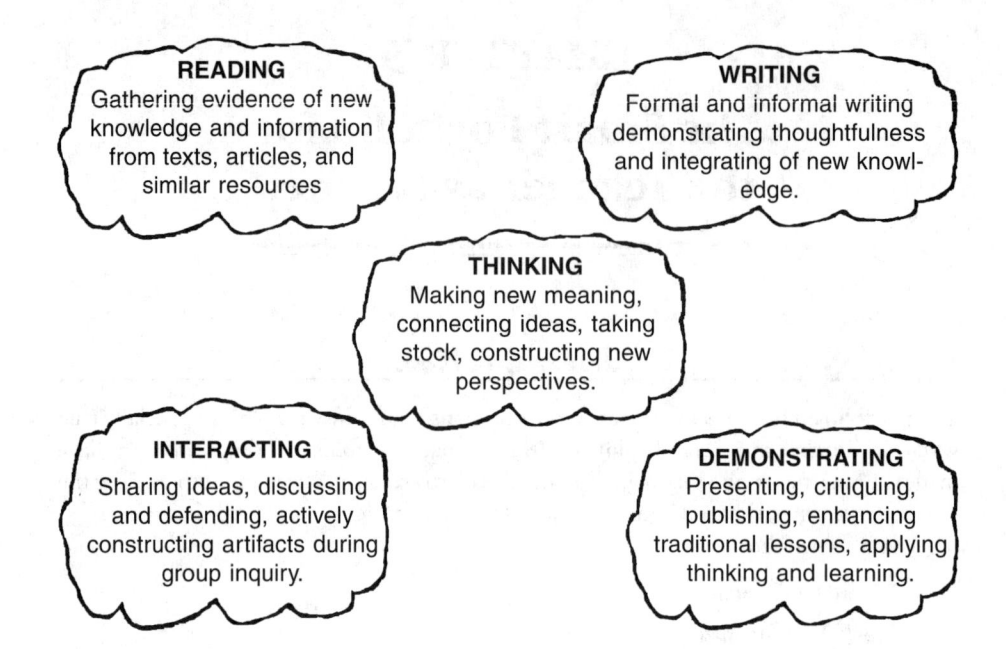

READING
Gathering evidence of new knowledge and information from texts, articles, and similar resources

WRITING
Formal and informal writing demonstrating thoughtfulness and integrating of new knowledge.

THINKING
Making new meaning, connecting ideas, taking stock, constructing new perspectives.

INTERACTING
Sharing ideas, discussing and defending, actively constructing artifacts during group inquiry.

DEMONSTRATING
Presenting, critiquing, publishing, enhancing traditional lessons, applying thinking and learning.

Thinking lies at the heart of the portfolio and infuses personal feelings into otherwise random thoughts and ideas, giving them momentum and bringing them to life. The Thinking journal in the Smart Portfolio is "a place where our thinking can become visible, a place where we toss around ideas, consider what others think, make connections between new and prior knowledge, examine our own thinking strategies, and judge our own learning" (Wilcox, 1997, p. 36). Taking stock and re-evaluating goals enables us to monitor and manage our own learning.

Interacting requires that we argue and defend our ideas. Whether the individual is involved in group projects as a requirement of a pre-service course or has already launched their student teaching role, teamwork with fellow teachers almost always leads to personal and professional growth. Interacting is fostered by peer assessments, memos from group activities, brainstorming sessions, arguments, problems and solutions, and position papers defending different points of view.

How do I organize my Portfolio? The Smart Portfolio is organized into 3 Main Sections.

Demonstrating is an important process in the Smart Portfolio and, combined with the other foundations, its artifacts are rich in the application and transfer of learning. Demonstrations include the text of classroom presentations, speeches, oral interpretations, formal presentations at conferences, and completed projects using multisensory exhibits.

Whether we desire a documented knowledge base, a recorded history of teaching and learning, or an accurate account of experiences and achievements, the evidence must be tangible. To produce a portfolio representing thinking and learning, which is often hidden or overlooked, artifacts must be clearly explained.

How Do I Organize My Portfolio?

In an effort to provide some organization, the Smart Portfolio for the Teacher as Learner contains folders for storing Collect-

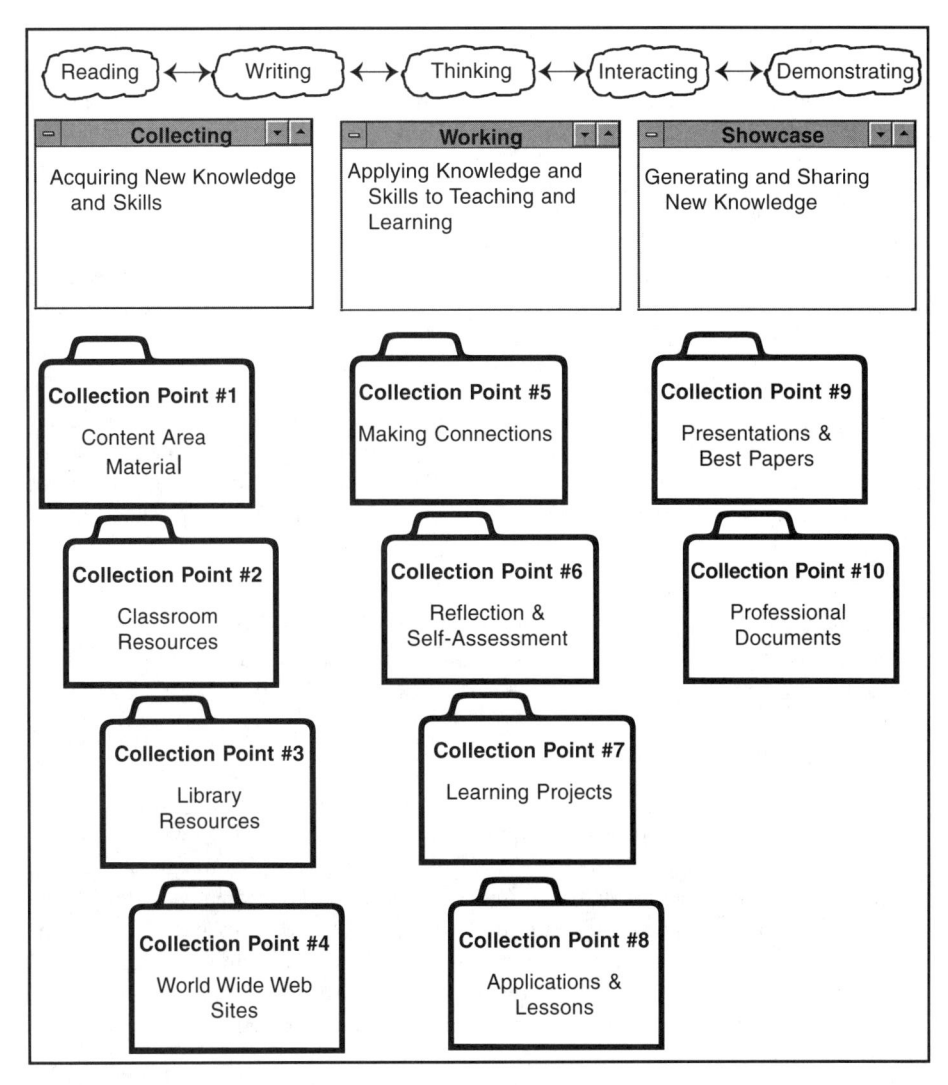

```
┌─────────────────────────────────────────────────────────────────────┐
│  (Reading)↔(Writing)↔(Thinking)↔(Interacting)↔(Demonstrating)       │
│                                                                       │
│  ┌─ Collecting ──┐   ┌─ Working ────┐   ┌─ Showcase ────┐            │
│  │ Acquiring New │   │ Applying     │   │ Generating and │            │
│  │ Knowledge and │   │ Knowledge and│   │ Sharing New    │            │
│  │ Skills        │   │ Skills to    │   │ Knowledge      │            │
│  │               │   │ Teaching and │   │                │            │
│  │               │   │ Learning     │   │                │            │
│  └───────────────┘   └──────────────┘   └────────────────┘           │
│                                                                       │
│  Collection Point #1   Collection Point #5   Collection Point #9     │
│  Content Area          Making Connections    Presentations &          │
│  Material                                    Best Papers              │
│                                                                       │
│  Collection Point #2   Collection Point #6   Collection Point #10    │
│  Classroom             Reflection &          Professional             │
│  Resources             Self-Assessment       Documents                │
│                                                                       │
│  Collection Point #3   Collection Point #7                            │
│  Library               Learning Projects                              │
│  Resources                                                            │
│                                                                       │
│  Collection Point #4   Collection Point #8                            │
│  World Wide Web        Applications &                                 │
│  Sites                 Lessons                                        │
└─────────────────────────────────────────────────────────────────────┘
```

ing, Working, and Showcase artifacts. The graphic above depicts how the portfolio might look with its Collection Points.

Collecting, Working, and Showcase folders include a number of Collection Points in which artifacts will be stored.

Collecting Folder

The focus for the Teacher as Learner is on acquiring knowledge and skills. Therefore, most of the evidence of learning will be housed in the *Collecting* Folder that comprises four Collection Points: Content Area Materials, Classroom Resources, Library Resources, and World Wide Web Sites. Artifacts are placed initially into one of these four collection points. Because of its importance to the Teacher as Learner, we have discussed the Collecting folder and its collection points in greater detail than the Working or Showcase folders.

Collection Point #1: Content Area Material
As a Teacher-Learner you have completed a rigorous course of study in preparation for the day when you will take the reins of your own classroom. Numerous sources of content area

materials will be encountered: subject matter presented in a methodology course, discipline-specific journal articles to consider, and course textbooks will become Collecting artifacts for your portfolio. Each item will form the basis for your development as an educator. Gather these items with sufficient care now, and they will serve you well throughout your career.

Collection Point #2: Classroom Resources
As you progress through the pre-service program, you will be exposed to the best in classroom-ready artifacts. Assessment tools, integrated thematic units, teaching and learning strategies, and affective and cognitive development exercises are just a few examples of artifacts that should be stored in this Collection Point.

Collection Point #3: Library Resources
The campus library is a familiar environment to many undergraduate educators. Bibliographies, CD-ROM journals and periodicals, and reserved materials are accumulated. Perhaps more than any other Collection Point, Library Resources become dated, and you must periodically add, replace, and delete materials to ensure that this Collection Point remains current.

Collection Point #4: World Wide Web Sites
The newest collection point for the Smart Portfolio, Web sites are fast becoming the favorite source of artifacts for today's technology-minded teachers. Particular attention must be placed, however, on the quality of artifacts gathered from the Internet.

Working Folder

As knowledge is applied and new skills acquired, you will be creating your own artifacts and placing them in the Collection Points of the *Working* folder. For the Teacher as Learner, four Collection Points are provided for this work-in-progress. They include: Making Connections, Reflections on Learning, Learning Projects, and Applications and Lessons. Artifacts taken from Collecting folders may be used here in the Working folder. A journal article once stored as Content Area Material may be transformed into a Learning Project in this area of the portfolio. As a result, new information is used to create new applications and extend thinking.

Showcase Folder

Some of your best Working artifacts document your growth and development as an educator. Following validation, these items are moved to one of the two Collection Points of the Showcase folder: Presentations and Papers and Professional Documents. Presentations at a conference or published papers are examples of Collection Point #9; documents such as teacher certification credentials, national teacher examination scores, and personal letters of reference are examples of Collection Point #10.

While each folder and Collection Point will come into play while using the Smart Portfolio, the emphasis for the Teacher as Learner remains on Collecting artifacts. Users of the Smart Portfolio must concentrate on building a strong knowledge base by accumulating artifacts.

The Teacher as Learner can begin immediately to organize artifacts into these Collection Points. It is recommended that an explanation for an artifact's inclusion be attached before it is placed into a folder. As an example, a formal paper written in response to a textbook or article may ultimately find its way into one of the Showcase folders. However, it may have started as an artifact in the Collecting folder and moved into and out of a Working folder several times. A paper trail of artifacts traces their movement within the portfolio and provides a reminder of where each item has been and how it has evolved. As new artifacts move in, other artifacts will move out ensuring the portfolio remains a living history.

Keep in mind that the Smart Portfolio is a tool for assessment, a tool for learning, and a tool for professional development. As a learning tool, it holds evidence of thinking and learning. As an assessment tool, it will be evaluated with both summative and formative appraisals. As a professional development tool, it will promote academic scholarship and sharing. These are the purposes of the Smart Portfolio.

At this point, the Teacher as Learner knows the sources of artifacts and how to organize them once they are generated. Our attention turns now to the question of how to decide which artifacts to include in the Smart Portfolio.

What do I collect? An "artifact" is evidence of knowledge, skill, and personal growth.

What Do I Collect?

Items stuffed in the pages of a course notebook, papers strewn about the top of your desk, and observations folded among the pages of a textbook typify the kinds of portfolio artifacts that the Teacher as Learner collects. Other artifacts include presentations and book reviews, test scores, transcripts, projects, and lessons. To assist the first-time user of the Smart Portfolio, Foley offers some specific examples of the artifacts that belong in each of the 10 Collection Points. Examine each Collection Point carefully to see what specific teaching and learning artifacts might be gathered.

Collection Point #1

Place your Content Area Materials in this folder.

Content Area Materials
Units of Study
Model Lessons
Professional Journal Articles
Teaching Videos
Booknotes

Classroom Resources
Monographs on Classroom Discipline and Learning
Sample Teaching Lessons
Higher Order Thinking Strategies for Children
Multiple Intelligence Exercises

Collection Point #2

Classroom Resources go in this folder.

Collection Point #3

This point will be chock full of materials—all from the library.

Library Resources
Pamphlet "How to Access the Card Catalog"
Personal Research Searches
Requests for Books, Articles, and Resources
Materials for Review

Collection Point #4

This point will house the Uniform Resource Locators (URLs) for your most exciting Web Pages.

World Wide Web Sites
- Search Engines
- Quick Retrieval
- Instructions
- Subject Matter Sites
- Lesson Plan Sites
- Collaborative Sites

Making Connections
- Responses and Reactions to Readings
- Journal Prompts
- Recording Class Discussions
- Lecture Interpretations

Collection Point #5

Making Connections means interacting with your artifacts and with peers.

Collection Point #6

When it's time for "Taking Stock" place these artifacts in this folder.

Reflections & Self-Assessment
- List of Personal Goals
- Self-Assessing Questions and Answers
- Reflections on Progress
- Tracking Standards

Learning Projects
- Plans for Instruction, Content and Assessments
- Learning Center
- Special Projects/Reports
- Topics and Ideas for the Classroom

Collection Point #7

Learning Projects should be standard fare for the Teacher as Learner. They go in this folder.

Collection Point #8

Put your efforts at developing classroom-ready lessons here.

Applications and Lessons
- Ready to Teach Units
- Student Teaching Lessons
- Exercises for the Classroom
- Assessments (Tests, Quizzes, Rubrics)

Presentations and Papers
- Publication-ready Reviews and Articles
- Proposals
- Formal Presentations
- Your Philosophy of Teaching and Learning

Collection Point #9

Remember, only finished artifacts, tested and reviewed, are moved into this folder.

Collection Point #10

This last folder will hold any artifact dealing with teaching credentials or classroom certification.

Professional Documents
- Transcripts
- NTE Test Scores
- Recommendations
- Honors, Recognitions, Awards
- Unique Experiences
- Resume

Even though the structure of the Smart Portfolio is established, the artifacts vary with portfolio keepers. Artifacts differ in purpose, meaning, and construction. The engagement and whole-hearted effort of the Teacher as Learner remains of paramount importance to the quality and relevance of artifacts.

One of the benefits of the Smart Portfolio is the way learning is fostered through an assessment process. With a comprehensive portfolio, Teachers as Learners experience learning through long-term, low-stakes assessments. These assessments allow students to learn from their mistakes without penalty, build on their strengths, and move to the point where they can advance on their own. This is why the process is more important than the product.

Who Will Assess My Portfolio?

Who will assess my work? Portfolios are assessed by peers, instructors, and you!

Who assesses the portfolio can be even more important than *how* it is assessed. The Smart Portfolio will be assessed by peer teacher-learners (informal assessment), by instructors (formal assessment), and most importantly, by you (self-assessment).

You will be the most important evaluator of your own learning. You will learn to analyze your portfolio and compare it with other portfolios. You will examine journals and lesson ideas and use checklists and self-generated questions to determine useful artifacts. These exercises will sharpen your critical-thinking skills. Assessment will offer insight into the process of using a portfolio and how it complements classroom instruction. You will develop a multidimensional view of assessment as a tool for learning and eventually transfer this knowledge to assess your own students when you become a classroom teacher.

Because it is a public document, your Smart Portfolio will be scrutinized by peers and instructors. Welcome the criticism and accept the constructive comments which can increase your learning and enhance your professional development—without becoming defensive.

The Portfolio Poster

To enhance the portfolio experience, we suggest an "Exhibition" to display your Smart Portfolio. The task of presenting a visual representation of thinking and learning at a public exhibition requires complex strategies for analytic, critical, and creative thinking. The poster should be able to stand on its own merit, but the "synergistic" approach is more powerful when learners articulate and defend what they know and how they came to know it. The poster gives the learner the opportunity to synthesize thinking and learning in a creative way, while showing evidence of engagement and reflection, deep understanding of content, meaningful (personal) connection, habits of mind, and skill in oral communications.

Notice that Collection Points #5 and #6 have been pulled from the other Working Folders (see page 38). They were placed at the top of the poster next to two Concept Papers that will be displayed for everyone to view. We consider your Philosophy of Teaching and Learning and your ability to assess your own progress as a Teacher-Learner deserving of special visual attention on the poster. Sort artifacts and display only your best work. Properly presenting the results of your portfolio will require careful analysis and synthesis of your thinking and learning as you progress through course work in teacher education.

Smart Portfolio for the Teacher as Learner

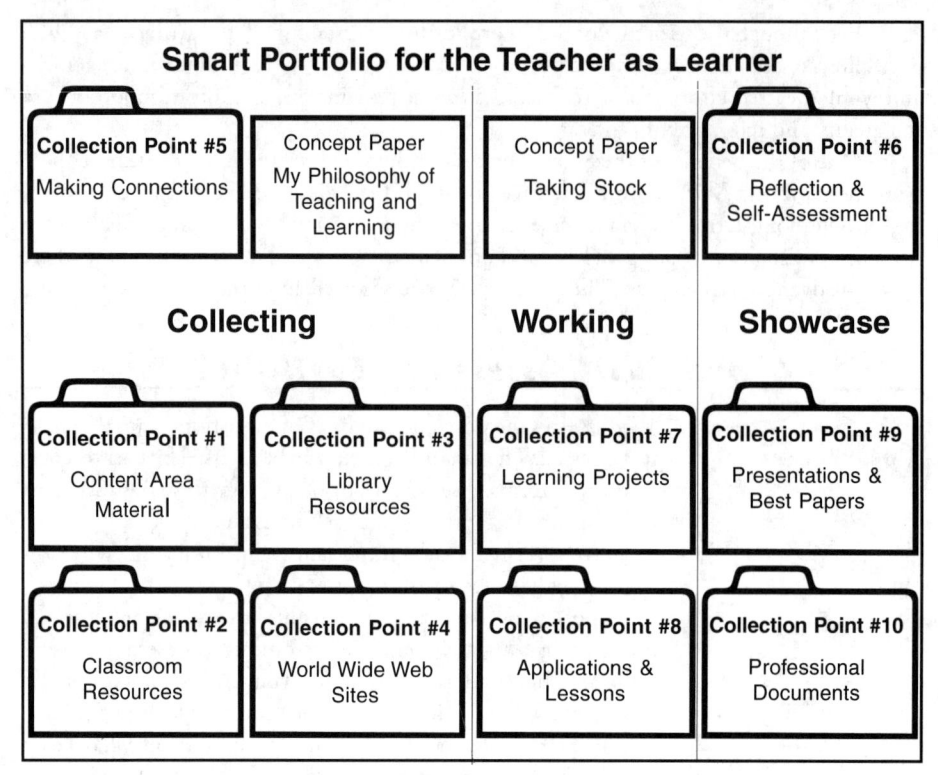

Collecting		Working	Showcase
Collection Point #5 Making Connections	Concept Paper My Philosophy of Teaching and Learning	Concept Paper Taking Stock	**Collection Point #6** Reflection & Self-Assessment
Collection Point #1 Content Area Material	**Collection Point #3** Library Resources	**Collection Point #7** Learning Projects	**Collection Point #9** Presentations & Best Papers
Collection Point #2 Classroom Resources	**Collection Point #4** World Wide Web Sites	**Collection Point #8** Applications & Lessons	**Collection Point #10** Professional Documents

A Posterboard View of the Smart Portfolio

Conclusion

The Smart Portfolio and the artifacts it contains contribute to your professional development and prepare you for responsibilities in the role of a classroom teacher. These artifacts represent your work, your learning, and your thinking. The Smart Portfolio process enhances teaching and learning, enabling you to master the levels of understanding from awareness to basic understanding to deep understanding. As you begin a life of learning and professional development, the Smart Portfolio tracks where you have been, and how you intend to go forward. Reaching goals will take you to the top of the ladder quickly and efficiently.

The Smart Portfolio and Your Professional Development

...Let Assessment and Learning move you up the rungs of professional development.

Showcase
Generating and Sharing Your New Knowledge and Skills

Working
Applying New Knowledge and Skills

Collecting
Acquiring Knowledge and Skills

The Teacher as Learner starts with an emphasis here...

Foley Tips

Here are some tips for a very professional Smart Portfolio.

Here are a few Tips from Foley to ensure that your Smart Portfolio is a viable tool for the Teacher as Learner.

1. **Teachers must be lifelong learners.** Once you define and articulate a philosophy and make a commitment to teaching and learning, personal goals fall into place.

2. **Teachers monitor and manage their own learning.** Through reflective self-assessment of artifacts, you will learn to adjust your own understanding of how you learn.

3. **Teachers record their own history of learning.** By collecting, selecting, and recording accurate accounts and evidence of teaching and learning, the Smart Portfolio can tell the story of your own learning throughout a career as an educator.

4. **Reading, writing, thinking, interacting, and demonstrating lead to more reading, writing, thinking, interacting, and demonstrating.** When we strengthen one aspect of the Smart Portfolio, all aspects are strengthened.

5. **Interacting keeps us mentally sharp and challenged.** Use the tools presented in this chapter to hone your skills and take opportunities for exchanging artifacts and ideas about portfolios.

6. **Ideas germinate and are nurtured in the Smart Portfolio.** Building on prior knowledge and thinking about new information transforms ideas into plans for lessons and presentations.

7. **Use a poster display to present your Smart Portfolio.** Exhibitions are a quick and easy way to share your learning and to see what others have learned.

8. **Consider the Intelligent Portfolio.** When you read Chapter Six, you will discover that the computer can provide excellent resources for the portfolio user, and the step-by-step approach makes the transition less daunting.

9. **Look ahead to the Smart Portfolio for the Teacher as Expert.** One day soon you will be a classroom teacher. The Smart Portfolio is designed to follow you throughout your career as an educator.

See you when you are ready to move to the Teacher as Expert version of the Smart Portfolio

References

Wilcox, B. (1997). Writing portfolios: Active vs. passive. *English Journal, 86,* 34–37.

CHAPTER 6
The Intelligent Portfolio for the Teacher as Learner

Introduction

If you have already successfully organized your Smart Portfolio, building the Intelligent Portfolio is a combination of three simple electronic tasks:

Step One: Creating Portfolio Folders for Reading, Writing, Interacting, Thinking, and Demonstrating,

Step Two: Populating Portfolio Folders with the most efficient and effective combination of software packages for the tasks at hand, and

Step Three: Organizing Folders and Collection Points to store the electronic artifacts that will be accumulated in your portfolio.

Foley will guide you through these three steps, so let's get started.

Step One: Creating Portfolio Folders

The only difference between the Smart Portfolio and its Intelligent Portfolio counterpart is the addition of automated hardware and software tools to collect, work, and showcase your artifacts.

Creating portfolio folders that take on a screen appearance requires some knowledge of how your computer desktop is generated (see the Figure on the following page). Whether you are working in Apple or Windows, creating folders specifically for the five foundations is not difficult. Here are the purposes of each folder:

Here's Step One: Creating Your Portfolio Folders.

Reading

The first foundation in the Intelligent Portfolio supports activities for the Teacher-Learner. Your Reading folder should contain software and hardware to access the Internet, selected libraries of your choice, and the World Wide Web.

Writing

The Writing folder should contain a word processor along with printing capability. Additional software, such as desktop publishing, is not recommended for this version of the Intelligent Portfolio. We do recommend that you concentrate your efforts on collecting materials, not how they are presented in their final form.

42 *Professional Portfolios for Teachers*

Collection Points	Reading	Writing

Thinking	Interacting	Demonstrating

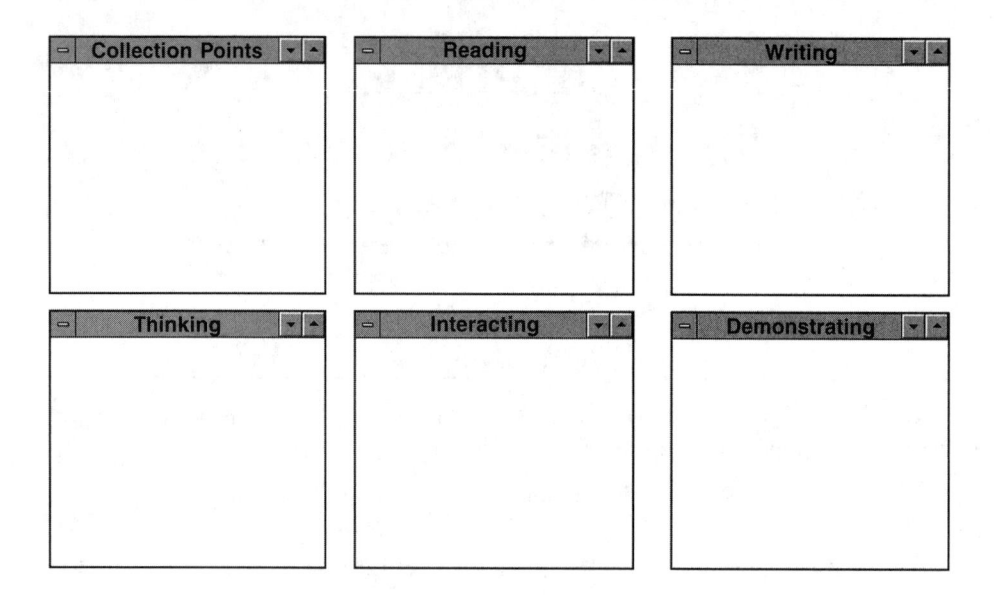

Thinking

Thinking is fostered by a host of tools for reflecting on the artifacts accumulated in the other portions of the Intelligent Portfolio. Using the software and hardware suggested in this folder, Teachers as Learners can gain a better definition of their own metacognitive skills.

Interacting

Teaching and learning are supported at this level by software that provides electronic mail, newsgroups, and Internet relay chat in addition to World Wide Web access. Perhaps the strongest use of computer technology in the Intelligent Portfolio will be in the component of Interacting—exploring one's discipline with others who share similar interests.

Demonstrating

Demonstration takes the form of preparing prototype classroom materials and developing class projects and presentations. The Teacher as Learner may present these materials in forums both inside and outside the classroom. This area of the Intelligent Portfolio will become the foundation for such presentations.

Ready for Step Two? Let's place some software and hardware into the folders...

Step Two:
Populating Portfolio Folders

With its emphasis on collecting, the Intelligent Portfolio for the Teacher as Learner consists of software that will support Reading, Writing, Thinking, Interacting, and Demonstrating artifacts emphasizing the teacher as a collector and knowledge builder. Foley will guide you through each of the portfolio folders suggesting the software packages and hardware components that make up the Intelligent Portfolio for the Teacher as Learner.

Reading Software

Network access along with some tried and true helper applications are required the primary features of the Reading foundation.

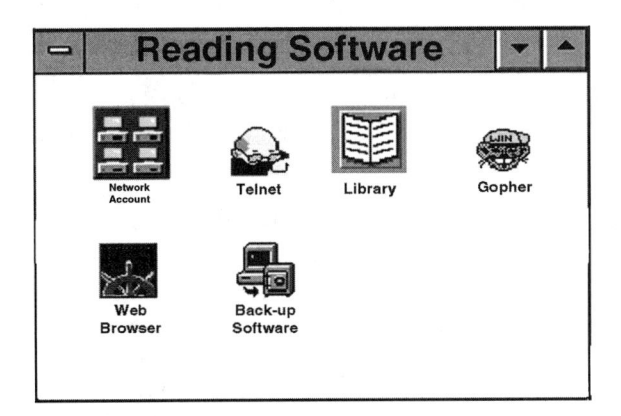

Add these packages to your Reading folder.

Network Account To add network capability to your Intelligent Portfolio, locate a service provider and apply for an account. America Online, Prodigy, and CompuServe are examples of such providers. Their costs range in the neighborhood of $20.00 per month for a specified number of connect-hours. Be careful not to exceed that limit unless you know in advance what the additional charges will be; some providers charge excessive fees to users exceeding these monthly ceilings.

You might wish to determine first if you are eligible for a free account. Many major universities and school districts provide such accounts to their teachers and students free of charge. In several states, intermediate units and school districts provide such accounts in addition to audiovisual materials, in-service training sessions, and programs for exceptional students. An increasing number of libraries, local governments, nonprofit organizations, and computer clubs also provide this service either free of charge or at minimal cost. If these complimentary sources are unavailable, use the Yellow Pages to locate a network provider, commonly referred to as an Internet Service Provider, or ISP. Closely scrutinize their costs to ensure you get the most access for your money at the times when you are most available for on-line work.

Telnet Communications Software The first of the actual software tools in your Reading folder is also one of the more popular software packages providing network access: Telnet. Telnet links a remote computer with other host computers on the network by emulating specific terminals. The remote computer services the user as though the connection were directly with the host machine. Log-ins using Telnet open the door to suites of powerful tools such as library card catalogs, databases, bulletin board systems, and other similar services. The software is easy to learn and simple to use and provides an excellent tool for Reading.

Library One of the most important options in the Reading folder will be on-line library access to electronic books and digital library files along with volumes of periodicals offered on CD-ROM. Electronic literature reviews require that educators learn on-line inquiry techniques. To obtain a library account, some association with a university library or a state-of-the-art public library is required. Registering for one of these accounts usually results in a special phone number, log-in user name, and password. Again, search for free access from public sources first before trying accounts which charge a fee.

Gopher Documentation Management This popular on-line documentation resource received its name from a well-known garden variety rodent: the Gopher. The Gopher system is a standard menu-based interface to information management systems and services and, like the tiny mammal, sets about locating text files and fetching them back to the user's "den." While its success in the text-based world is being rapidly overshadowed by the graphics-intensive World Wide Web, Gopher links are an abundant source of outstanding material for educators.

For example, at the top of most Gopher menus is a link to "All the Gophers in the World." Literally, information from thousands of Gopher sites in nearly every country of the globe is available, oftentimes in foreign languages. Teachers use the Gopher system to connect their students to high schools in Paris, France where students communicate with on-line "pen pals" in French, trading book reports, newspaper clippings, and general communications.

The Gopher system contains search engines, which make Gopher an excellent starting point for exploring subjects that can later expand to the graphics-based World Wide Web. A word of caution, however, goes along with the use of Gopher: Since so many sites are moving to the Web, locating current information may require some digging. Be sure to double-check the accuracy of any information obtained from these sources and the dates to make sure it is current.

Web Browser Software Virtual sojourns to tens of thousands of World Wide Web sites are possible. To make those visits a reality in the classroom, you'll need the latest World Wide Web browser software (such as Netscape). The Intelligent Portfolio must contain a Web browser that makes full use of the documents prepared using formatting, style, and color along with links to related documents which may contain images, sounds, and video files.

Back-up Software Select a back-up software package and use it at least weekly. Pick a day of the week and become devout in saving a complete copy of your hard drive medium. The Zip Drive, a high-memory disk drive, is recommended to store complete back-ups of all Collection Points. Backing up data files will be time well spent. The first time a hard drive goes bad, a directory is corrupted, or a file or group of files is inadvertently deleted, the effort expended to back up your system will pay off. Basic back-up software typically comes with the operating system of the computer. There are more elaborate packages available. For example, the Zip Drive comes with excellent back-up software. Regardless of which package or medium is used, Foley's recommendation is to use back-up software—and use it regularly.

Reading Hardware

To effect this suite of software capabilities, the Intelligent Portfolio requires a computer system with state-of-the-art technology. We will describe and recommend the minimum requirements for the processor, modem, and disk storage configurations of your Teacher as Learner Intelligent Portfolio.

Personal Computer. We recommend that you use a Laptop Computer for your Intelligent Portfolio. Desktop systems with similar capabilities are equal to the task, but portability and convenience make the laptop preferable. The computer you choose can be either Apple-compatible or Windows-compatible. Here are the specifications for each type:

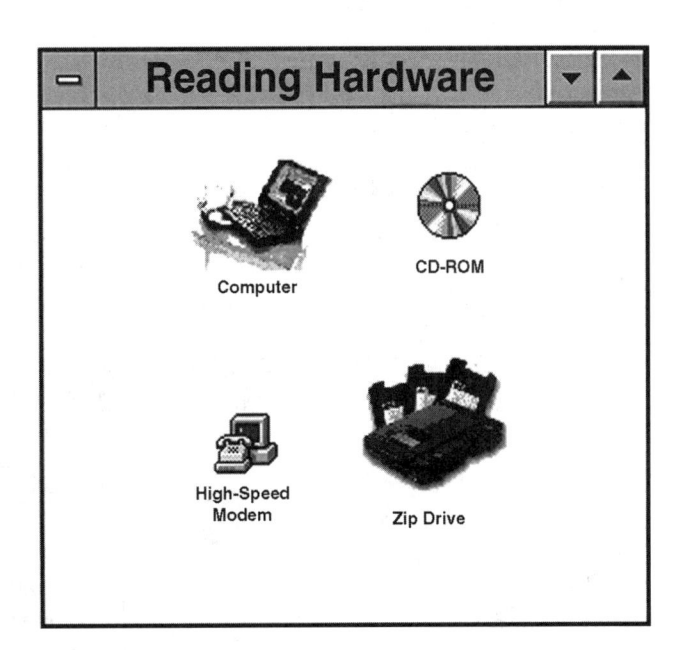

Reading Hardware

Here's what you've been waiting for...the Hardware Requirements of the Intelligent Portfolio!

- Computer
- CD-ROM
- High-Speed Modem
- Zip Drive

Apple-Compatible Systems. Macintosh with a 68060 microprocessor or better; at least 16 megabytes of random access memory (RAM) (32 megabyte recommended); a 1 gigabyte hard drive (2 gigabyte drive recommended); and the Macintosh Operating System 7.5 (Mac 8.0 OS recommended).

Windows-Compatible Systems. A personal computer (PC) with a Pentium microprocessor; at least 16 megabytes of random access memory (32 megabyte recommended); a 1 gigabyte hard drive (2 gigabyte drive recommended); and the Windows 95 (Windows 98 recommended) Operating System.

CD-ROM Player. A unique aspect of the Intelligent Portfolio will be its use of CD-ROM technology not only as an input medium for the thousands of applications that are being distributed via this medium, but also as the primary (and ultimate) storage target for all the artifacts to be accumulated in your Collection Points. Since many artifacts include video, image, and sound files in addition to large text files, the fastest-speed CD-ROM available is recommended.

High-Speed Modem You'll need a high-speed modem. Try to get the fastest modem affordable and compatible with your network if you will be accessing most resources from a telephone connection rather than a network connection.

Zip Drive Storage A Zip drive is a high-capacity storage device that operates like a traditional floppy disk drive. Physically, the Zip and floppy drives are approximately the same size; however, they are technically very different. The 3.5 inch floppy can store 1.4 megabytes of data, while the Zip disk can hold over 100 megabytes of data. The Zip has 70 times the storage capacity, while occupying only little more than twice the space. Speed is also a consideration. A Zip drive transfers data at a much higher rate than its floppy-drive counterpart, making back-ups much more palatable for the conscientious user.

A Final Note about Hardware Keep in mind that the hardware we just recommended will serve you well for this phase of the Teacher as Learner Intelligent Portfolio. However, newer more capable systems will undoubtedly be introduced throughout the period in which your portfolio will be in use. (We predict that newer technology will have been introduced while this book was in publication.) Keep abreast of these changes and take full advantage of the increased capabilities for your Intelligent Portfolio.

Writing Software

A capable word processor includes a growing number of helper applications such as a spelling checker, thesaurus, table of contents writer, template (boilerplate) forms maker, hyphenator, auto correction, word count and grade level calculator, and grammar checker.

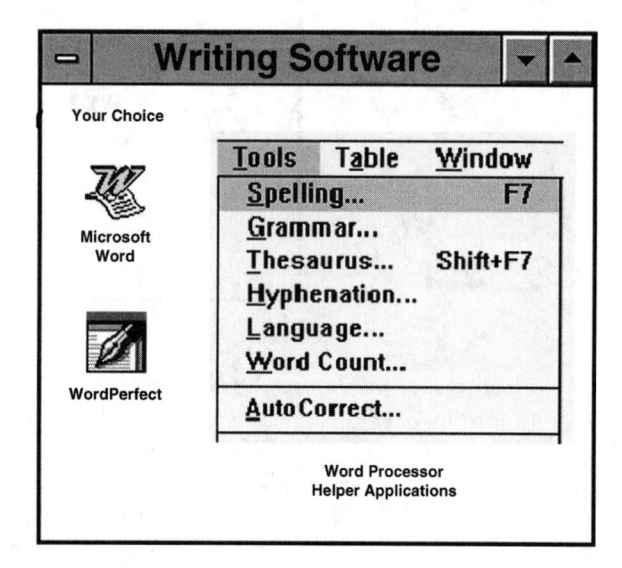

Word Processors In addition to basic text entry and editing, a capable word processor provides several easy-to-use helper applications.

- A word-count feature automatically and nearly instantly calculates the number of pages, words, characters, paragraphs, and lines within a document.
- Grammar checkers not only identify common grammatical errors, but also improve writing style by suggesting, for example, how to make writing more active.
- Spell checkers and an on-line thesaurus, which have been features of word processors for several years, are invaluable when composing classroom materials, preparing class projects and papers, and preparing draft lesson plans.
- Table of Contents (TOC) writers are relatively new and are not a standard feature in all word processors, but are a useful organizational tool. By the time the Teacher as Learner Intelligent Portfolio is completed, the amount of materials stored will be voluminous. A TOC writer with an index feature can assist in cataloging this material.
- Templates provide a standardized format for new documents. Think how many times you will be preparing papers for class, evaluating performances, and composing mock journal articles. A template significantly reduces the amount of for-

matting work by offering a method of creating the document format once and using it for all subsequent papers containing similar content.

- Hyphenators are not nearly as important; however, to conserve paper and to present a professional image, they are handy features and most word processors provide them.

- Finally, automatic corrections to commonly misspelled and mistyped words is a definite plus for word processors.

Writing Hardware

You'll need a good printer for your Intelligent Portfolio. We recommend either an inkjet or laser printer. The selection of which printer is most appropriate will depend more on cost than capability, since both printers produce acceptable hard copies.

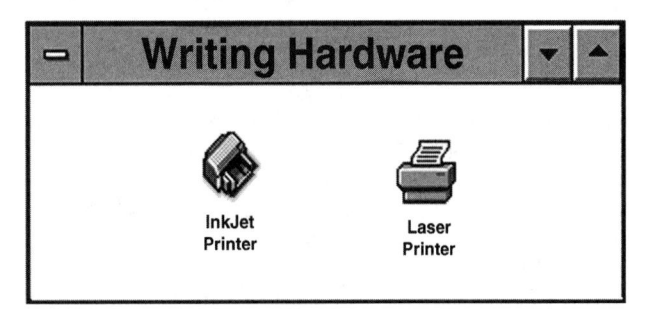

Inkjet Printer   The inkjet printer, because of its quality and low price, is recommended for the Teacher-Learner version of the Intelligent Portfolio. It delivers quality output, albeit more slowly than its laser cousin.

Laser Printer   If you can afford the more expensive laser printer, get one. The print is higher quality and it prints much faster. It also does a better job printing graphic images and multiple fonts.

Thinking Software

World Wide Web Helper Applications   Helper Applications enhance the exploration of the Internet and support new thinking in a technology-rich environment.

A robust suite of software applications is available to support your Thinking demands. The Intelligent Portfolio provides tools to explore the World Wide Web, generate new ideas, analyze data, and organize your artifacts.

Image Viewers, Sound Players, and Movie Players   Viewers and players assist in downloading and capturing files that will add to a Teacher-Learner's cache of future classroom resource materials. Maps, charts and graphs, instructional materials, lesson plans, and news videos—all prepared by professional educators—are readily captured in the expanding storage of your Intelligent Portfolio. Even personalized audio greetings from public officials can be found using these state-of-the-art tools.

Compression and decompression tools   (Sometimes called "zip" and "unzip") these tools are needed to handle some of the largest files available in compacted formats designed to facilitate speed in downloading and save space on the host system.

"Thinking about Thinking" Here are some excellent packages to support the Teacher as Learner.

Thinking Software

- Helper Applications
- Image Viewer
- Sound Player
- Movie Player
- Compression Tools
- Database
- Spreadsheet
- Idea Generator
- Statistics
- Organizer

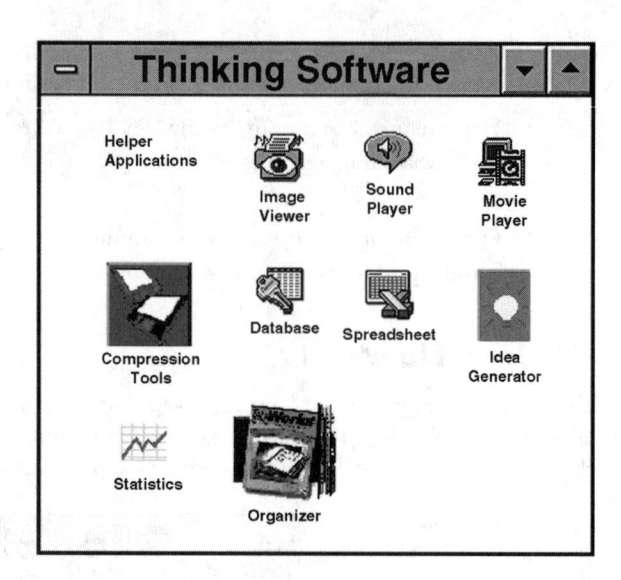

Database management software Database packages address the problem of managing the many phone numbers, personal and professional contacts, bibliographic references, and World Wide Web sites that will accumulate in the Intelligent Portfolio. Databases foster thinking by organizing information logically and aiding in the retrieval of that information.

Spreadsheet Software Spreadsheets tabularize numeric information, allowing the Intelligent Portfolio to electronically project "what if" scenarios based on data accumulated by the Teacher as Learner.

Idea Generator Software This software is a creative concept development tool. It integrates easy-to-use diagramming principles with powerful outlining capabilities to create the foundations for new thinking. Using this tool, the Teacher-Learner expresses ideas visually while simultaneously creating an organized outline. Ideas are captured quickly. Diagrams are updated automatically.

Statistics Packages Statistical software once provided little more than indicative data such as mean, median, mode, and standard deviations. Today's packages feature options such as a statistics coach, on-line help, a tutorial and on-line tour, glossary, and show-me screen. Tutorials provide examples that guide users through the program quickly. Tutorials run independently from start to finish or from within a procedure for a more in-depth look at specific operations. Context-sensitive help offers short cuts for operations, definitions, and rules of thumb for interpreting a particular statistic. A statistical glossary permits the user to highlight an object, press the mouse button for a definition of statistical terms, and display a graph of the data being examined.

Organizer Software Organizer tools make it easy to arrange everything on a hard drive with colorful, user-friendly graphics. Organizer tools transform desktop icons into a tabbed, three-ring notebook that systematically finds documents electronically by turning tabs and pages. Create as many notebooks as needed for your Intelligent Portfolio. There are no commands to remember, no directories to consider. Add or delete tabs and pages with a click of the mouse. Computer files are easy to see, easy to find, and very easy to use. Each notebook has a table of contents and an alphabetical index that lists everything in that notebook. The text search feature locates documents by name, date, location, or even specific text contained in the document.

Thinking Hardware

The collection of images, sound files, and video clips required in the Thinking folder will demand significant hard disk storage.

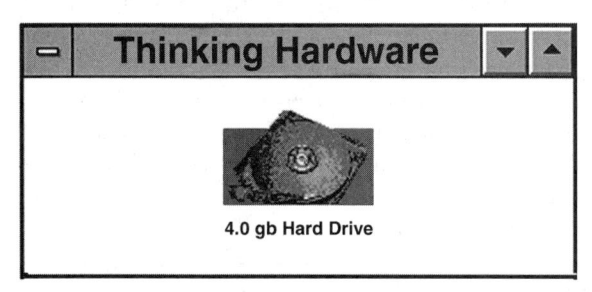

Hard Drive   At this point in the development of the portfolio, we recommend that the size of the hard drive be increased to 4 gigabytes to adequately handle both the back-up and mass storage requirements of the Intelligent Portfolio.

Interacting Software

Interacting means "communicating." The list of software packages to assist the Teacher as Learner is short but very important to the utility of the portfolio. Electronic mail, newsgroups, and Internet chat provide valuable connections to locations that foster interaction among peers and colleagues.

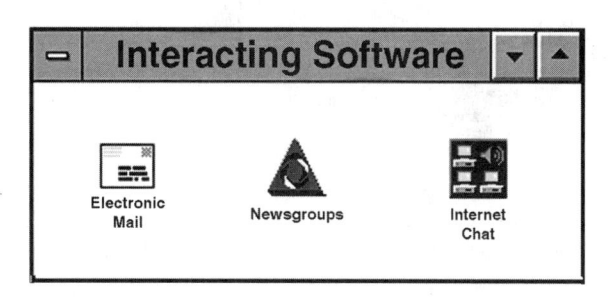

Electronic Mail   For the Teacher as Learner, the use of electronic mail (email) fosters communication with scores of educators at various levels of expertise. Email manages a list of fellow educators representing groups of common interest such as the psychology of learning or the teaching of science, math, or languages. Electronic mail tracks colleagues who share ideas, brainstorm new concepts, and assess learning objectives while they are still in the design phase. Network access, combined with email, opens doors for personal contacts in national and international arenas.

Newsgroups Software   Newsgroups circumvent some of the inconveniences of email (such as handling the sheer volume of mail that is generated and managing email address lists). A newsreader becomes part of the Intelligent Portfolio to provide access to literally thousands of specifically targeted interest groups. For example, a newsgroup focusing on social studies brings together educators interested in the general aspects of lesson planning, classroom presentations, and assessment. Newsgroups include a more focused scope of interested parties than email. Most often you will be sharing ideas with teachers, students, and renowned educators from around the world.

Internet Relay Chat For a more personalized discussion, **Internet Relay Chat (IRC)** provides a forum for communicating across vast distances with instant communication for the exchange of ideas and comments. IRC is analogous to a citizens band radio—the CB that nearly every trucker possesses as standard equipment on the open road. As with the CB, IRC opens channels of communications where interested parties choose to enter and leave at their discretion. Anyone can initiate a channel and invite or restrict membership to those sharing common interests. For the Teacher as Learner, IRC channels are relatively easy to locate—selecting channels worth your time and effort may prove somewhat more difficult. Several instructors at universities around the country use IRC to hold open forums with students physically separated from the classroom.

Interacting Hardware

Little additional hardware is needed to support the Interacting foundation. A computer with sufficient memory and disk storage to support Reading, for example, will also provide the necessary elements for this folder.

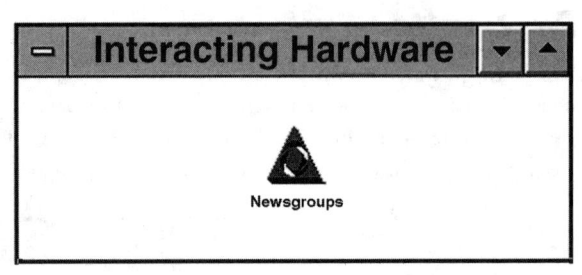

Not much new hardware is needed for Interacting.

Interacting Hardware

Newsgroups

The only additional requirements relate more to the following capabilities of the selected network account:

1. What is the size of the email account offered by your service provider? Insist on an account that provides at least 5 megabytes of storage on the host system as a minimum to ensure you can download messages containing large text files and graphics.

2. How many newsgroups does your service provider offer? Be selective in the specific news services as well—ensure that you can select from among educational, scientific, and content area groups as well as recreational and entertainment groups.

3. Does the service provider restrict access to Internet Relay Chat? This is sometimes the case when providers are forced to deal with the high overhead associated with users who log into channels and remain there for hours at a time.

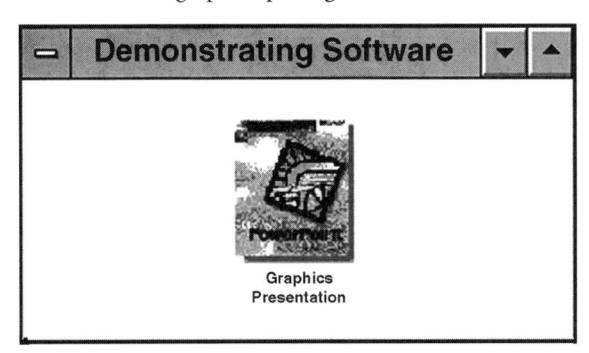

Demonstrating Software

For the Teacher as Learner, the demands for Demonstrating can be readily satisfied with a state-of-the-art graphics package.

One software package will be added for the Demonstrating Folder.

Graphics Presentation Software   A graphics presentation package enables you to combine materials containing images, sounds, text, and even video into a single multimedia-based presentation. Most graphics software supports a comprehensive list of development tools, including: expert slide construction and editing, a wide choice of template backgrounds, ease of formatting to include bullet and sub-bullets as well as automatic numbering, and font choices including style, size, and location on the slide. An easy-to-use viewer delivers classroom slides, transparencies, and printed handbooks.

Demonstrating Hardware

Color printing capabilities add a professional touch to the Demonstrating folder of the Intelligent Portfolio.

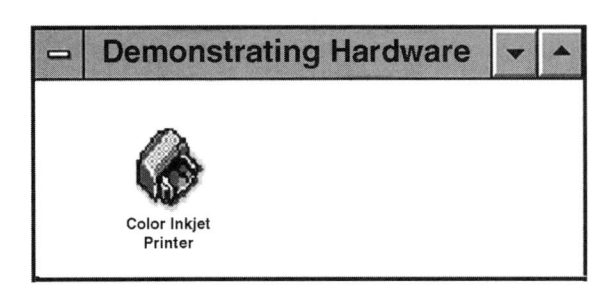

Let's add some color to your Portfolio...

Color Inkjet Printer   An inkjet printer with color capability is recommended to meet the demands of the Demonstrating folder. For the Teacher as Learner, graphics presentation software produces materials that are best displayed in color: transparencies and handouts may cost a little more to produce in color than in black and white, but they present a professional appearance. These larger color files will also increase the demand on your hard disk space. However, the 4 gigabyte hard drive already recommended will more than cover these demands.

Step Three: Organizing Folders and Collection Points

Step Three: Organize Your Artifacts into one of 10 Collection Points.

Now that you have created and populated the folders for the five Foundations, it's time to set up Collection Points to hold you artifacts. The quantity and content of artifacts are inherently different for the Teacher as Learner, Teacher as Expert, and Teacher as Scholar. The recommended proportions for each will be different as well. The Teacher as Learner can expect to store artifacts in approximately the proportions shown in Figure 6-2.

Over 50 percent of the Intelligent Portfolio artifacts for the Teacher as Learner will be for the accumulation of resources—the **Collecting Folder.** Collecting materials is paramount, and retrieving that information at a later date will be similarly critical. The **Working Folder** represents 25 percent of the Intelligent Portfolio for the Teacher as Learner. Its set of Collection Points will help the Teacher-Learner develop initial skills as a classroom teacher. While **Showcase Folder** artifacts comprise less than 25 percent of the overall target for this version of the Intelligent Portfolio. The Teacher as Learner is encouraged to exhibit readiness for teaching through periodic presentations of classroom-ready material.

Evidence of Learning for the Teacher as Learner

25% — Presentations / Best Papers / Professional Documents

25% — Learning Projects / Self-Assessment / Applications and Lessons

50% — Content Area Materials / Classroom Resources / Library Resources / Web Sites/Bookmarks

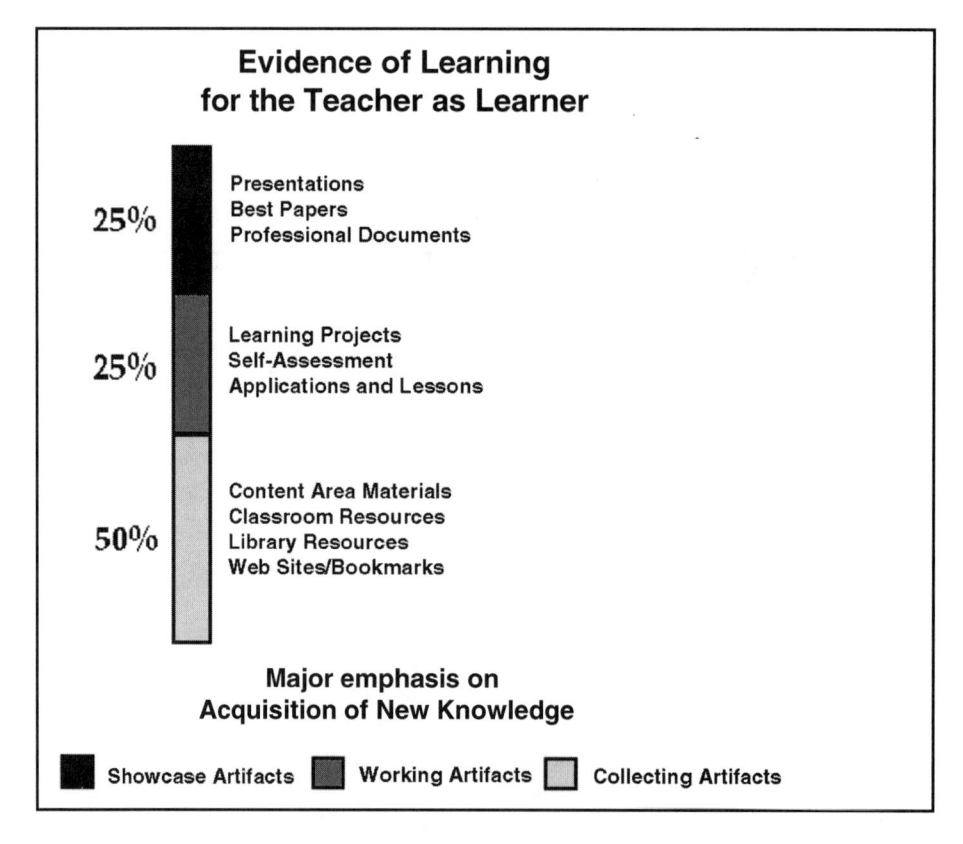

Major emphasis on Acquisition of New Knowledge

■ Showcase Artifacts ■ Working Artifacts ■ Collecting Artifacts

Figure 6-2. *This is what you'll be storing in your Intelligent Portfolio.*

Collecting Folder

The focus for the Teacher as Learner is on acquiring knowledge and skills. Four Collection Points will be electronically created on your computer to assist in this task: Content Area Materials, Classroom Resources, Library Resources, and World Wide Web Sites. By placing all your collecting artifacts in these four Collection Points, the task of locating resources later on is made significantly easier.

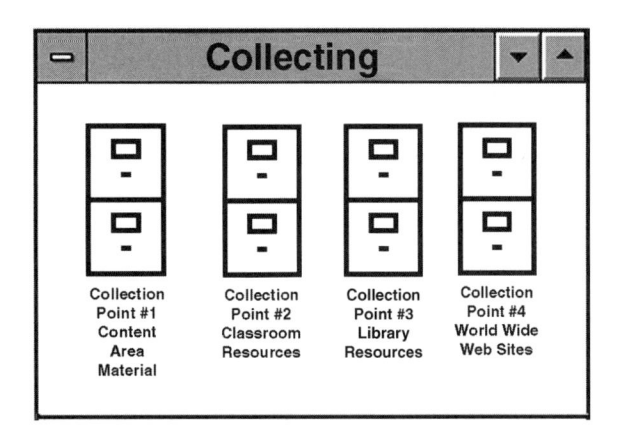

Create Four Collecting Collection Points. They can be Folders or Directories.

Collecting

Collection Point #1 Content Area Material

Collection Point #2 Classroom Resources

Collection Point #3 Library Resources

Collection Point #4 World Wide Web Sites

Collection Point #1: Content Area Material The majority of artifacts for the Teacher as Learner take the form of future classroom material gathered from various sources. Electronically prepared course notes; word processing documents used to prepare in-class assignments; graphic presentation handouts, transparencies, and graphic files supplied by instructors; and on-line projects produced in methods classes are only a few examples.

Collection Point #2: Classroom Resources Instructors and peers become prolific sources of material as you build the knowledge base supporting your professional development. It is not uncommon to accumulate shelves and shelves of notebooks filled with papers. Lesson plans developed after group explorations of Best Practices in teaching could be downloaded to this Collection Point, for example. *Alone,* you would never be able to accumulate this amount of material in a lifetime of classes. *Cooperatively,* a four-year undergraduate program or a two-year master's program will easily result in a wealth of material that can be optically scanned into electronic media.

Collection Point #3: Library Resources With the introduction of so many electronic books, journals, and CD-ROM-based material, gathering resources from the library is easy. Some of these newest media offer high-resolution graphics, sounds, text scanning, and downloading features in addition to sharing access to resources from around the world. Logging into one library is often a steppingstone to an unlimited array of on-line library sources. Access to libraries is typically accomplished via Telnet software already discussed in the Reading Software folder.

Collection Point #4: World Wide Web Sites A personalized list of Web sites is the hallmark of today's technology-oriented teacher. Locating educational sites dealing with particular subject matter areas has been a tedious and catch-as-catch-can process. With the advent of Web-based search engines, this daunting task is now easier.

We have a favorite analogy to share regarding Web-based research. One of the authors of this book recently moved to Pittsburgh, Pennsylvania. Arriving only a few days before starting a new position in a new city, one of his first tasks was to have phones installed at his new home. The telephone installer arrived late one afternoon and, after working for some 20 minutes, announced that the installation was complete, and the phones were in good working order. The Pittsburgh phone book, however, was not his responsibility. It would be mailed directly from the home office in 7–10 days. A new phone—with some 2.6 million subscribers within a 20-mile radius—but no phone book!

Web explorers experience a similar set of circumstances. Conservative estimates find 200–300 new Web home pages every few days. Building a personal "phonebook" of valuable sites begins with the first access of the Internet. Surfing the Web should be performed with a mouse in one hand and a notepad in the other. Collection Point #4 provides a place to store the Uniform Resource Locator (URL) addresses; it needs constant maintenance as new and better locations are found and outdated pages are deleted from the Internet.

Working Folder

As you create your own artifacts, they will be placed in *Working* Folders. For the Teacher as Learner, four Collection Points are provided as knowledge is applied and new skills acquired. They include: Making Connections, Reflections on Learning, Learning Projects, and Applications and Lessons. Artifacts taken from Collecting Folders are developed here in the Working Folder as new knowledge is created.

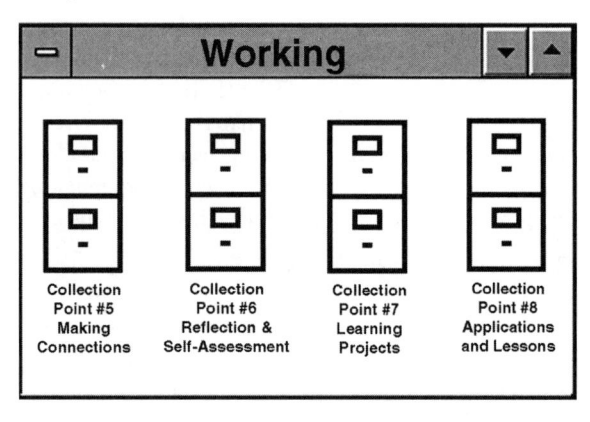

The next 4 Collection Points will store Your Ideas, Reflections, Projects and Lessons. They will be Your Thinking Areas.

Working

Collection Point #5 Making Connections

Collection Point #6 Reflection & Self-Assessment

Collection Point #7 Learning Projects

Collection Point #8 Applications and Lessons

Collection Point #5: Making Connections This collection point records your current thinking about new learning experiences and information. It offers a place to toss around ideas, fine-tune thinking, change and add ideas, or just imagine, problem solve, and brainstorm. Artifacts amassed in previous Collection Points are moved electronically into the Working area. Content resources, combined with library resources and journal articles, become the ingredients of new lessons. Learning requires that we synthesize new knowledge and prior knowledge.

Collection Point #6: Reflection and Self-Assessment An ongoing process of professional development calls for periodic self-assessment. This Collection Point will be used to house efforts at evaluating your own progress toward specific career goals. Artifacts in Collection Point #6 include "evidence" of learning or thinking from an initial awareness of ideas and topics affecting the classroom to a deeper understanding of the impact those ideas have on how we teach and how the student learns.

Collection Point #7: Learning Projects Developing classroom materials occurs in this Collection Point. Electronic bulletin boards, computerized units of study, programmed classroom activities, on-line student documents, and graphic overhead transparencies are a few of the specific artifacts created and shared by the Teacher as Learner. New materials will be tested in the safety of undergraduate methods courses. While under development, this new material will be kept in this Collection Point where it can be evaluated.

Collection Point #8: Applications and Lessons This Collection Point will house classroom-ready materials that have passed the scrutiny of a formal assessment. An integrated thematic unit on "Dinosaurs" would be an example of an artifact stored in this folder. The unit may combine images of the terrible lizards taken from the World Wide Web, maps of fossil locations captured during a geography lesson, and a video clip taken from an old movie about the creatures.

Showcase Folder

Your best electronic artifacts, assessed and validated, are stored in one of two Collection Points of the Showcase Folder. Your best automated lessons, learning projects, and classroom applications are housed in Presentations and Papers. Professional Documents holds scanned images of your teacher certification credentials, national teacher examination scores, and personal letters of reference.

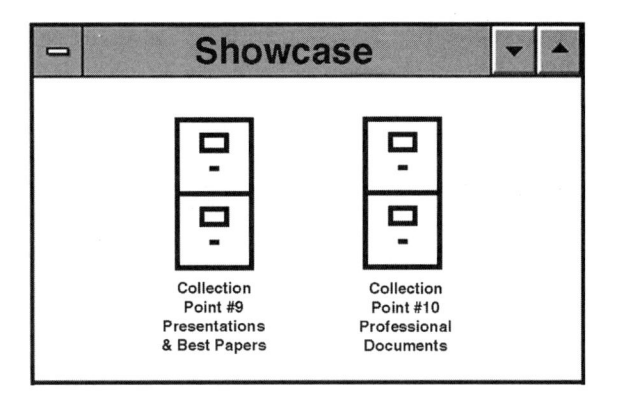

Collection Point #9: Presentations and Best Papers All validated materials not specifically destined for the classroom are stored in this Collection Point. Best Papers include the electronic text of manuscripts submitted for consideration. Draft reports, papers, and future publications are also artifacts of this Collection Point. Collection Point #9 houses numerous artifacts as diverse documents are combined, consolidated, and then trimmed to present new concepts.

Collection Point #10: Professional Documents The final Collection Point will house documents such as personal resumes, student teaching evaluations, and classroom clearance requests. We recommend that you review this Collection Point each semester. It should be updated regularly with evidence of accomplishments.

We have created all the Collection Points in three folders...

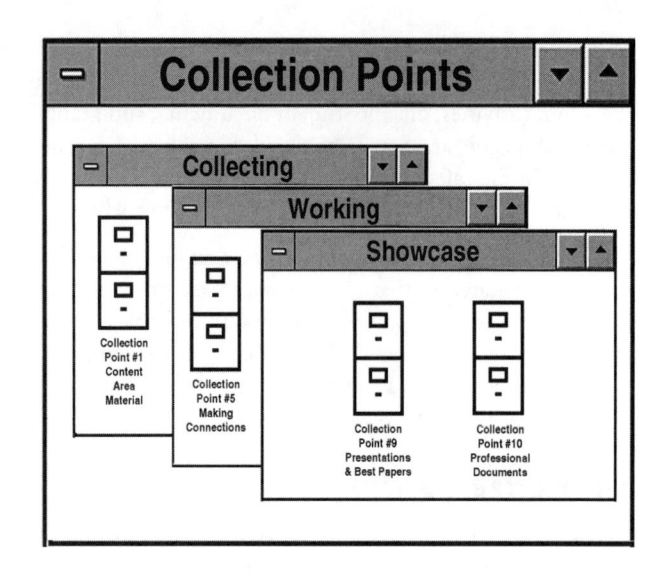

Collection Points

Collecting
- Collection Point #1 Content Area Material

Working
- Collection Point #5 Making Connections

Showcase
- Collection Point #9 Presentations & Best Papers
- Collection Point #10 Professional Documents

Conclusion

The Intelligent Portfolio is the electronic counterpart of the Smart Portfolio; it is recommended for the Teacher as Learner who acknowledges the advantages and potential of technology. It can also share certain Collection Points of the Smart Portfolio. Some Collection Points can be maintained electronically while others are captured manually. The final configuration of the portfolio is up to you.

Foley Tips

This tour of the Intelligent Portfolio for the Teacher as Learner will conclude with a few timely tips from Foley.

1. **Collecting is the focus of the Intelligent Portfolio for the Teacher as Learner.** Do not clutter your computer with software or hardware that does not contribute directly to the collection of artifacts. For example, desktop publishing, while an excellent tool for the preparation of papers and personal publications, is superfluous for the Teacher as Learner. Word processors are more than capable for now; desktop publishing will appear in later versions of the Intelligent Portfolio.

    Here are a few simple Tips for the Teacher as Learner Intelligent Portfolio.

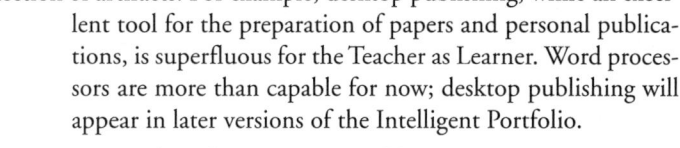

2. **Visit each Collection Point weekly.** As you progress through a pre-service program, revisit the artifacts collected, culling out the extraneous materials before becoming overwhelmed by data rather than information.

3. **Solicit opinions about your artifacts.** Periodically seek the opinions of your instructor as well as your class peers regarding the artifacts being collected. A "cooperate and graduate" attitude will help ensure excellence and thoughtful development of your personal teaching skills.

4. **Continue to upgrade the Intelligent Portfolio.** Stay alert to the latest versions of operating systems, software, and hard-

ware. Remember that the Intelligent Portfolio is a tool for a lifetime of professional development.

5. **Continue to explore.** Don't limit the search for electronic artifacts. Search all avenues of resources in pursuit of the best materials.

6. **Seek artifacts on the World Wide Web.** The future is on the Internet. Items captured on-line via the Web will be technically easier to store and incorporate into the Intelligent Portfolio. You will not find it difficult to identify content area material on the Internet. The challenge is to select only the most pedagogically sound materials.

7. **Look ahead to the Intelligent Portfolio for the Teacher as Expert.** Ensure that the migration to the next version of the Intelligent Portfolio is not hampered by limitations to hardware or software. The best way to do that is to prepare now by understanding how the Intelligent Portfolio will change once your focus shifts from student to teacher in the classroom.

8. **Begin the migration to the Teacher as Expert Intelligent Portfolio immediately following your student teaching.** Make that migration gradual. There will be a tendency to believe that the further "up" the continuum of portfolios, the "better" the portfolio—that the Teacher as Scholar portfolio is the ultimate goal. That is simply not true. Migration to another form of portfolio should occur only when additional capabilities are required and the focus of the portfolio has evolved.

9. **Take inventory of your Intelligent Portfolio usage.** The Intelligent Portfolio relies on the premise that professional development is a lifelong process which integrates reading, writing, interacting, thinking, and demonstrating in proper measure. Each element of the Intelligent Portfolio should be used periodically. Too much emphasis in any one area could indicate a neglect of other important factors of your professional development.

10. **Add Collection Points to your Intelligent Portfolio.** Identify other repositories for your artifacts to supplement the basic Collection Points presented in this chapter. Personalize the Intelligent Portfolio by creating new Collection Points according to your needs. For example, you may wish to include a Collection Point for particular subject matter areas, such as science, language, and social studies. Since these are all Classroom Resources (Collection Point #2), they should be added to the Collecting Folder.

See you when you are ready to move to the Teacher as Expert version of the Intelligent Portfolio.

CHAPTER 7

Portfolios in Transition: The Teacher as Learner Perspective

The Smart and Intelligent Portfolios were initially conceived to address the development of undergraduate and graduate students seeking professional certification as classroom teachers. Many portfolio versions appear in the literature, but none come close to capturing the breadth of features needed by career educators. Even our own earlier versions looked very different from the final implementation. The evolution from the initial design of the Smart and Intelligent Portfolio to a professional development model, has been the result of prototype studies, countless evaluations, and numerous re-designs to arrive at the version you see in these chapters.

Two volunteers agreed to participate in a prototype study on portfolios and the Teacher-Learner. This chapter relates the efforts of those students who took upon themselves the additional challenges of first developing a Smart Portfolio and then making it electronically "intelligent." They participated in an initial training tutorial which introduced them to the concepts of the Smart and Intelligent Portfolio including the basic principles of artifacts, folders, and collection points. Both James and Jason (not their real names) were already computer literate, although they were still novices at keeping portfolios.

During the first few weeks of the semester, both students worked to establish the Collection Points that would hold their artifacts. As each student was presented with materials from his course instructor, he would categorize the item as Collecting, Working, or Showcase and transfer that artifact, at least temporarily, to its respective envelope. As their Smart Portfolio began to take form sometime during the fourth or fifth week of the semester, James and Jason met again with the authors, this time to receive their introduction to the concepts of the Intelligent Portfolio.

Ownership of a personal computer was one of the original criteria for admission into the prototype study. Each student used his own system as the Intelligent Portfolio platform. James owned a Macintosh PowerMac 6100 with 16 megabytes of memory and a 1 gigabyte hard drive. Jason preferred the PC-compatible Dell 466/L with 8 megabytes of memory and a 500 megabyte hard drive. Both students had internal modems to connect to their University-provided email account which kept them in touch with each other and the authors.

They were taught how to use two computer systems located in a campus computer laboratory and configured with the recommended software, hardware, and Collection Points. James and Jason were encouraged to keep the systems as similar as possible to their own machines. The lab computers enabled James and Jason to present the Intelligent Portfolio to other students in the class. After students received a formal critique of their portfolio presentation using the poster format of the Smart Portfolio, James and Jason were given additional class time to present the results of their efforts with the Intelligent Portfolio.

The following paragraphs share the research surrounding the development, evolution, and implementation of the Smart Portfolio and Intelligent Portfolio as a professional development tools for Teacher as Learner. Keep in mind that this prototype study served to evolve the concepts of the Smart and Intelligent Portfolio and does not contain all of the elements which comprise the final implementation.

The Results of James's Efforts

From the outset, James had a clear picture of how his portfolio would look. His enthusiasm and desire to experiment remained unbridled for most of the semester, as we continued to gather important lessons which culminated in the final versions of both portfolios. At the conclusion of the semester, James's Smart Portfolio contained the following artifacts depicted below.

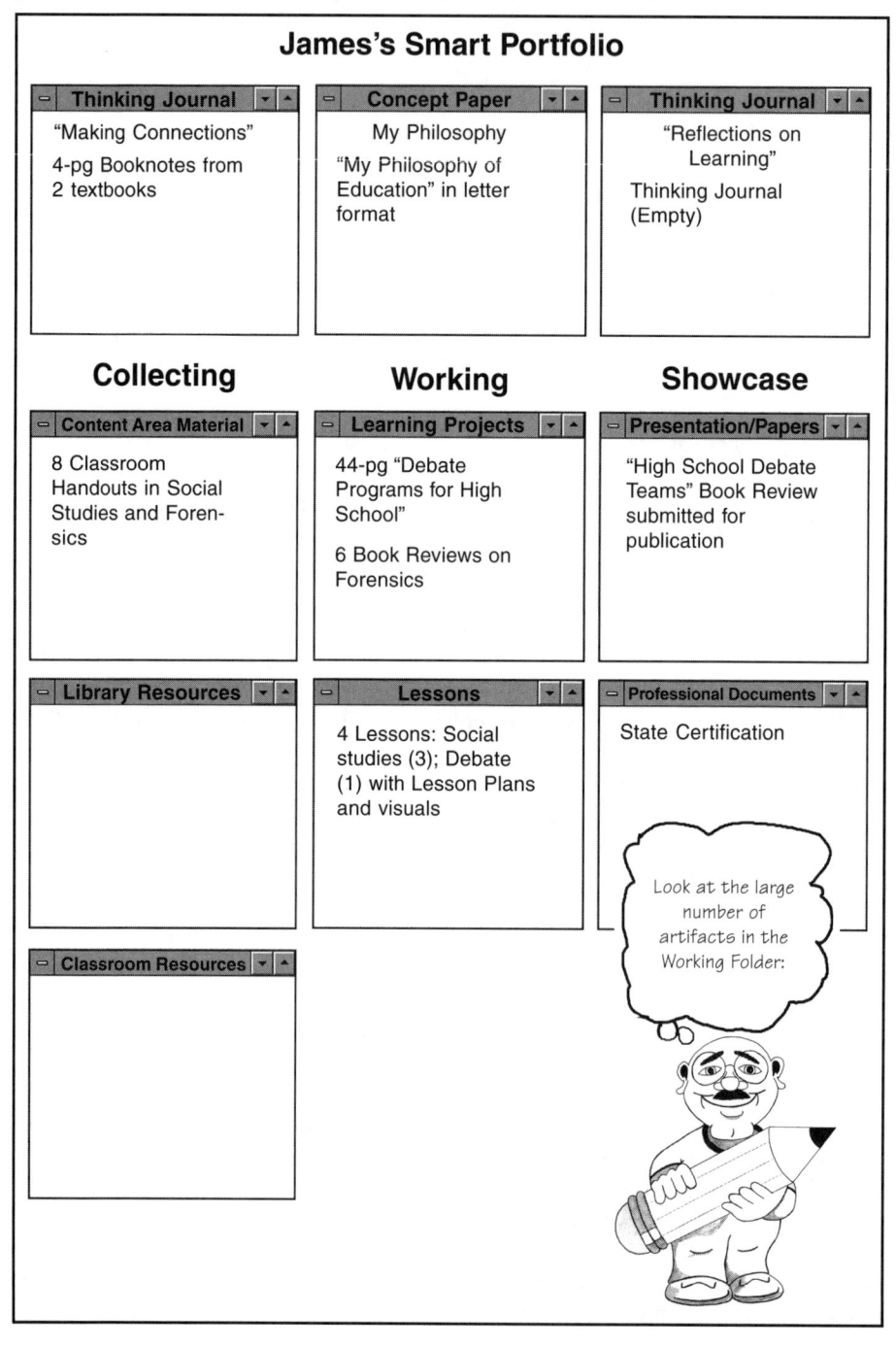

James's Smart Portfolio

Thinking Journal
"Making Connections"
4-pg Booknotes from 2 textbooks

Concept Paper
My Philosophy
"My Philosophy of Education" in letter format

Thinking Journal
"Reflections on Learning"
Thinking Journal (Empty)

Collecting | Working | Showcase

Content Area Material
8 Classroom Handouts in Social Studies and Forensics

Learning Projects
44-pg "Debate Programs for High School"
6 Book Reviews on Forensics

Presentation/Papers
"High School Debate Teams" Book Review submitted for publication

Library Resources

Lessons
4 Lessons: Social studies (3); Debate (1) with Lesson Plans and visuals

Professional Documents
State Certification

Look at the large number of artifacts in the Working Folder:

Classroom Resources

The Smart Portfolio

James based his Smart Portfolio on the assumption that its primary purpose was to accumulate vast amounts of work and that assessing the value of the portfolio in light of professional development for the Teacher as Learner must necessarily be based on the weight and volume of artifacts collected. James did an excellent job of locating and gathering artifacts which he placed judiciously in the correct Collection Points. He recognized the need to add a Collection Point for professional documents in which he stored such items as requests for background investigations and security checks required by the state. This Collection Point was added to the Smart and Intelligent Portfolios.

But James did not spend enough time establishing a firm foundation for teaching. He moved too quickly beyond Collecting, focusing instead on the Working and Showcase aspects of the portfolio. As a result, he gathered artifacts more appropriate for a classroom teacher than the Teacher as Learner.

The Intelligent Portfolio

James did a very credible job identifying the most useful suite of software packages, making effective use of the computer to store his artifacts, and recommending several software packages and hardware additions that would take the Intelligent Portfolio to a new level. Let's examine closely his first efforts with the Intelligent Portfolio.

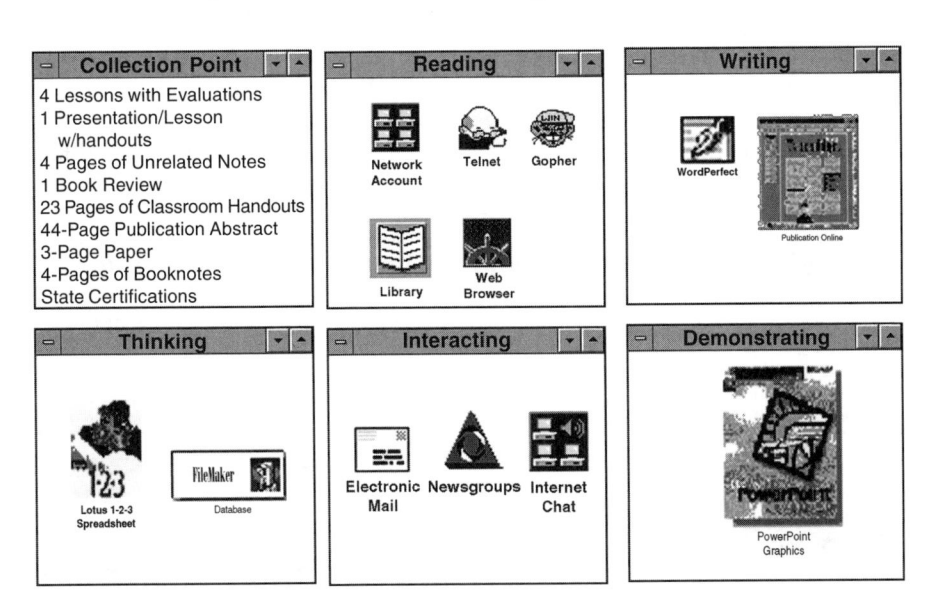

Collection Point	Reading	Writing
4 Lessons with Evaluations 1 Presentation/Lesson w/handouts 4 Pages of Unrelated Notes 1 Book Review 23 Pages of Classroom Handouts 44-Page Publication Abstract 3-Page Paper 4-Pages of Booknotes State Certifications	Network Account, Telnet, Gopher Library, Web Browser	WordPerfect Publication Online

Thinking	Interacting	Demonstrating
Lotus 1-2-3 Spreadsheet, FileMaker Database	Electronic Mail, Newsgroups, Internet Chat	PowerPoint Graphics

The artifacts in James's prototype Intelligent Portfolio were primarily copies of the products he had collected in his Smart Portfolio. He did add several original items captured directly from the Internet, mostly graphic images and lesson plan documents. Even so, James often expressed frustration when trying to locate articles he knew he had collected but he forgot which disk or folder contained the documents. He ignored one of the earliest lessons regarding portfolios: **storing information must support its subsequent retrieval.**

It was interesting to note that his own self-assessments continually referenced artifacts as "stuff" and work as "data" as though to discount electronic artifacts as a conglomeration of files rather than resources for thinking and learning.

James neglected our initial counsel to create separate Collection Points, relying instead on a single gathering location for all his Collecting, Working, and Showcase artifacts. Coincidentally, the original framework of the Intelligent Portfolio also called for a single Collection Point, believing that one location would be more easily indexed and searched. The disadvantages of this original viewpoint became vividly apparent throughout this prototype effort.

At the conclusion of the semester, James provided an outstanding presentation of the value and shortcomings of the Intelligent Portfolio. During his briefing to the other students, he applauded the use of standardized software and hardware as a means of sharing ideas. James recommended the addition of three network-related capabilities: Newsgroups, Internet Relay Chat, and the Gopher documentation management system. Each of his suggestions was ultimately accepted by the authors and incorporated into the final version of the Intelligent Portfolio.

James also was highly critical of certain aspects of the Intelligent Portfolio, most notably the lack of organizational software to better manage his artifacts. As a result, James opted to place all artifacts in a single Collection Point which, as already discussed, made it difficult for him to retrieve single items. It was interesting to note that Jason solved this problem with specialized organizer software. But, his solution was not available to James because their computer systems were incompatible.

Portfolio Assessment

The evaluation of James's portfolios was based on accumulated artifacts, presentation format, and evidence of reflective thinking. He was awarded an Overall Evaluation of **Excellent** for his efforts with the Smart Portfolio; his implementation of the Intelligent Portfolio earned him a **Satisfactory**. Specific assessments in each of the major areas of the portfolios were awarded as follows:

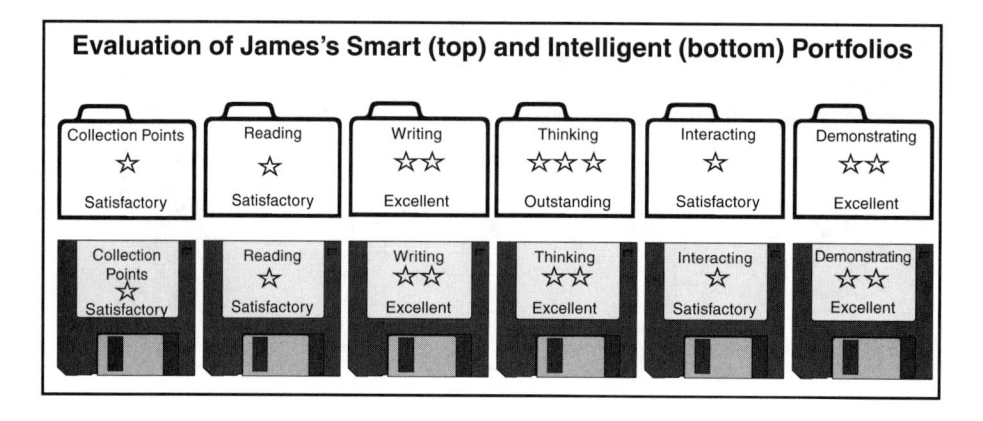

Evaluation of James's Smart (top) and Intelligent (bottom) Portfolios

	Collection Points	Reading	Writing	Thinking	Interacting	Demonstrating
Smart	☆ Satisfactory	☆ Satisfactory	☆☆ Excellent	☆☆☆ Outstanding	☆ Satisfactory	☆☆ Excellent
Intelligent	☆ Satisfactory	☆ Satisfactory	☆☆ Excellent	☆☆ Excellent	☆ Satisfactory	☆☆ Excellent

The Results of Jason's Efforts

Jason enjoyed more success with his implementations of both portfolios. Throughout the 15-week semester, both students frequently discussed their progress with each other and with the authors. However, the differences in their philosophies regarding portfolios resulted in an inability to share ideas and solutions to many common problems. These issues served to further the cause for standardizing certain important features of portfolio design. A look at the contents of Jason's Smart Portfolio shows how well Jason understood the

Jason's Smart Portfolio

Thinking Journal
"Making Connections"

70-pg Booknotes from 6 different textbooks

18-pg Journal Responses

Concept Paper
My Philosophy

"My Philosophy of Education" in letter format

Concept Paper
Self-Assessment

"My Portfolio—Smart and Intelligent: Lessons Learned"

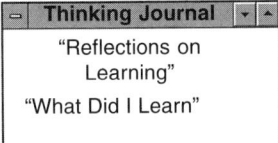

Thinking Journal
"Reflections on Learning"

"What Did I Learn"

Collecting

Content Area Material
4 Lesson Ideas (Web)

23 Classroom Handouts in Math, Learning, Multiple Intelligences

Library Resources
How to Use ERIC

70-pg ERIC Search of Teaching w/Technology

This is better... Jason's portfolio concentrates more on Collecting artifacts. Exactly what the Teacher as Learner needs.

Classroom Resources
Published Thematic Units: Math, Learning & Intelligences

Collection of 23 Lesson Plans

Web Sites
Comprehensive List of 112 Education Web Sites

Working

Learning Projects
Puzzle Demo with 2 Cooperative Learning Groups

Lessons
5 Math Lessons

1 Lesson on Multiple Intelligences

Showcase

Presentations/Papers
"The Thinking Classroom" Book Review for publication

concept that half of the Intelligent Portfolio for the Teacher as Learner should be concentrated in Collecting Folders.

The Smart Portfolio

Contrary to James's approach, Jason spent the majority of his time and effort gathering content area material, library resources, and classroom products that would one day make him a better teacher. Jason also proposed a new Collection Point: World Wide Web Sites. He "surfed" the Web energetically, and many of the resources he would ultimately present at assessment time were gathered directly from Home Pages downloaded from the Web. Indeed, he had so many hard-copy outputs from these sources, that we agreed to the addition of a new Collection Point folder specifically to hold Web addresses and documents. His Smart Portfolio would contain an outstanding accumulation of resource materials that would be the envy of any classroom teacher.

The Intelligent Portfolio

At the beginning of the prototype study, only the six Collection Points recommended by the authors were available to Jason. Jason created the recommended Collection Points as the first step in his Intelligent Portfolio. However, after using the portfolio all semester it became clear that more Collection Points were needed. As a result, the authors added four new Collection Points.

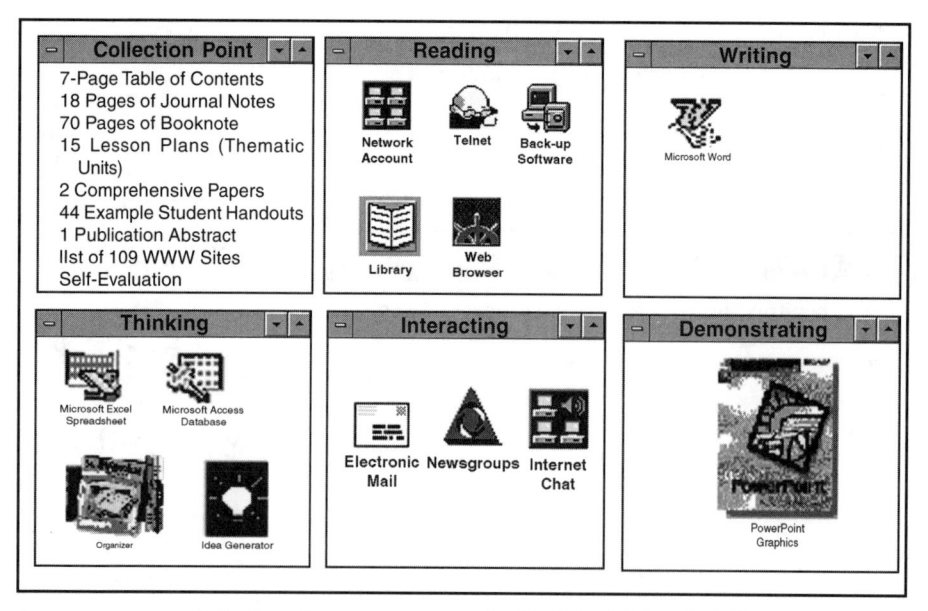

Collection Point	Reading	Writing
7-Page Table of Contents 18 Pages of Journal Notes 70 Pages of Booknote 15 Lesson Plans (Thematic Units) 2 Comprehensive Papers 44 Example Student Handouts 1 Publication Abstract llst of 109 WWW Sites Self-Evaluation	Network Account, Telnet, Back-up Software, Library, Web Browser	Microsoft Word
Thinking	**Interacting**	**Demonstrating**
Microsoft Excel Spreadsheet, Microsoft Access Database, Organizer, Idea Generator	Electronic Mail, Newsgroups, Internet Chat	PowerPoint Graphics

Jason recommended several new features and added 2 additional Collection Points to the Intelligent Portfolio for the Teacher as Learner.

Jason was instrumental in further changes to the look and feel of the original Intelligent Portfolio. He suggested a method to index and search the portfolio which gave rise to the Organizer software that appears in the Thinking Software folder. He identified an excellent software package for generating ideas, which also was added. His interaction, or rather the lack of it, with James resulted in a standardized number of Collection Points.

During the initial creation of the folders and directories that were to comprise the Intelligent Portfolio, a hard disk failure resulted in the loss of every file Jason had created: both applications and data. It took many hours to reconstruct the artifacts that had preceded the failure. His only consolation was that the disaster occurred early in the semester. A similar failure weeks later would have resulted in the loss of many artifacts. As a result of that experience, back-up software was added to the list of vital software and particular emphasis was placed on making regular back-ups.

Portfolio Assessment

Jason received higher marks for both portfolios. He was awarded an Overall Evaluation of **Outstanding** for his Smart portfolio. The Intelligent Portfolio earned him an **Excellent**. Individual assessments are depicted in the following graphic:

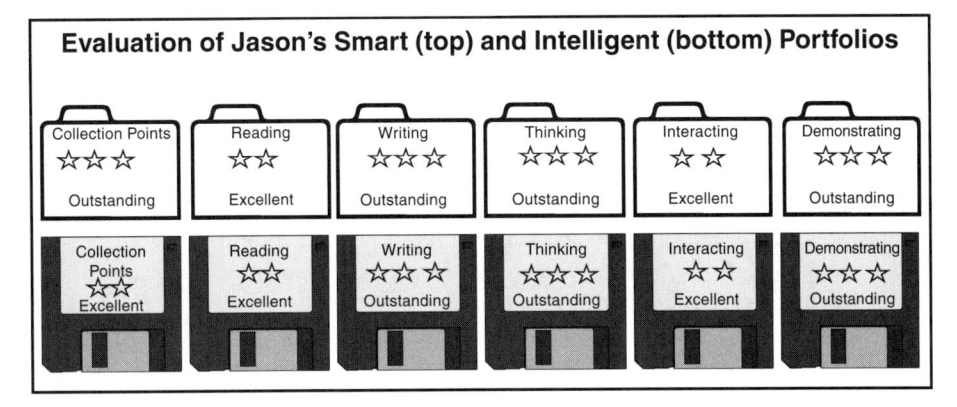

Evaluation of Jason's Smart (top) and Intelligent (bottom) Portfolios

Collection Points	Reading	Writing	Thinking	Interacting	Demonstrating
☆☆☆	☆☆	☆☆☆	☆☆☆	☆☆	☆☆☆
Outstanding	Excellent	Outstanding	Outstanding	Excellent	Outstanding

Collection Points	Reading	Writing	Thinking	Interacting	Demonstrating
☆☆☆	☆☆	☆☆☆	☆☆☆	☆☆	☆☆☆
Excellent	Excellent	Outstanding	Outstanding	Excellent	Outstanding

Summative Results of the Study

Several important issues ensued from this study. They are discussed below.

- *The Impact of Technology* As expected, technology immediately impacted the development of both students' portfolios. Motivation soared. Jason and James were determined to move beyond the mandatory expectations set. However, more was not always necessarily better. The original Intelligent Portfolio suggested automating processes that should have remained manual. These are clearly identified in the revised Teacher as Learner portfolio. For example, James chose to work with Desktop Publishing software instead of a word processor, spending an inordinate amount of time and effort learning the intricacies of columnar design, placement of graphics, and indentation. His time could have been better spent collecting artifacts that are available to the pre-service student only during this short period of professional development. These findings prompted us to move the more sophisticated hardware and software packages to later versions of the Intelligent Portfolio.

- *Portfolio Models* The Teacher as Learner may be exposed to several portfolio models during a pre-service program, many of which propose a "catch-as-catch-can" approach that leaves the final construction of the portfolio largely to the discretion of the learner. This unstructured approach oftentimes results in a babel of folders and artifacts, computer files and directories, that make the shaping of new ideas difficult. The Teacher as Learner should recognize that the merits of the

Smart and Intelligent portfolio model depend upon its usefulness as the teacher matures as expert and scholar.

- *Common Platforms, Common Capabilities*   The most efficient and effective use of portfolios presupposes common platforms with common capabilities. Variations in James's and Jason's Intelligent Portfolios guaranteed that they could not help one another master this newest technology. While the recommended software packages are available for both the PC-compatible and Macintosh-compatible hardware, incompatible memory, hard disk capacity, and data storage formats precluded sharing of word processing, database, spreadsheet, and application files.

- *Software*   Finally, the prototype study identified several new software packages that would become important additions to one or more of the Intelligent Portfolio software folders. Back-up software was added to the Reading folder; Organizing and Brainstorming software were placed in the Thinking folder; and, Newsgroup, Gopher, and Internet Chat packages were made part of the Interacting folder. In addition, several new Collection Points were added.

Concluding Remarks

Without benefit of a prototype study, the Teacher as Learner portfolio, be it Smart or Intelligent, would depend entirely on theory. In this realistic environment, packages were added and deleted, Collection Points were validated, and the focus on Collecting as the domain of the Teacher as Learner was confirmed.

PART IV
Portfolios for the Teacher as Expert

Constructing a portfolio can be a challenge, especially for the busy classroom teacher. But once you get started, you will wonder why you didn't do it sooner. So, what are you waiting for?

Chapters 8, 9, and 10 will guide you through the construction of the Smart and Intelligent Portfolios for the Teacher as Expert.

Chapter 8	Chapter 9	Chapter 10
The Smart Portfolio for the Teacher as Expert	*The Intelligent Portfolio for the Teacher as Expert*	*Portfolios in Transition: The Teacher as Expert Perspective*
Chapter 8 explains the change in focus from the Collecting folders to the Working folders for the Teacher as Expert. Constructing the Smart Portfolio is detailed step-by-step.	This chapter introduces the electronic steps to construct an Intelligent Portfolio that will aid the classroom teacher in locating, developing, and delivering instruction.	Read Chaper 10 to see how Jennifer learned to organize her artifacts electronically and how she helped to move both the Smart and Intelligent Portfolios to their present configuration for the classroom teacher.

CHAPTER 8
The Smart Portfolio for the Teacher as Expert

Introduction

The primary difference between the Smart Portfolio for the Teacher as Learner and Teacher as Expert is its focus on the application of knowledge and skills through classroom exercise, constant practice, and personal reflection. As a role model for students, classroom teachers promote learning not as a destination but rather as a journey. The Smart Portfolio contains artifacts that demonstrate excellence in teaching, illustrate thoughtfulness and sharing, and indicate a disposition toward lifelong learning.

Foley will continue to guide the development of the Smart Portfolio by answering the same four questions proposed in Part III to produce a fully functioning portfolio for the Teacher as Expert:

(1) Where Do I Begin,
(2) How Do I Organize the Portfolio,
(3) What Do I Collect, and
(4) Who Will Assess My Work?

It's Foley again. If you are ready, we will create the Smart Portfolio for the Teacher as Expert by answering these four questions...

Where Do I Begin?

You begin—as did the Teacher-Learner—with the five essential foundations: Demonstrating, Interacting, Thinking, Writing, and Reading. For the Teacher as Expert, these foundations remain stable; however, their emphasis shifts as the classroom teacher employs the portfolio for distinctly different purposes. Take a close look at how the foundations work together.

Where do I begin? If you already use the Smart Portfolio, this will be a refresher. If not, look over Part III before going further.

The foundations for the Teacher as Expert remain organized around the pivotal element of Thinking—as with all implementations of the Smart Portfolio. However, in this version of the portfolio, Demonstrating emerges as the predominant foundation.

Demonstrating involves the application of what a teacher knows and how instruction is presented. Artifacts created in direct support of teaching constitute the focus of the portfolio for the Teacher as Expert. Formal lessons with student workbooks, handouts, evaluations, and visual aids are generated as Demonstrating artifacts. Communications with students, parents, colleagues, and scholars are appropriate as well. Student assessments, documented committee work, and formal reports are

DEMONSTRATING
Presenting, critiquing, publishing, enhancing traditional lessons, applying thinking and learning.

INTERACTING
Sharing ideas, discussing and defending, actively constructing artifacts during group inquiry.

THINKING
Making new meaning, connecting ideas, taking stock, constructing new perspectives.

WRITING
Formal and informal writing demonstrating thoughtfulness and integrating new knowledge.

READING
Gathering evidence of new knowledge and information from texts, articles, and similar resources.

further examples. Demonstrating will certainly become the most popular source of artifacts for the Teacher as Expert.

Interacting for the teacher is always a challenge because of the inherent nature of schools. Teachers are often isolated in classrooms with little time for cooperative work and peer problem-solving. The importance of Interacting is well documented in the research. Brainstorming, defense of personal ideas, arguments in support of professional beliefs, new ways of teaching—each of these interactive episodes offers new perspectives to extend the limits of thinking. Because interacting is such an indispensable component of an expanding knowledge base, classroom teachers must make opportunities to interact with other Teacher-Experts.

Thinking remains the pivotal foundation of the Smart Portfolio. Thinking is a prerequisite for classroom learning, and teachers must make it "second-nature" by teaching thinking strategies to their students. The Smart Portfolio can serve as the impetus for consistent and self-directed thinking.

Writing, both private or public, actively promotes thinking. Teachers who write are often better teachers. As writers, they share their lessons and units of instruction with other teachers. They encourage writing in their classroom, and serve as role models for lifelong learning. The Smart Portfolio holds the teacher's Writing artifacts for a lifetime of professional development.

Learning begins with **Reading**. In all implementations of the Smart Portfolio, book notes, journal articles, casual reading, book reviews, and periodicals build a knowledge base that will extend supplement, and rejuvenate the Smart Portfolio with new artifacts.

So, while the foundations of the portfolio remain the same, the priorities and sequencing of the foundations change for the Teacher as Expert. If you began using the Smart Portfolio as a Teacher-Learner, you have undoubtedly accumulated numerous artifacts. First-time users may have far fewer to synthesize. For either user, organizing the Smart Portfolio is the next issue to be addressed.

The Smart Portfolio for the Teacher as Expert

How Do I Organize the Portfolio?

Collecting, Working, and Showcase Folders provide the structure for the Smart Portfolio. As with the foundations, the emphasis for the Teacher as Expert shifts—from the *Collecting Folder* to the *Working Folder*—since the focus is now on the **application** of knowledge and skills and the discovery of useful and practical ways to put artifacts into practice. Take a look at how this version of the portfolio is organized.

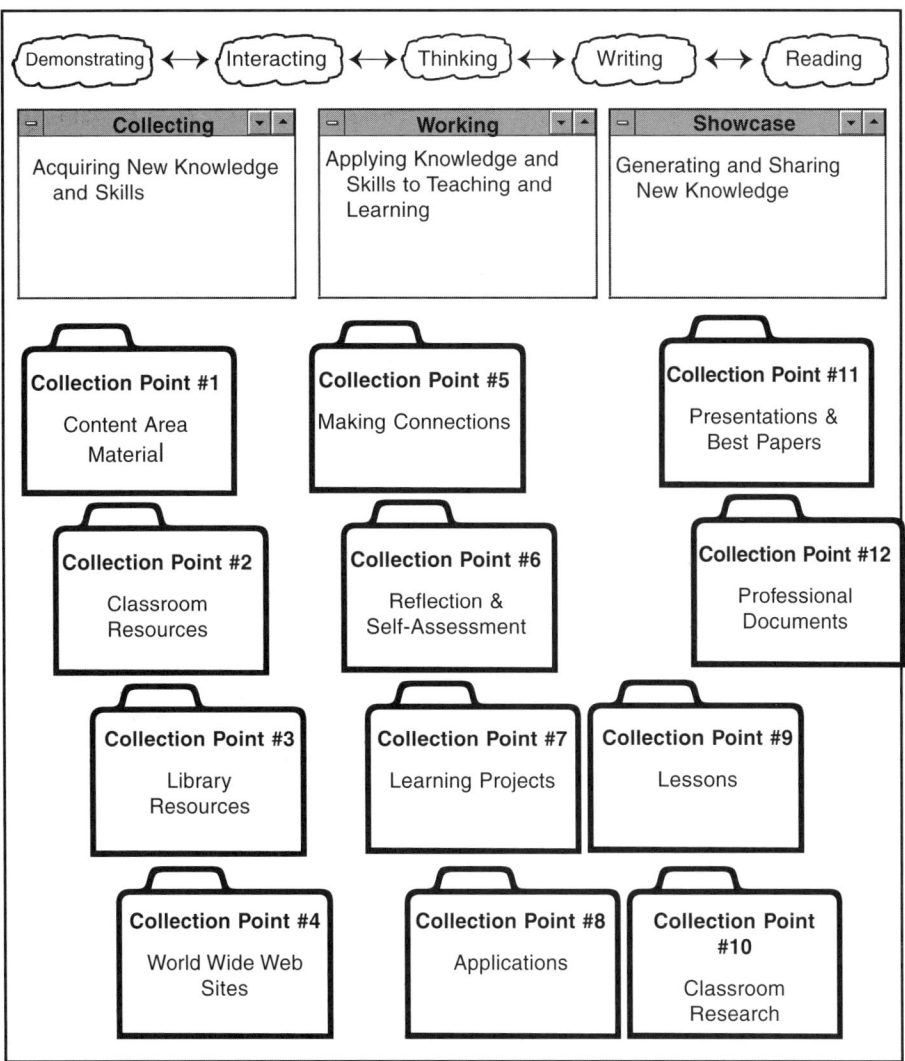

How do I organize my portfolio? The elements of the Smart Portfolio will produce artifacts that will be organized into 3 main sections.

Demonstrating ↔ Interacting ↔ Thinking ↔ Writing ↔ Reading

Collecting: Acquiring New Knowledge and Skills

Working: Applying Knowledge and Skills to Teaching and Learning

Showcase: Generating and Sharing New Knowledge

- Collection Point #1 — Content Area Material
- Collection Point #2 — Classroom Resources
- Collection Point #3 — Library Resources
- Collection Point #4 — World Wide Web Sites
- Collection Point #5 — Making Connections
- Collection Point #6 — Reflection & Self-Assessment
- Collection Point #7 — Learning Projects
- Collection Point #8 — Applications
- Collection Point #9 — Lessons
- Collection Point #10 — Classroom Research
- Collection Point #11 — Presentations & Best Papers
- Collection Point #12 — Professional Documents

Collecting Folder

Content Area Materials, Classroom Resources, Library Resources, and World Wide Web Sites hold artifacts acquired by Reading and Interacting. If you have been using the Smart Portfolio, it should be overflowing with *Collecting* artifacts. Although still the domain of the Teacher-Learner, Collecting remains critically important in all aspects of portfolio use to ensure the availability of up-to-date resources that will continue to generate new thinking.

Working Folder

As the Teacher as Expert begins to apply the collected artifacts, new evidence of thinking is produced and transferred to the Working folder. One new and two revised collection points make their appearance in this version of the Smart Portfolio. Because of their importance to the Teacher as Expert, these Collection Points will be discussed in more detail.

Collection Point #5: Making Connections Making Connections holds new classroom teaching strategies. Ideas and information gleaned from artifacts stored in Collecting folders are brought forward by the classroom teacher and evaluated in light of daily instructional practices. Successful attempts to produce new lessons and projects along with failures afford opportunities for better practice.

Collection Point #6: Reflection and Self-Assessment Reflection and Self-Assessment contribute to the growth of the educator in the classroom. Evaluating one's own effectiveness results in setting personal goals and objectives. Reviewing a video of your teaching or asking students what they learned contribute to a deeper understanding of the benefits of these kinds of assessment tools.

Collection Point #7: Learning Projects Field trips, visits to museums, history timelines, science projects, and other in-class works are stored in this Collection Point until they are needed in the classroom. Then they are moved intact to the Lessons folder.

Collection Point #8: Applications This Collection Point holds all validated classroom materials including lesson plans, student handouts, subject-specific activities, and course assessment tools until they are needed in the classroom. At that time, they too are moved to the Lesson folder and placed within one of the course subfolders that we will discuss next.

Collection Point #9: Lessons The Lessons Collection Point is the most active repository for the Teacher as Expert. It is the only Collection Point with subfolders—one for each current class being taught. A subfolder is established for each subject area. If a teacher teaches more than one class of a subject area, a folder is created for each class period. As active folders, these components will be accessed by the teacher on a daily basis. Each subject-class folder will store grades, rosters, lesson plans, classroom activities, and tests and quizzes.

Grades. A grade sheet is maintained either manually or electronically on a spreadsheet. A hard copy of the report is stored in this subfolder. Each student is listed in alphabetical order with grades for homework assignments, group projects, tests, and quizzes. Remember, in this example the subfolder will contain grades only for 8th period Language Arts.

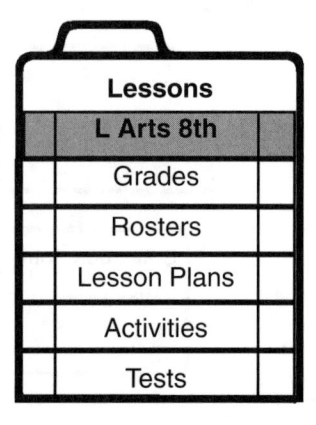

Lessons
L Arts 8th
Grades
Rosters
Lesson Plans
Activities
Tests

Rosters. Class rosters are created at the start of each academic period and serve as a temporary seating chart until the teacher can determine the most appropriate arrangement for the students. Rosters track attendance, student participation in special activities, parent-teacher conferences, and measurements of classroom performance.

Lesson Plans. Validated lesson plans are moved to this subfolder when the teacher begins the academic period. When not supporting an active class, Lesson Plans are stored either in Applications or Learning Projects.

Classroom Activities. Any scheduled activity during the grading period is included in this subfolder. An agenda for a field trip to a nearby museum, a college production of Romeo and Juliet, or a guest speaker invited for a school-wide convocation during National Drug Awareness Week are examples of activities. Itineraries, points of contact, local facilitators, and critiques and evaluations from previous visits also reside here.

Tests and Quizzes. Any and all assessment tools associated with this academic period are held in the Tests subfolder. Until they are needed, validated tests and measurements are co-located with other lesson plans in the Applications Collection Point.

Collection Point #10: Classroom Research New teaching strategies, the latest educational technologies, and investigations of thematic units are stored here to be tested and validated. If the artifacts prove viable as usable classroom material, they are moved to the Applications Collection Point for temporary storage, then on to Lessons when they are ready to be used in the classroom.

Showcase Folder

The two Showcase Collection Points have plenty of room for contributions from the Teacher as Expert. Presentations at national, regional, or local conferences, artifacts from parent-teacher meetings, and publications are placed in the Presentations & Best Papers Collection Point. Updated course transcripts, certificates of completion for in-service credits, letters of recommendation, and special recognition or awards go into the Professional Documents Collection Point.

It is recommended that an explanation as simple as "I wrote this paper to strengthen my content knowledge" be attached to each artifact before it is placed into a folder. An article manuscript may ultimately be stored in one of the Showcase folders. However, it probably started as an artifact in the Collecting folder and moved into and out of a Working folder several times. A paper trail of artifacts trace movement within the portfolio and provides a reminder of where each item has been and how it has evolved. As new artifacts move in, other artifacts will move out ensuring the portfolio remains a living document.

Keep in mind that the Smart Portfolio is a tool for assessment, a tool for learning, and a tool for professional development. As a learning tool, it holds evidence of thinking and learning. As an assessment tool, it will be evaluated with both summative and formative appraisals. As a professional development tool, it will promote academic scholarship and sharing. These are the purposes of the Smart Portfolio.

At this point, the Teacher as Expert has many sources of artifacts, and we have presented a detailed plan for organizing them. We now turn our attention to the question of deciding which artifacts to include in the Smart Portfolio.

What Do I Collect?

What to keep and what to throw away is a practical question that deserves a thoughtful answer. A Letter of Recommendation may be important enough to store in the Smart

What do I collect? An "artifact" is evidence of knowledge, skill, and understanding.

Portfolio. However, a reminder of an upcoming meeting, even if it is from the district superintendent, may not. Grade reports can be discarded when you receive a final transcript. Evaluations of student teaching by supervisors become less important after years of teaching. On the other hand, if you were to rewrite an activity to give it a problem-solving emphasis, that artifact would be added to the portfolio along with an explanation to support the changes. A book review for publication would include a final draft, the editor's letter, and the published copy; each of these artifacts should be retained.

To assist the user of the Smart Portfolio, Foley will offer some specific examples of the possible artifacts that might be stored in each Collection Point. Some of them will be similar to the previous Teacher-Learner implementation.

Collection Point #1

This folder should already be filled with artifacts. Any new content material should be addded or replaced.

Content Area Materials
Journal Articles
Subject Matter Books
Textbooks
Raw Lesson Plans taken from the Internet.

Classroom Resources
Monographs on Classroom Discipline and Learning
Sample Teaching Lessons
Higher Order Thinking Strategies for Teaching
Multiple Intelligence Exercises

Collection Point #2

Classroom Resources go in this folder.

Collection Point #3

Remember not to limit your library resources to only your own school library.

Library Resources
Requests for Books, Articles, and Resources
Audiovisual Resources
Library Reference/Reserve Materials

Collection Point #4

URLs for the Teacher as Expert consist of sites that promote teaching and learning for students as well as teachers.

World Wide Web Sites
Search Engines
Subject Matter Sites
Online Presentations
Student-oriented Research
Content Specialties
Education E-Zines

Making Connections
Points of Contact
Mental Maps
Book notes
Insight into Classroom Issues/Problems
Unresolved Questions

Collection Point #5

Interacting with your own artifacts and with colleagues and students.

Collection Point #6

Self-Assessment help the educator improve teaching and better the profession.

Reflection & Self-Assessment
Self-analysis of Lessons
Results of Student Surveys
Discipline Problems
Personal Philosophy of Teaching and Learning

Learning Projects
Videos of Past Student Projects
Parents' Nite Program
Itinerary for Field Trips
Instruction for Senior Research Paper
Student Science Handouts

Collection Point #7

If you use it in the classroom, store it in this Collection Point.

Collection Point #8

Here's one of the new Collection Points . . . sort of a "parking lot" until you need the artifact in the classroom.

Applications
Next Semester's Units of Study
Enhancement Exercises
Thematic Units
Assessments Activities

Collection Point #9

The second new Collection Point, your active Lessons, will all be placed in this folder with 5 subfolders.

Lessons
- L Arts 8th
- Grades
- Rosters
- Lesson Plans
- Activities
- Tests

Collection Point #10

Here's the last new Collection Point. Any new ideas that deserve further investigation should go here.

Classroom Research
Experiential Teaching
Design for Study
Background Research
Student Survey of Teacher Effectiveness

Collection Point #11

Your Best Works go here. We moved this collection point up two notches to number 11.

Presentations and Best Papers
Submitted Reviews
Proposed Lesson Ideas
Teacher In-Service
   Workshops

Collection Point #12

The last folder for the Teacher as Expert continues to hold a growing number of professional artifacts.

Professional Documents
Graduate Transcripts
Teacher Evaluations
Test Scores
Honors, Recognitions,
   and Awards
Letters of Recommendations

Artifacts vary with each portfolio user. Even though the structure of the Smart Portfolio is established, artifacts differ in purpose, meaning, and construction. The amount of time and effort given to the portfolio are the responsibility of the Teacher as Expert and often determine the quality and relevance of artifacts.

With a comprehensive portfolio, Teachers as Experts experience learning through in-class self-assessments. These assessments allow teachers to adjust their teaching methods to address individual student weaknesses. Assessment is a critical component of any teaching career based on a professional portfolio. This leads us to consider our fourth and last question: "Who will assess my work?"

Who Will Assess My Work?

Who will assess my work? Assessment will be very different for the classroom teacher.

An undergraduate student is given numerous assessment opportunities in a structured, non-threatening, long-term environment. Not so for the Teacher as Expert whose successful classroom evaluation may be based on a limited number of satisfactory in-class observations. Portfolio assessments—formal or informal—provide a more holistic appraisal of teacher performance.

Formal assessment is the purview of the school principal and, on occasion, external evaluators such as school accreditation teams. Some principals consider portfolio assessment more valuable than classroom observation. Artifacts subject to evaluation include all Collection Points as evidence of growth and development. Teachers, too, are finding the portfolio a more authentic assessment of their teaching and learning.

Informal assessments, originating from fellow teachers, students, parents, and personal examination, represent a significant aspect of the professional portfolio. Peers and colleagues provide valuable and timely feedback on classroom activities. Students and parents contribute to teacher collected artifacts when indicators of success are produced through letters, surveys, and other kinds of classroom assessments. Finally, informal assessment incorporates curriculum vita, your philosophy of teaching and learning, any proposals for publication, and professional development plans. As these artifacts change and develop, they move in and out of various Collection Points in your Smart Portfolio.

The Portfolio Poster

To enhance the portfolio experience, we suggest an "Exhibition" to display the results of the Smart Portfolio. Presenting a visual depiction of thinking and learning requires analytic, critical, and creative thinking. The poster should be able to stand on its own merit, but the "synergistic" approach is more powerful when teachers get a chance to articulate and defend what they know and how they came to know it. The poster not only provides the opportunity for the Teacher-Expert to synthesize thinking and learning in a creative way, but also shows evidence of the teacher's engagement and reflection, deep understanding of content, meaningful personal connections, habits of mind, and skill in oral communication. Collection Points #5 and #6 are separated from the other Working folders. They are placed next to your Philosophy of Teaching and Learning worthy of special visual attention on the poster.

The Smart Portfolio Poster for the Teacher as Expert

Collecting

- Collection Point #5 — Making Connections
- Collection Point #1 — Content Area Material
- Collection Point #2 — Classroom Resources
- Collection Point #3 — Library Resources
- Collection Point #4 — World Wide Web Sites

Working

- Concept Paper — My Philosophy of Teaching and Learning
- Concept Paper — Taking Stock
- Collection Point #7 — Learning Projects
- Collection Point #8 — Applications
- Collection Point #9 — Lessons
- Collection Point #10 — Classroom Research

Showcase

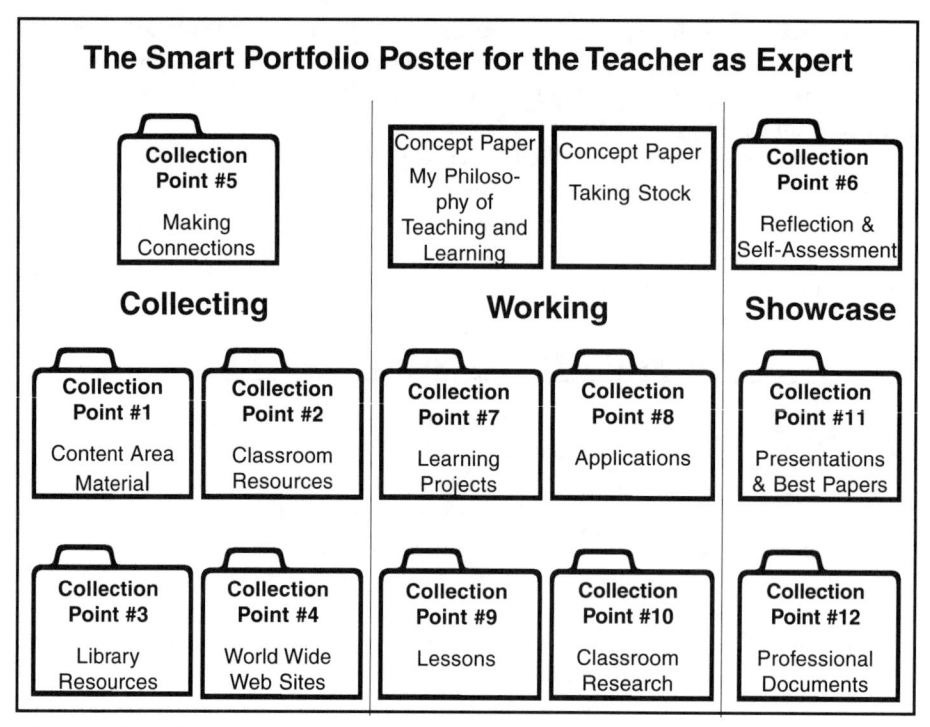

- Collection Point #6 — Reflection & Self-Assessment
- Collection Point #11 — Presentations & Best Papers
- Collection Point #12 — Professional Documents

A Posterboard View of the Smart Portfolio

Conclusion

The Smart Portfolio adapts to the evolving needs of the Teacher as Expert. By expanding Working Collection Points, the Smart Portfolio houses artifacts applied directly to classroom teaching. Grades, rosters, activities, lesson plans, and assessments are stored in the respective subfolders of Collection Point #9. Classroom Research (Collection Point #10) is added as a repository for new classroom-directed investigation.

In the Teacher as Expert Portfolio, Working artifacts focus the teacher's attention on the more immediate aspects of applying knowledge and skills, but collecting must always play a role in portfolio development: New artifacts are the lifeblood of personal growth. Showcase artifacts, too, continue to provide evidence of professional development. Perhaps Foley summarizes it best with his tips for using the Smart Portfolio for the Teacher as Expert.

The Smart Portfolio for the Teacher as Expert   79

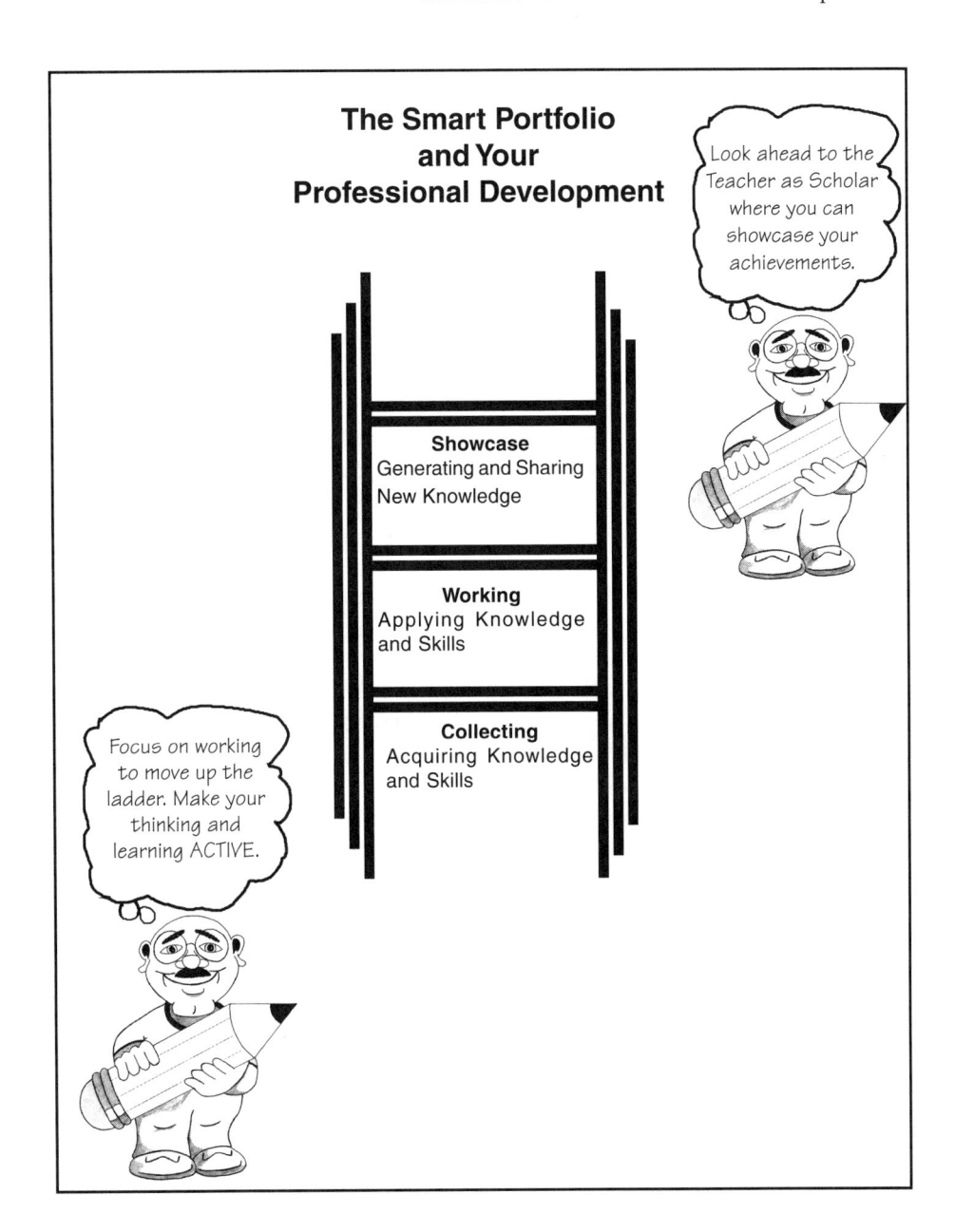

The Smart Portfolio and Your Professional Development

Look ahead to the Teacher as Scholar where you can showcase your achievements.

Showcase
Generating and Sharing New Knowledge

Working
Applying Knowledge and Skills

Collecting
Acquiring Knowledge and Skills

Focus on working to move up the ladder. Make your thinking and learning ACTIVE.

Foley Tips

Here are a few final tips from Foley to ensure that the Smart Portfolio remains a valuable tool for the Teacher as Expert.

Here are some tips for you.

1. **Teachers are lifelong learners.** Use the Smart Portfolio to explore new ideas and test new discoveries. Your Philosophy of Teaching and Learning should continue to change.

2. **Emphasize the Working Folder.** The Working folder is the focus for the Smart Portfolio for the Teacher as Expert. Collecting must be ongoing, and Showcase must be advanced, but Working remains the emphasis.

3. **Review Collection Point #9, Lessons.** Much of the Smart Portfolio's success is centered on the idea of using the subfolders presented in this chapter. The Smart Portfolio addresses one of the most critical resources for the classroom teacher: time.

4. **Collect, collect, collect.** The old must give way to the new. Artifacts must be re-examined periodically. Foley suggests reviewing them at least twice a year: once in December at mid-year, and again in June at the end of the school year. Remove old artifacts and replace outdated items with new content material, classroom and library resources, and Web site addresses.

5. **Keep interacting.** Interacting will keep you mentally sharp and challenged: Defend what you think, argue for what you believe, and justify how you teach. Join the "professional conversation" and publish!

6. **Consider the Intelligent Portfolio.** Now that you understand the structure of the Smart Portfolio for the Teacher as Expert, making your portfolio electronic might facilitate the portfolio process.

When you are ready to move on to the Teacher as Scholar Portfolio, I'll be waiting for you.

CHAPTER 9
The Intelligent Portfolio for the Teacher as Expert

Introduction

The Intelligent Portfolio combines the folders and Collection Points of the Smart Portfolio with computer technology to construct an electronic version of the portfolio. This is accomplished with three simple electronic tasks:

Step One: **Creating Portfolio Folders** for Demonstrating, Interacting, Thinking, Writing, and Reading,

Step Two: **Populating Portfolio Folders** with the most efficient and effective combination of software packages, and

Step Three: **Organizing Folders and Collection Points** to store electronic artifacts.

Step One: Creating Portfolio Folders

Here's Step One: Creating Your Portfolio Folders.

Creating portfolio folders requires some knowledge of how your computer desktop is generated. Both Apple and Windows users should find it relatively simple to create folders such as those shown in the graphic at the top of page 82. The purpose of each folder is explained in the following paragraphs.

Demonstrating

The Demonstrating folder supports the majority of activities for the Teacher-Expert. In the Teacher as Learner Portfolio, the Demonstrating folder was used to prepare instructional materials, class projects, and presentations. For the Teacher as Expert, Demonstrating is more proactive. This folder adds several software packages and additional hardware components to help the classroom teacher design more complex classroom materials.

Interacting

Often the casualty of an overextended school day, Interacting is critical for the Teacher as Expert. To promote sharing ideas, the Interacting folder of the Teacher as Expert provides two new software packages in addition to electronic mail, newsgroups, and Internet Relay Chat of the previous portfolio.

Thinking

The Thinking folder also expands under this implementation. Databases, spreadsheets, and organizers continue to be very useful. Additional software provides for student evalua-

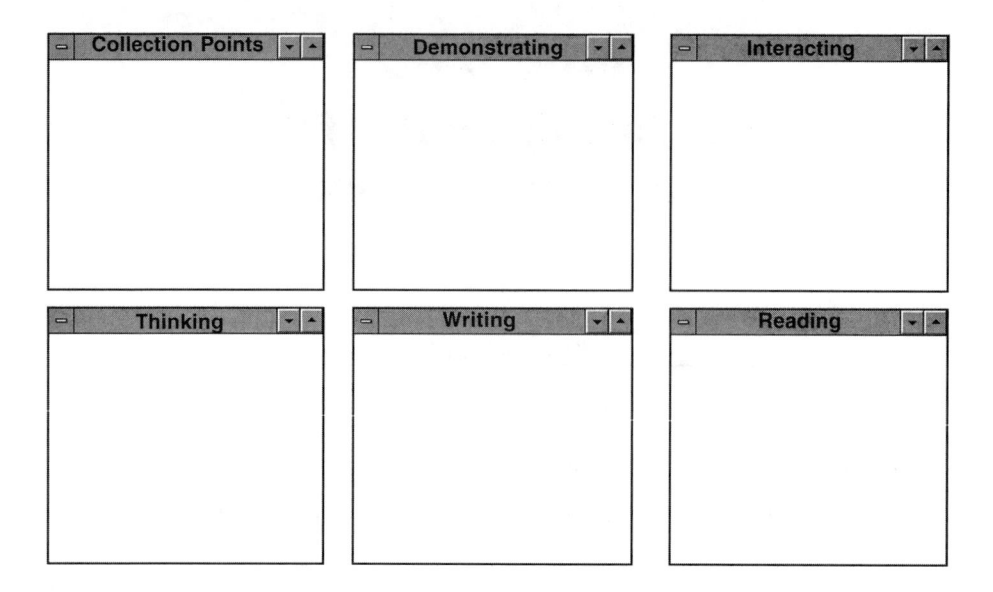

Collection Points	Demonstrating	Interacting

Thinking	Writing	Reading

tion, and new hardware is added to enable the teacher to import image and text-based subject matter.

Writing

The Writing folder takes on increased prominence for the Teacher as Expert and should contain a full-featured word processor along with high-quality color printing capability. Preparing volumes of class material, assessment tools, and lesson plans is very important for the teacher in the classroom.

Reading

The Reading folder contains software and hardware to access libraries and the World Wide Web. This shift in focus from the Teacher as Learner implementation is not intended to diminish the value of reading to the practicing teacher. It places the emphasis of the portfolio on other aspects of professional development. The recommended software and hardware continue to support your need to read.

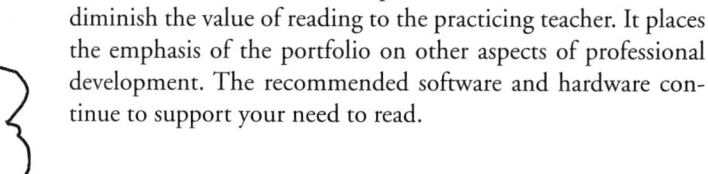

Ready for Step Two? Let's place some software and hardware into the folders...

Step Two: Populating Portfolio Folders

The emphasis of the Intelligent Portfolio for the Teacher as Expert shifts to the working aspects of the teacher in the classroom. This version of the portfolio contains software that supports the hands-on design, development, and application of artifacts so important for the practicing teacher. Foley will begin by examining the components of the Demonstrating folder for the Teacher as Expert.

Demonstrating Software

A graphics presentation package supports the design and development of classroom-ready materials. With a growing array of helper applications, the teacher can integrate images, sounds, text, video, and clip art into multisensory presentations. A Web Design package is new for the Teacher as Expert and is highly recommended for building Internet-based educational sites to hold lesson objectives, lesson plans, and assessments.

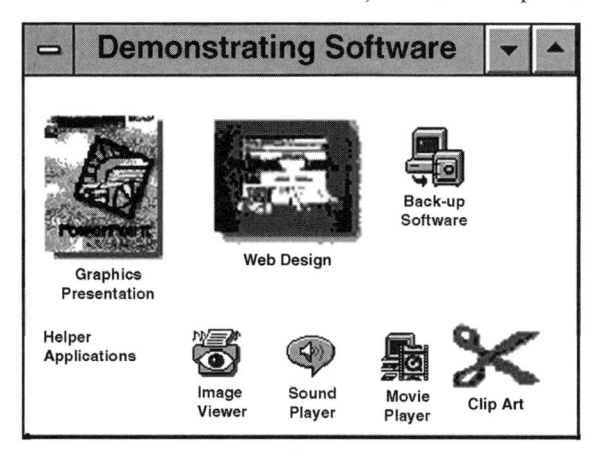

Web design is added to the Graphics Package for our Demonstrating Software.

Graphics Software A state-of-the-art graphics presentation package provides a toolkit of capabilities for expert slide construction and editing, templates, formatting styles, font choices including style, size, and location on the slide. An easy-to-use viewer delivers classroom slides, transparencies, and printed handbooks.

Web Design Software Teachers in the 21st century will be developing new course material on the World Wide Web. Lesson plans, assessment tools, reading assignments, and classroom projects that are Web-based open new horizons for distance learning. Just as important, the Teacher as Expert will be afforded new opportunities to use multisensory experiences in an effort to bolster individual learning strategies. Web design packages simplify programming; incorporate images, sounds, and video; and, create links to the best the Web has to offer.

Back-up Software Back-up software should be used at least weekly to save a complete copy of your hard disk. The Zip Drive captures Collection Points, application programs, and data files in only a few minutes. The first time a hard drive goes bad, a directory is corrupted, or files are inadvertently deleted, you will appreciate the discipline of regular system back-ups. The recommended software comes with the operating system of your computer; however, there are more elaborate (and easier to use) packages available. The Zip Drive itself comes with excellent back-up software.

Demonstrating Hardware

Basic hardware support for the Demonstrating folder includes a computer system with state-of-the-art technology. Minimum requirements for our Teacher as Expert portfolio address processor speed, printing, CD-ROM, and hard disk storage. Additional technology will be recommended to support more ambitious efforts.

Since Demonstrating is our first folder, it will contain the basic hardware for the Intelligent Portfolio.

Demonstrating Hardware

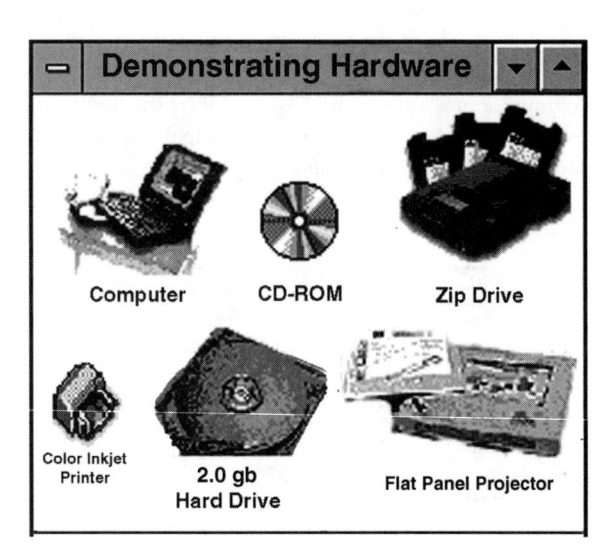

- Computer
- CD-ROM
- Zip Drive
- Color Inkjet Printer
- 2.0 gb Hard Drive
- Flat Panel Projector

Laptop Computer   Because of its portability and convenience, a laptop computer is the platform of choice for the Intelligent Portfolio. Desktop systems with comparable capabilities are acceptable. Either way, the system must have the following capabilities:

Apple-Compatible Systems.   Macintosh with a 68060 microprocessor or better, 32 megabytes RAM, a 1 gigabyte hard drive (2 gb recommended), and the Macintosh Operating System 7.5 (Mac 8.0 OS recommended).

Windows-Compatible Systems.   A personal computer with a Pentium microprocessor, 32 megabytes random access memory (RAM), a 1 gigabyte hard drive (2 gb recommended), and the Windows 95 Operating System (Windows 98 recommended).

CD-ROM Drive   The Intelligent Portfolio uses CD-ROM technology not only as an input medium for the thousands of applications distributed via this medium, but also as the primary storage device for all the artifacts to be accumulated in the various Collection Points. Since artifacts will include video, image, and sound files in addition to large text files, we recommend that you purchase the fastest CD-ROM that you can afford.

Zip Drive   A Zip drive is a high-capacity storage device that can be used to store documents and back up critical files and directories. It operates much like a traditional floppy disk drive. The Zip and floppy disks are approximately the same size. Technically, however, they are very different. The 3.5 inch floppy can store 1.4 MB of data, while the Zip disk can hold 100 MB of data. And Zip drives transfer data at a much faster rate.

Inkjet Color Printer   The Demonstrating Hardware folder includes the inkjet printer with **color** capability for printing classroom materials and professional-looking handouts.

2-Gigabyte Hard Drive   Graphics presentations require large files, which increases the demand for hard disk space; therefore, a 2-gigabyte hard drive is highly recommended.

Flat Panel Projector   We suggest acquiring a flat panel projector to display lessons directly from the computer to an overhead screen. If this peripheral is not in the budget, you can print your materials or produce overhead transparencies and slides.

Interacting Software

Electronic mail and newsgroups foster interaction among peers and colleagues. File Transfer Protocol (FTP) software moves electronic lesson plans, student materials, and other discipline-specific documents from a host computer system to your portfolio. With so much material already accessible, these few Interacting software packages provide a wealth of resources that can rapidly fill a Collecting folder with current artifacts.

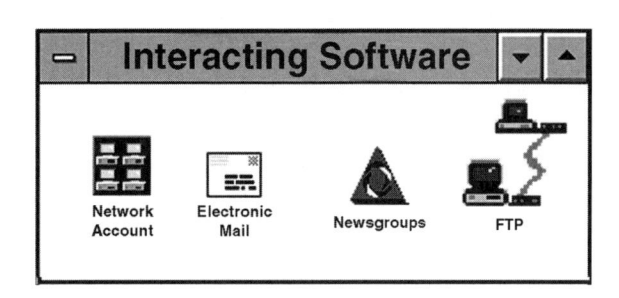

Interacting Software includes network applications for the Teacher as Expert.

Interacting Software

Network Account | Electronic Mail | Newsgroups | FTP

Network Account Network service providers typically charge about $20.00 per month for a specified amount of on-line connect time. Be careful not to exceed that limit since some providers charge exorbitant fees to users exceeding their monthly ceilings. Most major universities (and now even some elementary and secondary schools) provide accounts to their students free of charge. Some of the larger universities also provide accounts to neighboring public and private school teachers. In several states, Intermediate Units and consolidated school districts provide these resources. Finally, an increasing number of libraries, local governments, nonprofit organizations, and computer clubs provide free service. If these sources are not available, the local Yellow Pages™ provides the next best source of possible network providers, sometimes called an Internet Service Provider, or ISP. Compare costs to ensure you get the most access for the money—at times when you are most available for on-line work.

Electronic Mail Email offers on-line communications with fellow teachers sharing similar experiences and exploring common interests. A single email request can result in a flood of ideas and suggestions regarding classroom experiences. Using email as a platform for interacting, teachers transmit reading assignments and return graded homework from their distant students. With today's technology, email is fast becoming routine at all levels of education.

Newsgroups Newsgroups provide an expanded vehicle for sharing ideas among teachers and students. Most newsgroups services provide personalized newsgroups—created and modified by individuals interested in hosting their own electronic forums. The Teacher as Expert should consider the possibilities of sponsoring newsgroup forums for their own school. One advantage over email is the elimination of overhead tasks such as tracking addresses, participation, and routine maintenance. Once the newsgroup is created, students with access to the Internet and a newsserver can participate in the electronic message board forum. They create, post, respond, and share new thinking. With only limited guidance from the classroom teacher, this style of teaching can produce innovative lessons.

File Transfer Protocol (FTP). For the classroom teacher, FTP provides immediate access to materials on the Internet. Entire units of instruction are available on host FTP servers. Most files are either freeware (no cost) or shareware (minimal remuneration) for surprisingly excellent material. Math tutors, science projects, and English composition can be found at FTP sites serving specific educational disciplines, while electronic grade books and attendance routines are available for managing administrative aspects of the classroom. File transfer works to the advantage of both the provider and recipient if both remain committed to distributing only the best education-ready materials.

Interacting Hardware

For the most part, the Interacting folder will utilize the hardware that already has been included in the Demonstrating folder. The only new requirement for the Teacher as Expert is for faster communications using a high-speed modem.

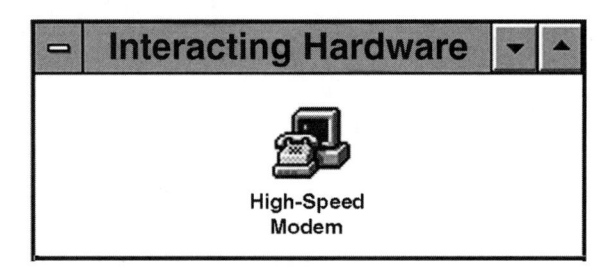

High-Speed Modem Network accounts, electronic mail, newsgroups, and file transfer require high-speed communications. We encourage the Teacher as Expert to use the fastest modem affordable to ensure satisfactory communication over telephone lines.

Thinking Software

A list of idea-generating, data managing, and desktop organizing tools supports the Teacher as Expert both in the classroom and in the management of the Intelligent Portfolio. A spreadsheet program will allow you to collect and organize data in different ways for your research projects. An organizer will keep track of your goals and successes.

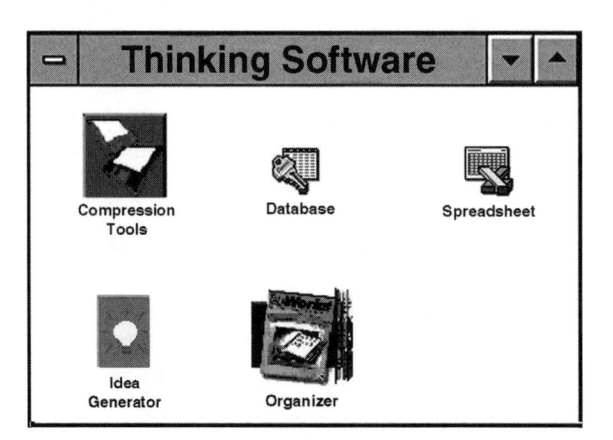

Compression and decompression tools   These tools are designed to handle the storage and transfer of very large files. Also known as "zip" and "unzip", Internet users should seek compressed files to make downloading faster. Compression also saves significant storage space. These "zip" files are "unzipped" after they are downloaded.

Database software   Databases help the Teacher as Expert manage the myriad of phone numbers, personal and professional contacts, bibliographic references, and potential World Wide Web sites that they have collected. Databases encourage thinking by organizing information into logical structures and aiding in its retrieval.

Electronic spreadsheets   Spreadsheets are powerful mind tools that enhance and extend our thinking. They play a dual role in the Intelligent Portfolio for the Teacher as Expert. As a management tool, a spreadsheet serves as the foundation for a class grade sheet to calculate averages and assign letter grades, create class rosters, and track classroom participation. As a creative tool, a spreadsheet also can be integral to learning. "What If" lesson objectives are a natural extension of spreadsheets as simple changes to data are quickly transformed into new information.

Thinking software   Idea-generating software utilizes diagramming and outlining paradigms for developing new ideas. These packages visualize thinking processes, transforming them into a graphical outline of interrelationships among processes, variables, and events. This package creates concept maps, process flows, knowledge flowcharts, and other visually-oriented diagrams.

Organizer software   An organizer program uses graphics to arrange files on the hard drive. It transforms the computer desktop into a virtual notebook that organizes, searches, and locates documents by "turning tabs and pages." For the Teacher as Expert, organizer tools provide for computer-managed instruction. Multiple notebooks create individual classes with computer files stored by name, date, location, and text contained in the document. Organizer software typically provides a table of contents and an alphabetical on-line index that lists every artifact in the portfolio.

Thinking Hardware

The rapidly expanding collection of images, sound files, and video clips requires significant hard disk storage.

4.0-Gigabyte Hard Drive   To support the demand for both back-up and mass storage, we recommend a 4-gigabyte hard drive for the Intelligent Portfolio.

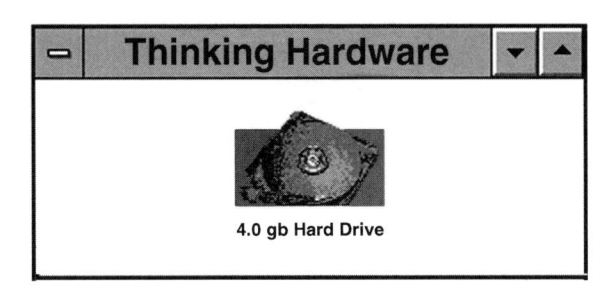

Thinking Hardware

4.0 gb Hard Drive

Writing Software

A full-featured word processor, teamed with an array of tools and formatting options, continues to serve as the recommended Writing software package for the Teacher as Expert.

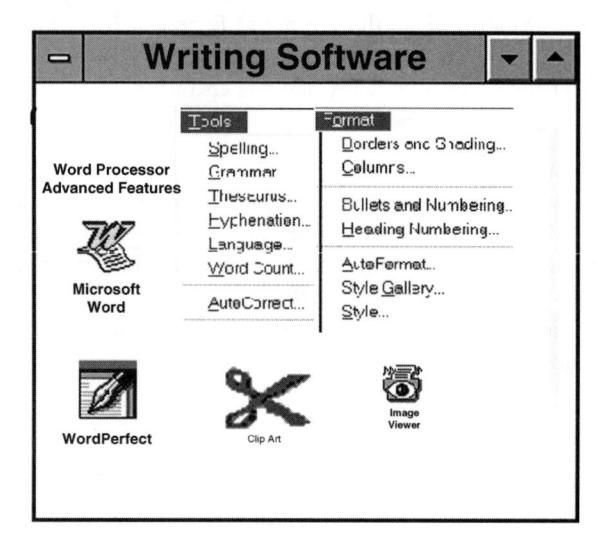

Word processors The Teacher-Expert will prepare classroom materials using a powerful word processor outfitted with tools such as a spell checker, thesaurus, hyphenator, automatic word correction, word count and grade level calculator, and grammar checker. Select a word processor that offers advanced formatting features such as column design, bullets or numbering of lists, headings and footers, and automatic formatting based on standard templates for preparing documents such as lesson plans.

"Visuals" software package Teachers integrate visual material into student handouts, study guides, and workbooks. Incorporating graphics or clip art into a document requires additional helper applications.

In the Intelligent Portfolio for the Teacher as Learner, we recommended that you select the word processor offered in your program course of study. If you are using the Teacher as Expert portfolio for the first time, you may wish to select the word processor which meets the local standards of your school. In both

Consider this if you are using the Intelligent Portfolio for the first time.

cases, the rationale is to aim for compatibility with the system in which you are working.

Writing Hardware

Material of classroom caliber demands higher-quality printing than a dot matrix or black-and-white inkjet printer affords. For this implementation of the Intelligent Portfolio, color

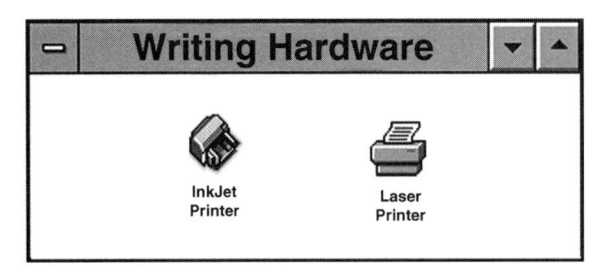

printing is recommended. If it is not available or affordable, a black-and-white laser printer is the next best thing.

Color inkjet printer Because of its quality and rapidly decreasing price, we recommend a color inkjet printer. The inkjet printer delivers an acceptable product for classroom use. After the initial purchase, the major cost centers around the color ink modules that must be replaced periodically. Search for a printer that uses two individual cartridges: one for black-and-white printing, the other for color. This feature is considerably less expensive when printing mostly black-and-white documents. Teachers should be alert, however, that inkjet printers—especially color models—can be painfully slow when they print. Do not wait until the last minute to prepare classroom materials.

Laser printer If you are a procrastinator (or a stickler for quality), the more expensive laser printer is a better option. Color laser printing is probably not affordable for most practicing teachers. Black-and-white laser, however, is priced considerably less, and the quality of print and throughput speed are quite acceptable. Laser printers also handle image printing much better than inkjets because they typically come with larger memory capacity for storing graphics files.

Reading Software

Reading is vital to lifelong learning. Although the Reading folder no longer takes on the prominence it held for the teacher-learner, it remains an indispensable source of artifacts. The network account is now in the Interacting folder and backup software is in the Dem-

onstrating folder. However, Library, Telnet, Gopher, and Web Browsers continue to provide avenues for Reading and the collection of new artifacts.

Telnet Communication Software Telnet is one of the more popular software packages connecting a remote computer with host resources. Telnet emulates an on-line terminal so that the host system accepts the link as though it were directly connected. For the Teacher as Expert, Telnet access is used for electronic mail, databases, on-line bulletin boards, library card catalogs, and other similar services.

Library Account Library access is one of the most important capabilities in the Intelligent Portfolio across all three implementations. Users of the portfolio must remain vigilant in their efforts to continually update Collecting artifacts—Smart or Intelligent. Libraries are the best source of this updated material. Teachers must make a concerted effort to go beyond the limited resources of their own local school plant to nearby colleges and universities that possess the collections from which new classroom thinking can grow and mature. Telnet software is the door, a library account is the key, and the Intelligent Portfolio is the vehicle for acquiring up-to-date artifacts.

Gopher The Gopher application is losing its pre-eminence as a popular text-based documentation management system. However, a wealth of material still remains in the system for the persistent researcher. Unfortunately, many of the original creators of this information are unavailable to transfer their works to a Web-based format. Until such time, if ever, that Gopher sites disappear entirely from the Internet, they continue to provide valuable materials, free for the taking. Since much of this material initially supported education, classroom teachers would be remiss if they did not check these sites when searching for discipline-specific artifacts. Gopher sites remain too numerous and easily accessible to be ignored simply because they do not provide the glamour of the World Wide Web. They can be accessed via Telnet or directly from many Web browsers.

World Wide Web Browser Use of the Internet takes on a dual purpose for the Teacher as Expert: as a research tool and as a teaching aid. Web browser software is placed in the Reading folder because its primary focus is to gather new Collecting artifacts. As a research tool, the teacher explores countless sites from which to choose the best lesson plans, student materials, and assessment alternatives. A Web browser accesses electronic journals and on-line magazines. It searches for the latest in classroom applications that help teachers remain current in the pedagogy of their subject-matter discipline.

In addition, the teacher has a new reason to use the Web. As a teaching tool, the Internet is only now being recognized for its potential in the classroom. Web-based courses and distance learning incorporates the pedagogical advantages of the World Wide Web into new programs for teaching. Multisensory graphics, cooperative learning, and active teaching techniques are realized with the help of this tool.

Reading Hardware

Reading Hardware

Desktop Scanner

Many of the Reading artifacts with which teachers come in contact on a daily basis involve printed material. The technology of the desktop scanner translates text and graphics into electronic artifacts for permanent storage in the Intelligent Portfolio. Without a scanner, it would not be possible to capture printed material electronically, without re-entering it as word processing text or graphics.

Desktop Scanner   Many schools already have scanners. Teachers consider them invaluable tools for converting text and graphics into machine-readable artifacts. A scanner translates analog light into digitized data, recording the amount of light reflected by the item being scanned. For the Teacher as Expert, the scanner is a valuable tool for capturing text-based artifacts and storing them in an electronic Collection Point.

Step Three: Organizing Folders and Collection Points

The Folders and Collection Points for the Intelligent Portfolio reflect the changing Teacher as Expert.

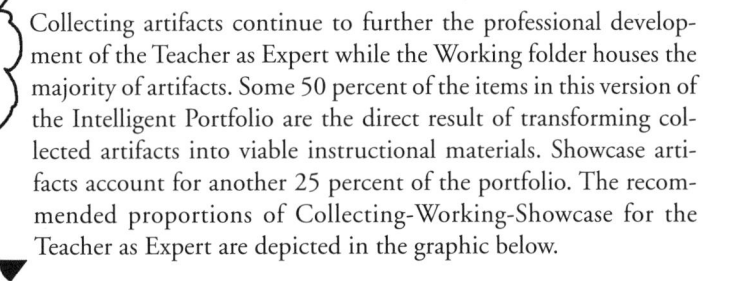

Collecting artifacts continue to further the professional development of the Teacher as Expert while the Working folder houses the majority of artifacts. Some 50 percent of the items in this version of the Intelligent Portfolio are the direct result of transforming collected artifacts into viable instructional materials. Showcase artifacts account for another 25 percent of the portfolio. The recommended proportions of Collecting-Working-Showcase for the Teacher as Expert are depicted in the graphic below.

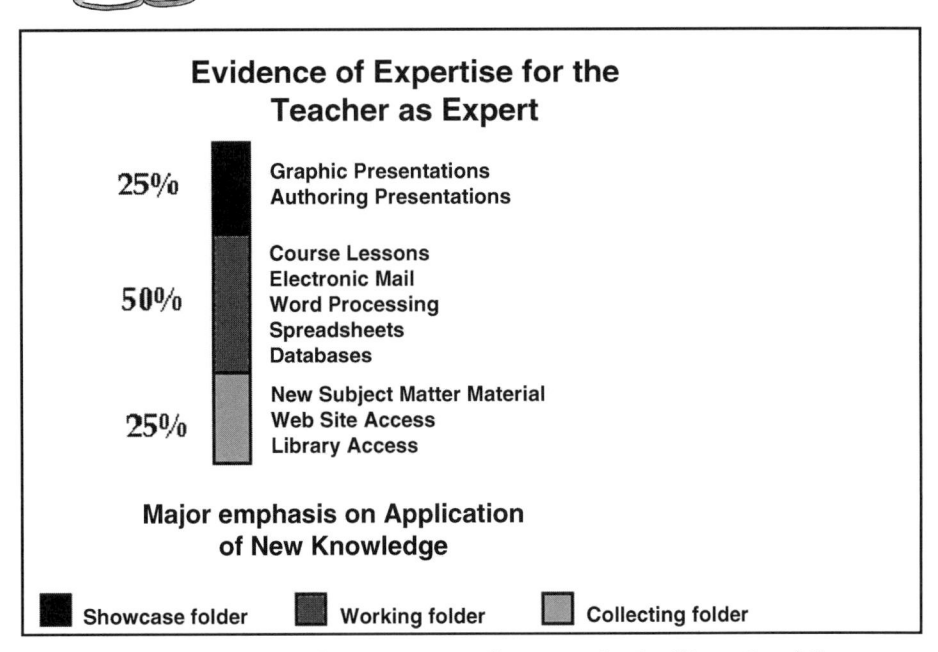

Evidence of Expertise for the Teacher as Expert

25%		Graphic Presentations Authoring Presentations
50%		Course Lessons Electronic Mail Word Processing Spreadsheets Databases
25%		New Subject Matter Material Web Site Access Library Access

Major emphasis on Application of New Knowledge

■ Showcase folder   ▩ Working folder   ▢ Collecting folder

Take a look at what the Teacher as Expert will store in the Intelligent Portfolio.

Collecting Folder

The Collecting artifacts that were gathered in the previous version of the Intelligent Portfolio provide a valuable source in the development of new classroom material. Although the Teacher as Expert will continue to use all four Collection Points, the Collecting folder becomes primarily a repository to aid in the development of working artifacts.

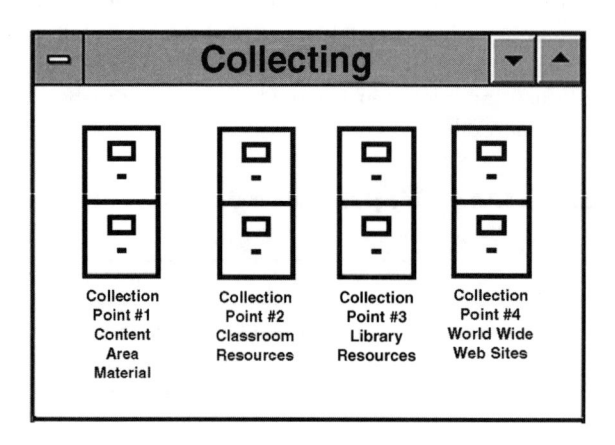

Collection Point #1: Content Area Material   As the instructional leader of the classroom, teachers accumulate a wealth of science handouts, math articles, creative writing ideas, and geography lessons. These artifacts continue to replace or augment existing teaching materials and contribute to better teaching. As a practitioner, the Foundations of Reading, Writing, and Interacting produce most of the materials for this Collection Point. Never stop gathering artifacts.

Collection Point #2: Classroom Resources   Of all the Collecting folders, Collection Point #2 continues to be the most popular target for newly acquired classroom assets. Textbook publishers, Web site creators, and curriculum designers, as well as contributing teachers offer predesigned lesson plans, tests, review notes, study guides, and lesson objectives simply for the asking. Unvalidated materials should not be placed directly into a Working folder. Instead, place them in this Collection Point until they are validated against particular learning objectives.

Collection Point #3: Library Resources   The content of this Collection Point changes little throughout the various implementations of the Intelligent Portfolio. Library Resources continues to house pertinent information regarding access to educational materials. For the Teacher as Expert, the school library adds a wealth of artifacts. In addition to books and journals, laser discs, videotape, audio selections, and cable television programs are available to the classroom teacher.

Collection Point #4: World Wide Web Sites   New Web site addresses for education-related Internet sites continue to be added to this Collection Point. The Teacher as Expert focuses on sites that provide subject matter material, locations that offer ready-made lesson plans and classroom projects, and home pages that present concepts that can be integrated into an existing lesson. Here are some example World Wide Web sites that meet these criteria:

Subject Matter Specialists

Government

http://www.whitehouse.gov	White House Web
http://www.law.cornell.edu/constitution/constitution.overview.html	US Constitution

Science

http://sln.fi.edu:80/biosci/	Outstanding Tour of the Human Heart
http://seds.lpl.arizona.edu/nineplanets/nineplanets/nineplanets.html	Tour of the Solar System
http://www-itg.lbl.gov	Interactive Frog Dissection Kit

Social Studies

http://www.historychannel.com	History Channel
http://www.halcyon.com/howlevin/social.studies.html	Social Studies Lesson Plans
http://rs6.loc.gov/amtitle.html	The American Memory: Titles and Topics
http://www.webcorp.com/sounds/index.htm	Historical Speeches Archive
http://www.uscivilwar.com	Civil War stories, maps, discussion groups and games

Mathematics

http://olmo.swarthmore.edu/dr-math/dr-math.html	Ask Dr. Math!
http://www.c3.lanl.gov/mega-math/	Mega Math (Los Alamos)

Language Arts

http://www2.southwind.net/~frsttchr/old/rubric.html	Mr. Boline's Handwriting Rubrics
http://the-tech.mit.edu/Shakespeare/works.html	Complete Works of Wm Shakespeare

Art

http://cnam.fr/louvre/paint/auth	Louvre Museum, Paris France
http://www.mcae.k12.mn.us/gallery/artgal.html	The Art Gallery

Working Folder

To assist in the storage of Working artifacts, two new Collection Points have been added to the Intelligent Portfolio. The first results from the partitioning of Lessons and Applications in the previous Teacher as Learner portfolio into two separate folders. The second is an entirely new Collection Point labeled Classroom Research.

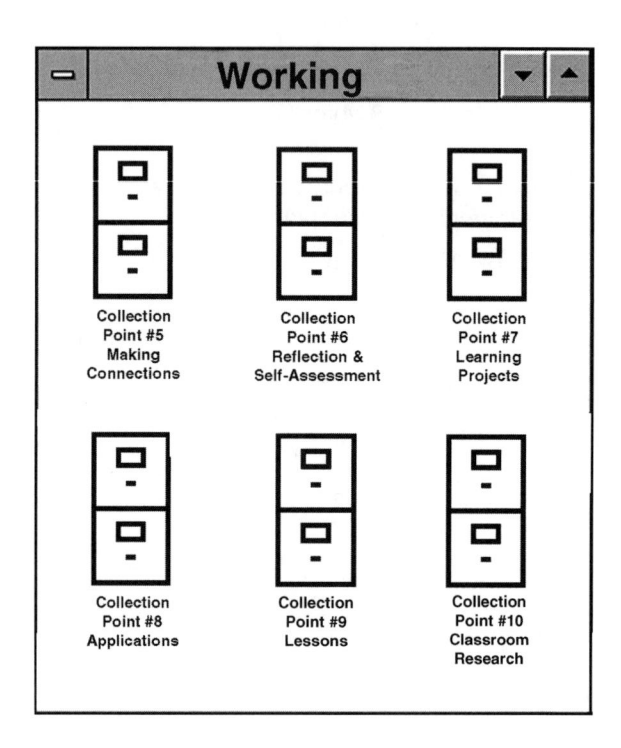

For the Teacher as Expert, create your next 6 Working Collection Points like these. There are two new Points in this Portfolio.

Working

- Collection Point #5 Making Connections
- Collection Point #6 Reflection & Self-Assessment
- Collection Point #7 Learning Projects
- Collection Point #8 Applications
- Collection Point #9 Lessons
- Collection Point #10 Classroom Research

Collection Point #5: Making Connections Making Connections takes on an expanded role as teachers share classroom practices common to their specific grades and subject matter areas. This Collection Point contains mindmaps and drawings where ideas begin to form. Ideas from reading mix with conversations with colleagues to extend thinking and integrate new knowledge.

Collection Point #6: Reflection and Self-Assessment This Collection Point tracks progress toward individual career goals. As a teacher in the classroom, these artifacts include in-class evaluations conducted by mentors, department heads, and principals. It also includes annual evaluations scanned electronically to become part of your permanent record. Many novice teachers prefer to keep an electronic journal of their experiences and thinking. Notations might include a reflection of the day's activities: what went right and what went wrong, lessons learned, tasks that resulted from a particular lesson, possible questions for an upcoming teacher-made test, and so on.

Collection Point #7: Learning Projects Individual learning projects take an active role in this version of the Intelligent Portfolio. Discovery learning activities, cooperative exercises, and group learning materials are a few of the artifacts to be stored here. To be included in this Collection Point, the project must have been successfully used in actual classroom situations. Material should be tested prior to placement in this Collection Point.

Collection Point #8: Applications For the Teacher as Expert, a majority of the Working artifacts shift to the development of lesson materials and their use in actual classroom presentations. The Integrated Thematic Unit (ITU) is an excellent example of an Application artifact that can be developed and maintained in this Collection Point. New artifacts are created when Content Area Materials are combined with Classroom Resources to create classroom-worthy exercises.

Collection Point #9: Lessons A simple rule of thumb for the Teacher as Expert: "If you use it in the classroom, store it in this Collection Point." Lessons constitute the single most used repository in this version of the Intelligent Portfolio. The only Collection Point with its own subfolders, Lessons provides one subfolder for each course session to be taught during the academic year. After considerable research and testing, these self-contained subfolders were found to provide the most logical approach to storing in-use classroom artifacts. Since this Collection Point lies at the heart of the Intelligent Portfolio for the Teacher as Expert, let's examine its contents in greater detail.

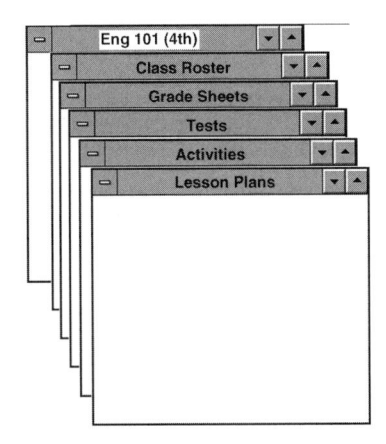

```
Eng 101 (4th)
  Class Roster
    Grade Sheets
      Tests
        Activities
          Lesson Plans
```

Teaching fourth period English requires an electronic subfolder such as the one pictured above. If the user of the Intelligent Portfolio teaches 7 different subjects, then 7 separate subfolders are contained in Collection Point #9. Each subfolder will house....

....**Rosters** reflecting the names and information of each student in the class. The database software proposed in the Thinking folder is recommended for this task. If a digital camera is available, this subfolder may also hold a pictorial student roster and a graphical seating plan.

....**Grade Sheets** created using another Thinking folder application: the electronic spreadsheet. Using this automated tool, numeric scores can be tracked, averaged, and translated into letter grades automatically at the end of each grading period.

....**Tests and Quizzes** created using the word processor in the Writing folder, and modified and printed as needed throughout the academic year. Other test-related statistics are kept here as well, including item analyses of specific test questions, and alternative forms of each test.

....**Classroom Activities** including digitized agendas to annual field trips, word-processed letters inviting special guest speakers, and electronic games, Web site contests, and computer exercises.

....and **Lesson Plans.** Only lesson plans that will be used in this specific class during the current academic year are maintained in this Collection Point. Otherwise, they should reside in the Applications Collection Point.

These five elements: class rosters, grade sheets, tests, activities, and lesson plans comprise the Lessons Collection Point. For the Teacher as Expert, these artifacts represent the culmination of an educator's dedication to excellence in teaching and learning in the classroom and lifelong professional development.

Collection Point #10: Classroom Research Do some of your artifacts propose a new approach to classroom teaching? Do they point out areas of instruction that deserve special attention? Do they address a particular psychology of learning that merits further exploration? If so, this Collection Point might explore new ways to combat sexual bias in the classroom, best practices in an advanced math class, or the conduct of a successful science project for secondary students. Collection Point #10 promotes teacher inquiry and effective student learning by exploring new ideas and instructional approaches.

Showcase Folder

The teacher in the classroom has ample opportunity to display the results of new thinking. Showcase Collection Points store artifacts representing the best efforts of the Teacher as Expert.

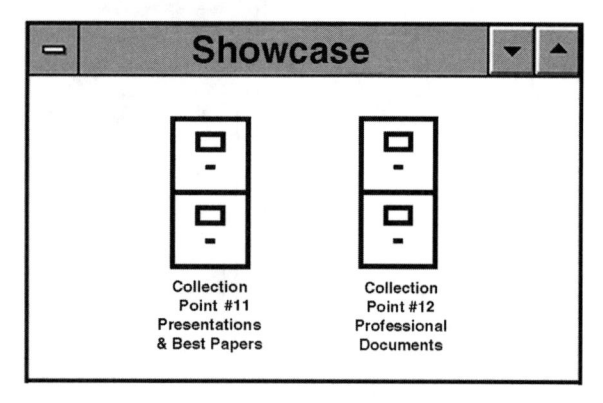

Collection Point #11: Presentations and Best Papers Education-related materials not specifically destined for the classroom are stored in this Collection Point. Best Papers include the text of manuscripts submitted for professional publication. Draft reports, papers, and future articles are prepared and saved as artifacts in this Collection Point. A wealth of diverse documents aimed at presenting new concepts are combined, consolidated, focused and stored here.

Collection Point #12: Professional Documents The educator's list of professional documents grows almost daily. The Intelligent Portfolio offers the convenience of storing electronic artifacts that can be easily retrieved; this is particularly important with respect to professional documents. Included in the Teacher as Expert Intelligent Portfolio is an updated vita of classroom experiences—even if that experience encompasses only a year or two of teaching. It holds artifacts such as state teaching credentials, scores from the National Teacher's Examination, personal background checks, academic transcripts for completed and in-progress coursework, and letters of recommendation. Finally, this Collection Point holds copies of any personal evaluation received during the academic year, career objectives and short-term goals, documentation required by the district or local school administration, and certificates of completion for continuing education courses taken in support of classroom teaching.

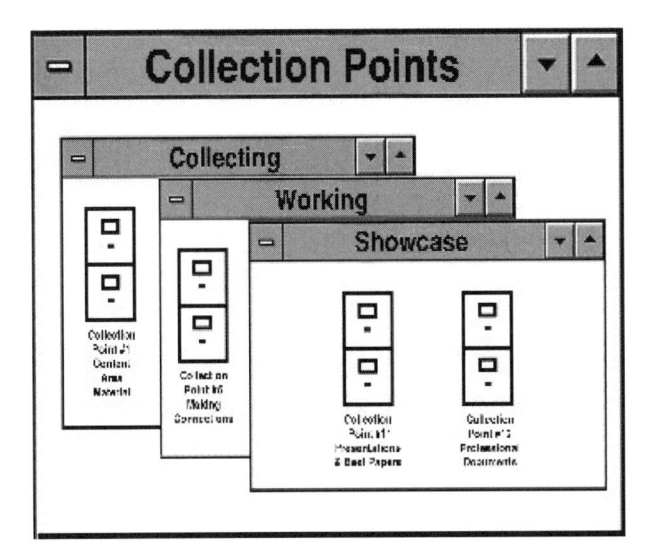

The Intelligent Portfolio for the Teacher as Expert 97

Thought bubble: We have created all the Collection Points in three folders.

Conclusion

The focus for the Teacher as Expert shifts to the Working folder of the Intelligent Portfolio. Electronic artifacts continue to be collected, but the emphasis is now on the development of those artifacts into new thinking that will play out in the classroom. Technology provides an excellent tool for the portfolio user. Let Foley offer a few final tips for using the Intelligent Portfolio.

Foley Tips

1. **Working is the focus of the Intelligent Portfolio for the Teacher as Expert.** Do not clutter your computer with software (or hardware for that matter) that does not contribute directly to the development of new artifacts.

Thought bubble: For the Teacher as Expert, here are a few tips when using the Intelligent Portfolio.

2. **Visit each Collection Point periodically.** Revisit artifacts regularly, especially those used in the classroom. Ineffective artifacts should be returned to their original Collection Points or disgarded, while tested and validated artifacts remain in the Working folder or are moved to a Showcase location.

3. **Continue to upgrade your Intelligent Portfolio.** Remain alert to the latest versions of operating systems, software, and hardware. Remember that the Intelligent Portfolio is a tool for a lifetime of professional development and requires routine upgrades.

4. **Continue to collect artifacts.** The Teacher as Expert depends on interacting and thinking skills to locate new artifacts. It is incumbent upon the educator to seek out artifacts that reflect current thinking and pedagogy in order to make informed decisions affecting classroom instruction.

5. **Capture new artifacts from the World Wide Web.** The future is on the Internet. The Teacher as Expert requires access to the Internet. If your school does not provide this tool, the teacher should obtain connectivity from home. It is *that* important. Downloading files from the World Wide Web will nearly always be the easiest form of collecting new artifacts. Exploring the vast resources of the Web is time well spent if that information results in improved educational instruction.

6. **Migrate gradually to the next phase of the Intelligent Portfolio.** Begin this gradual migration when you begin to see beyond the classroom. There is a tendency to believe that the further "up" the ladder of portfolios the "better." That is simply not true. Migration to the final Teacher as Scholar portfolio should occur only when you need the features of the next portfolio.

7. **Look ahead to the Intelligent Portfolio for the Teacher as Scholar.** The migration to the next portfolio should not be hampered by limitations to hardware or software. The best way to ensure that this does not happen is to prepare now by understanding how the Intelligent Portfolio will change once your focus shifts from classroom teacher to Teacher-Scholar.

8. **Enroll in technical classes which support the Intelligent Portfolio.** Each package recommended includes features far exceeding those suggested in the discussion of the Intelligent Portfolio. Most colleges and universities offer computer courses for the beginner and the expert. Take advantage of them as you seek advanced courses throughout your teaching career.

9. **Stick with the recommended software.** If the recommended package gets the job done, stay with it unless there are mitigating circumstances such as local support or better pricing that make other packages more attractive. Avoid changing software packages because of persuasive advertisements.

10. **Add Collection Points to your Intelligent Portfolio.** If you can identify other categories of artifacts that make sense, do not restrict your portfolio to the basic Collection Points proposed. However, do not remove any of the recommended repositories unless you are genuinely convinced that they are unnecessary.

CHAPTER 10

Portfolios in Transition: The Teacher as Expert Perspective

Introduction

By the time Jennifer stepped into her first teaching position, she had already successfully constructed several portfolios. As an undergraduate English major, she had maintained a writing portfolio throughout most of her upper-class college years. In fact, Jennifer had so many artifacts stuffed into shoeboxes and drawers that she took on the formidable task of organizing these items early in her academic career, well before anyone handed her the design of a Smart Portfolio. She used several drawers in a home filing cabinet to store the accumulated treasures she felt had merit. They would become an invaluable resource for her first teaching assignment and her eighth grade, third period, Creative Writing class.

Jennifer's portfolio contained proof that she was well-prepared for her new role as a teacher. One of the drawers held her treasured state teaching certificate along with copies of college transcripts, a publication piece that made it as far as a refereed journal committee, a validated lesson plan complete with student materials, a one-page philosophy of learning that her last professor insisted would be important some day, and several of her best works evidencing mastery of subject content knowledge.

It had taken a deliberate effort on Jennifer's part to reorganize materials into a Showcase exhibition for her first interview at a local junior high school. Fortunately for Jennifer, committee members were supervised by an avid proponent of teacher portfolios. From the beginning, Jennifer was encouraged to share her artifacts, although at times this became a logistical nightmare. Loose-leaf papers, floppy diskettes, and hard-copy handouts did not readily lend themselves to the teacher interview process.

The interview was a success, and Jennifer's first year in the school system was marked by her continued personal exploration of portfolios. Resources, in the form of time and money, were available and she found herself at the forefront of a school-wide campaign to raise the consciousness of portfolios in the school — for both teachers and students.

As she worked through many different models, Jennifer became adept at recognizing differences in purpose, organization, and audiences in the portfolio process. Since she was also technologically literate, these personal characteristics combined with her natural curiosity led her to explore the Smart and Intelligent Portfolios.

A Teacher-Expert

A recent graduate, classroom teacher, proponent of technology, and experienced portfolio user—Jennifer was a natural for this study.

Jennifer was the ideal candidate to validate the Teacher as Expert portfolio:

• She had experience with portfolios as a student;

• She was a recent graduate of a teacher preparation program that used portfolios for assessment;

• Her school environment adopted portfolios for lifelong learning; and

• She had expressed an interest in technology and its applications in portfolio design.

    Jennifer enrolled in a graduate-level course that put her in touch with the designers of the Intelligent Portfolio. The rest, as they say, is history. She agreed to translate her undergraduate portfolio into the suggested Smart Portfolio format. To convince her to move to the Intelligent Portfolio, a student aide was hired to convert her hard-copy documents into scanned text files, charts and handouts into graphic images, and reports into word processing documents.

    Jennifer was introduced to the principles of the Smart Portfolio. The Working focus of the Teacher as Expert and the experiences of James and Jason (presented in Chapter 7) were shared. As with the previous prototype study, her contributions and recommendations resulted in important changes to the ultimate design of both portfolios. The remainder of this chapter presents the results of her efforts to implement the Teacher as Expert portfolio.

Jennifer's Smart Portfolio

Collecting, Working, and Showcase Folders were constructed, and the accumulated artifacts of several years of pre-service teacher education quickly filled the empty repositories.

    At the outset of the study, Jennifer concentrated on Collecting artifacts including Content Area, Classroom, and Library Resources. Although her Web site products were limited, Jennifer continued to augment this Collection Point with URL addresses specific to her English subject matter area.

    Showcase folders contained the fewest artifacts for Jennifer's portfolio – appropriate for this point in her career. She produced several items worthy of consideration by peers, colleagues, and fellow students. In Presentations and Papers, Jennifer displayed the transparencies of her portfolio session given as in-service training to teachers in her school. Also, she held onto the Demonstrating artifacts shared with the interview team that approved her present appointment. Professional Documents contained many more artifacts. She transferred her teaching certificate, course transcripts, and background investigations, along with paperwork from the first meeting with school district administrators into an electronic format. Her Showcase folder was growing, but the emphasis of the Teacher as Expert portfolio would remain strongest in the Working aspects of the Smart Portfolio.

    From the outset, Jennifer felt the need to expand the original 10 Collection Points established in the previous Teacher as Learner portfolio. Focusing as she should on Working artifacts, she found too many classroom-related items to fit comfortably into only four Collection Points. So, she added three more Collection Points to the original Working Folder:

Jennifer's Smart Portfolio

Thinking Journal
"Making Connections"
Contacts for Language
Contacts for Writing

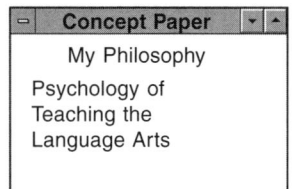

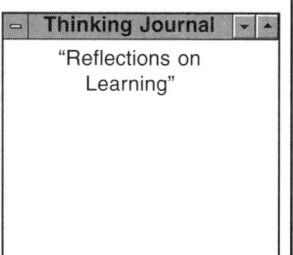

Concept Paper
My Philosophy
Psychology of Teaching the Language Arts

Thinking Journal
"Reflections on Learning"

Collecting

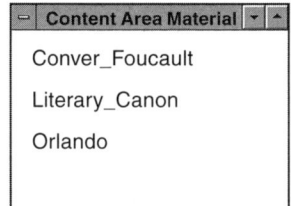

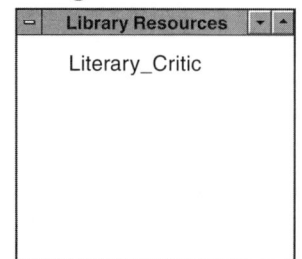

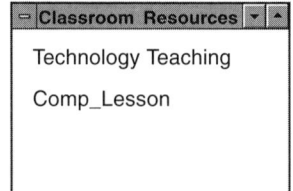

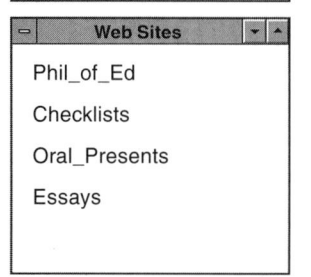

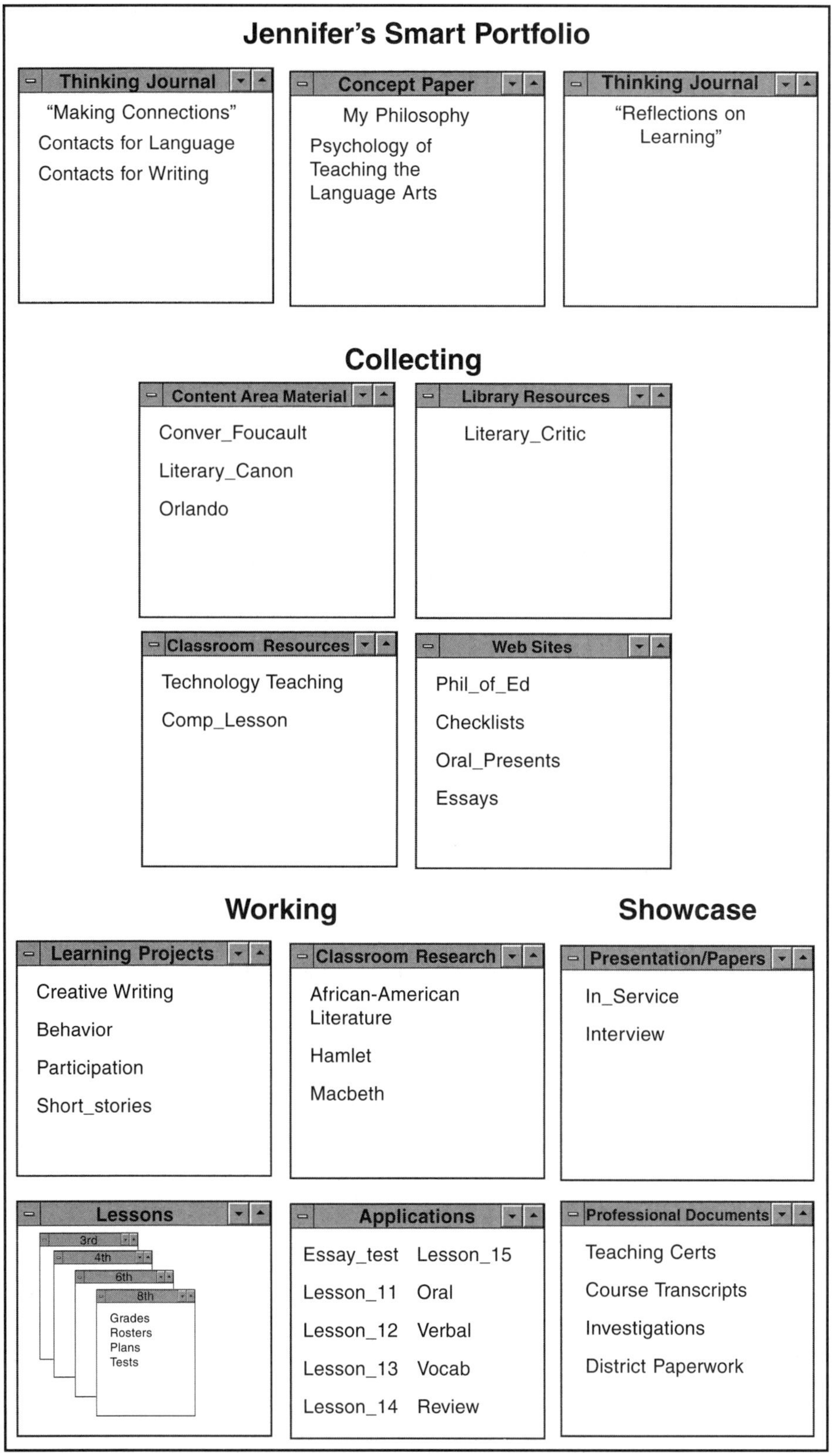

Content Area Material
Conver_Foucault
Literary_Canon
Orlando

Library Resources
Literary_Critic

Classroom Resources
Technology Teaching
Comp_Lesson

Web Sites
Phil_of_Ed
Checklists
Oral_Presents
Essays

Working

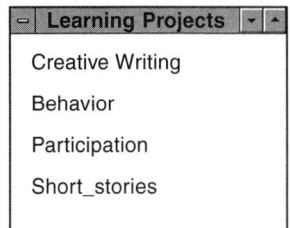

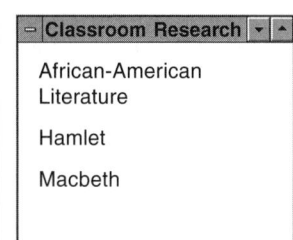

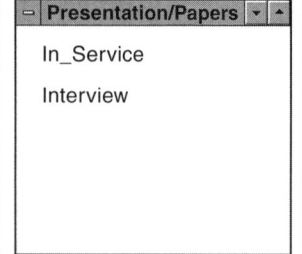

Learning Projects
Creative Writing
Behavior
Participation
Short_stories

Classroom Research
African-American Literature
Hamlet
Macbeth

Showcase

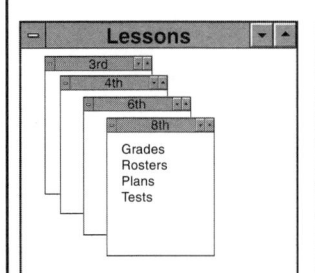

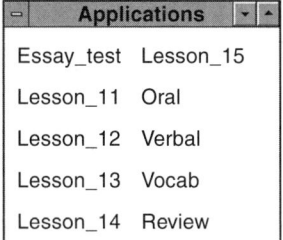

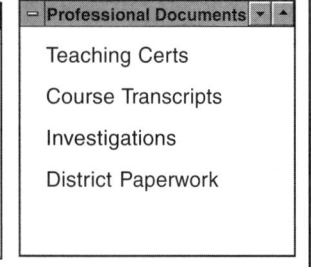

Presentation/Papers
In_Service
Interview

Lessons
3rd
4th
6th
8th
Grades
Rosters
Plans
Tests

Applications
Essay_test   Lesson_15
Lesson_11   Oral
Lesson_12   Verbal
Lesson_13   Vocab
Lesson_14   Review

Professional Documents
Teaching Certs
Course Transcripts
Investigations
District Paperwork

Classroom Research

Untested, incomplete, but promising ideas were relocated to one of the new Collection Points proposed by Jennifer. Considered an area always "under construction," she stored classroom materials that would need additional work before being incorporated into an actual lesson.

Classroom Research was one of the three new folders Jennifer recommended.

Applications

Applications and Lessons become separate Collection Points for the Teacher as Expert.

The Applications Collection Point houses only validated, classroom-ready artifacts that have passed the test of successful classroom presentation. These lessons measured up to the standards of excellence Jennifer expected of herself and matched her style of classroom teaching. Some of these artifacts were simple one-objective learning activities; others were more involved, multiday units of instruction that incorporated all the tools in her teaching repertoire. Classroom-ready materials stay in this Collection Point until placed in the Lessons folder.

Lessons

Jennifer's most prominent contribution to the Smart Portfolio (and later the Intelligent Portfolio) was the Lessons Collection Point. To adequately store all the various materials she would need in the classroom, Jennifer considered two alternative forms of "subfolders." The first subfolder contained "object-specific artifacts" for the classroom. The second stressed a focus on "self-contained entities."

Option One: Object-Specific Subfolders   When this option was first discussed, its title scared even the authors. Jennifer found that to function in a classroom, a teacher needed to tie together five key elements:

- Roster of Students
- Grade Sheets
- Assessment Tools
- Classroom Activities
- Lesson Plans

Jennifer identified 5 key elements needed to manage a classroom.

Whether the teacher used greenbar accounting paper or computer software, the Lessons Collection Point must contain these five elements to satisfactorily manage a classroom. Initially, Jennifer decided to create the subfolders according to the 5 elements as shown at the top of page 103.

Her thinking at the time was based on the formidable task of capturing artifacts. Rosters were placed in a single subfolder,

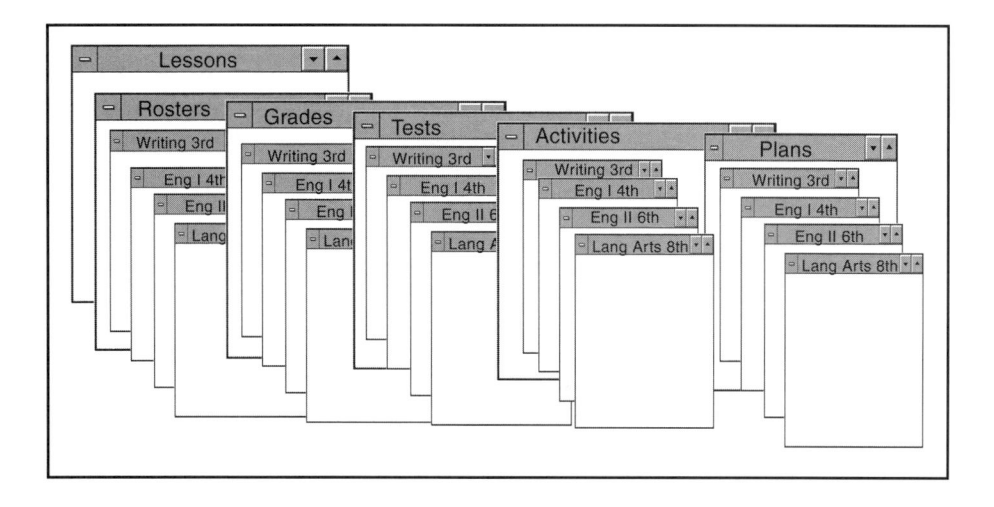

[Figure: Option One organization showing Lessons folder containing Rosters, Grades, Tests, Activities, and Plans subfolders, each with Writing 3rd, Eng I 4th, Eng II 6th, and Lang Arts 8th class entries]

grades is a second subfolder, and so on. To catalog the impressive number of artifacts she already possessed, Jennifer found this format to be most effective.

However, for purposes of retrieving these artifacts during her first teaching semester, she discovered this option to be particularly cumbersome. This option required her to move among the five subfolders for nearly every classroom activity. A simple chapter assessment demanded that she first flip through the *Test* subfolder to locate the appropriate quiz. Recording the scores called for a search through the *Grades* subfolder to find the spreadsheet for her third-period class. She checked the answer sheets against a class *Roster* to identify absent students and annotate an upcoming date for make-up tests. For this single classroom evaluation, three separate subfolders were involved. Clearly, Jennifer's portfolio confirmed that capturing artifacts is not as important as their retrieval.

Option Two: Class-Specific Entities After several discussions, Jennifer reorganized her portfolio by class periods. Results were far more promising, and, with only minor modifications, Jennifer's efforts became the model for the Teacher as Expert portfolio. The graphic below depicts the reorganized Lesson Collection Point:

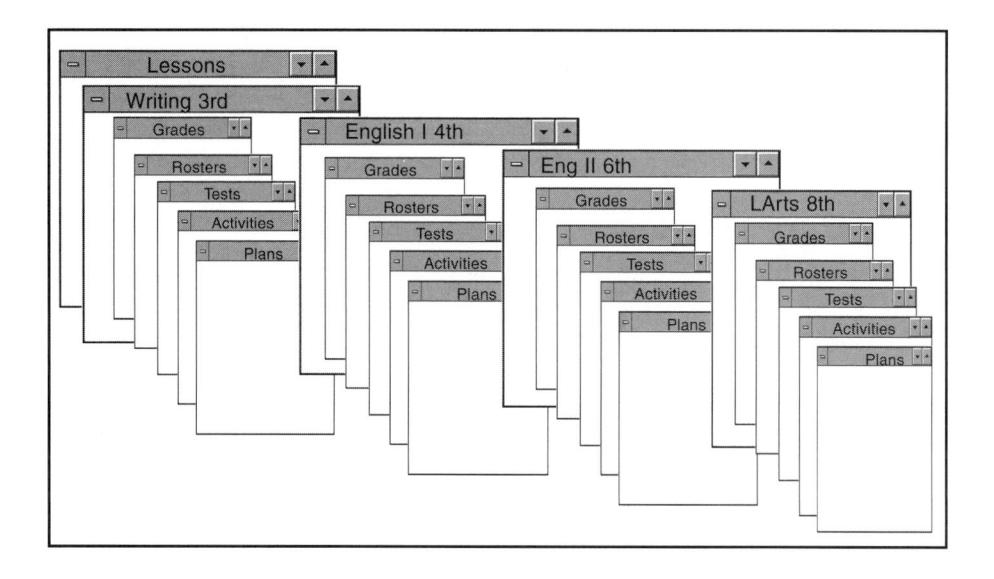

[Figure: Option Two organization showing Lessons folder containing Writing 3rd, English I 4th, Eng II 6th, and LArts 8th class folders, each with Grades, Rosters, Tests, Activities, and Plans subfolders]

104   *Professional Portfolios for Teachers*

Jennifer placed all artifacts related to each of her ongoing classes into a single subfolder. Storing new artifacts took longer, but the speed of retrieval was much faster. Grades, rosters, tests, classroom activities, and lesson plans were grouped together for each class. As semesters changed, creating a new suite of class-specific artifacts was made easier by using a boilerplate document Jennifer discovered in one of her undergraduate courses in Tests and Measurement. It contained an excellent format to apply in her own classroom situation. Lesson Plans were pulled from Applications and Learning Projects to keep the material fresh for both students and teacher. New class rosters were quickly created. The second option became an instant success, and these simple modifications were quickly incorporated into the final version of the Teacher as Expert portfolio.

Jennifer's Intelligent Portfolio

With her Smart Portfolio firmly established in everyday classroom use, Jennifer turned her attention to the full implementation of the Intelligent Portfolio. Excited about the possibilities of automating the cumbersome collection of artifacts, she readily accepted the offer of a student aide to help her convert the volumes of documents, spreadsheets, reproduced articles, and other artifacts into computerized files.

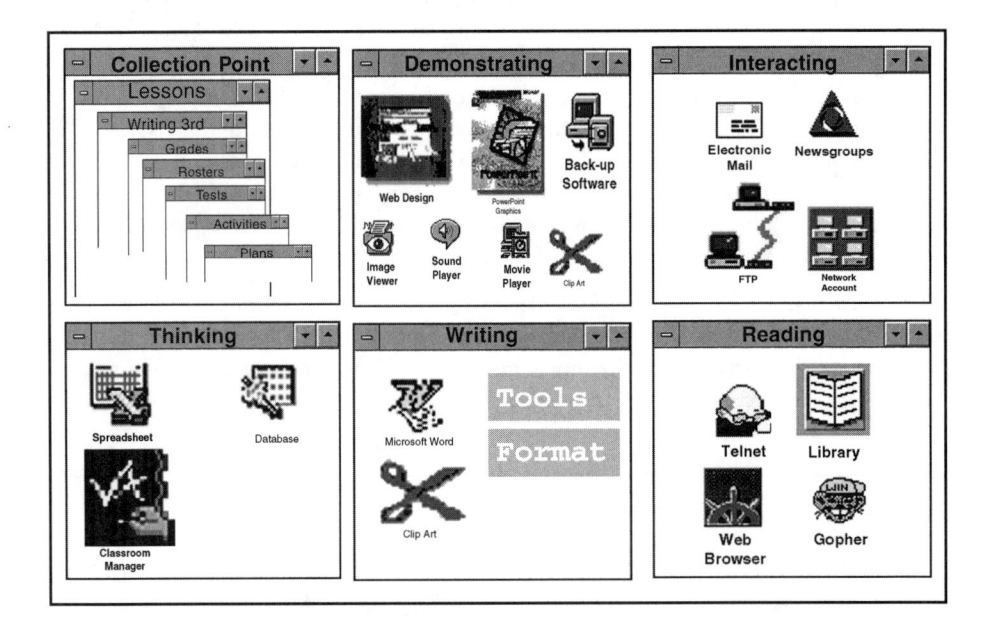

Portfolio Folders

Jennifer owned a laptop computer running Windows. Her first step in the prototype study was to format the desktop screen to resemble the Demonstrating, Interacting, Thinking, Writing, and Reading Folders of the Smart Portfolio.

The **Demonstrating** folder was installed first and included a course writing package that combined graphics presentation and back-up software. It provided a series of common templates for creating lesson plans, student handouts, visual aids, and teacher-made assessment tools in addition to other classroom management features. A suite of helper applications integrated image, sound, and video files into documents and graphic presentations. Clip Art was added during the study. Jennifer researched the World Wide Web until she found utility routines that would aid in the design of Internet-based lessons: editors, HTML primers, and scripting tools were introduced to the Demonstrating folder.

The **Interacting** folder contained most of the same hardware and software features of the previous Teacher as Learner portfolio. Exceptions included a file transfer package to download files from educational sites offering lesson plans, journal articles, and significant quantities of visual aids with Language Arts application.

Jennifer validated a new classroom management software package for the **Thinking** folder. The package provided a teacher gradebook to track and report student progress on a range of assignments. She used the software to store student test and assignment information as well as calculate student final letter grades and other statistics. Her positive reviews resulted in the inclusion of the package in the Intelligent Portfolio.

The **Writing** folder included a robust word processor with a host of tools and formatting features that would support the production of hardcopy student handouts and study guides.

Reading tools included what had become the standard suite of utilities such as Library access, Telnet and Gopher access, and World Wide Web locations.

Hardware consisted of a Pentium laptop computer with 32 megabytes of memory and a 1 gigabyte hard drive. Jennifer stored many of her artifacts on a Zip drive, especially those which she did not place into immediate classroom use. During in-service demonstrations, a flat panel projector displayed images onto a six foot by eight foot screen for her audience.

Portfolio Collection Points

Initially, Jennifer attempted to organize her artifacts using the directories and file structure with which she was most familiar. She converted the opening screens of her portfolio to hold the following folders:

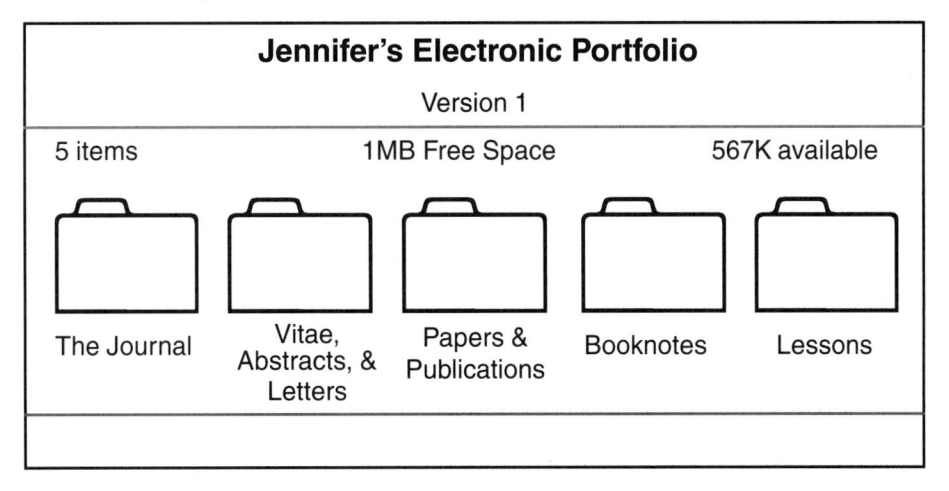

Jennifer's Electronic Portfolio
Version 1

5 items	1MB Free Space	567K available
The Journal	Vitae, Abstracts, & Letters	Papers & Publications	Booknotes	Lessons

A close-up examination of the contents of several folders attests to the fact that Jennifer understood the purpose of portfolios from the very start. In her initial **Lessons** folder, she captured the following artifacts:

Jennifer's Electronic Portfolio				
Lessons		Version 1		
8 items		1MB Free Space		567K available
	Size	File Type	Last Modified	
African-America_Lit	17K	sub-folder	Jan 22	7:55 PM
Creative_Writing	36K	sub-folder	Mar 05	7:25 AM
Hamlet	123K	sub-folder	Feb 21	8:59 AM
Laughing_Boy	46K	sub-folder	Jan 23	10:42 AM
Macbeth	61K	sub-folder	Feb 14	9:42 PM
Mythology/Heroes	22K	sub-folder	Jan 30	11:18 AM
Romeo & Juliet	111K	sub-folder	Mar 01	8:10 PM
Merchant_of_Venice	84K	sub-folder	Mar 11	12:10 PM

Vitae, Abstracts, and Letters held all of her Showcase artifacts:

Jennifer's Electronic Portfolio				
Vitae, Abstra . . .		Version 1		
		1MB Free Space		567K available
	Size	File Type	Last Modified	
Abstracts	61K	sub-folder	Feb 21	11:18 AM
Ed Vitae	111K	sub-folder	Mar 01	7:55 PM
Job Letters	36K	sub-folder	Feb 14	7:25 AM
Pub Corresp	22K	sub-folder	Jan 30	8:59 AM
Other Letters	17K	sub-folder	Mar 11	9:42 PM

And, her **Booknotes** folder was the primary repository of her growing array of Collecting items.

Jennifer had the makings of a viable suite of Collection Points. Each artifact in her electronic portfolio was identified as a Collecting, Working, or Showcase item and placed in one of the three collecting points. To her credit, Jennifer quickly recognized the shortcomings of using only a few Collection Points: they were too restrictive, did not separate teacher responsibilities, and made locating important artifacts cumbersome.

Jennifer's Electronic Portfolio

Booknotes   Version 1

81 items   1MB Free Space   567K available

	Size	File Type	Last Modified
Coover_Foucault	17K	file	Jan 22 7:55 PM
Literary_Canon	22K	file	Mar 05 7:25 AM
Orlando	12K	file	Feb 21 8:59 AM
Phil_of_Ed	11K	file	Jan 23 10:42 AM
Technology	9K	folder	Feb 14 9:42 PM
Literary_Critic	14K	file	Jan 30 11:18 AM
Responsive_Teaching	26K	file	Mar 01 8:10 PM
Checklists	116K	folder	Mar 11 12:10 PM
Oral_Presents	243K	folder	Jan 23 10:42 AM
Essays	21K	folder	Feb 14 9:42 PM
Comp_Lesson	32K	file	Jan 22 7:55PM

▼ More ▼

When the full suite of Collection Points was explained, Jennifer accepted the new organizational structure for her own portfolio. She did have some reservations about the Working folder as the most important container for the Teacher as Expert; her first inclination was to favor Showcase artifacts. She recommended that Lessons and Applications, formerly a single Collection Point, be divided into two separate folders. Also, she felt that another point was needed specifically for storing content area research with specific classroom potential.

After several iterations, Jennifer decided on a final configuration for the Teacher as Expert Intelligent Portfolio:

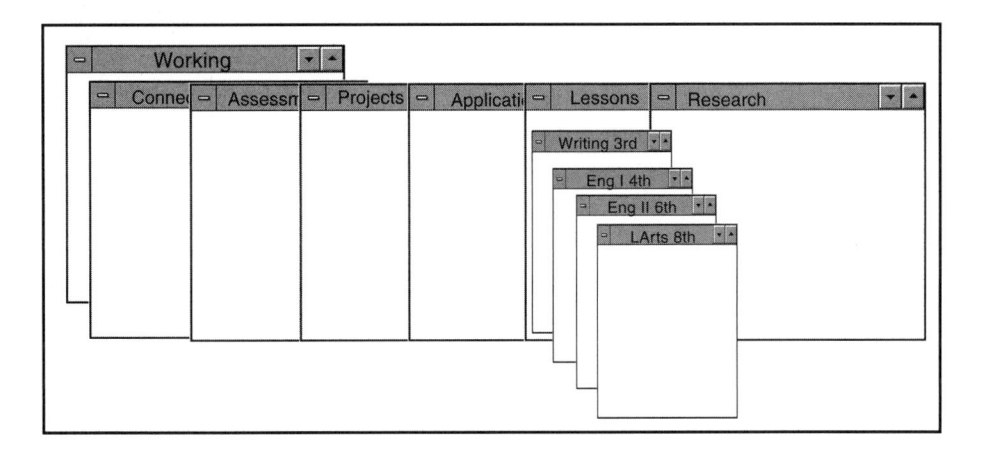

Working | Connec | Assessm | Projects | Applicati | Lessons | Research

Writing 3rd
Eng I 4th
Eng II 6th
LArts 8th

It is important to note that each of the artifacts originally stored in her electronic portfolio found their way into a Collection Point in the new Intelligent Portfolio. The new format reorganized her collection more efficiently and brought to light some of the shortcomings of her original thinking about portfolios for the classroom teacher.

Results of the Study

By category, here are some of the most salient findings of the study:

Growing Up with Portfolios

For Jennifer, portfolios have been a way of academic life since her early undergraduate days. The tool was a natural extension of her personal need for organization first as a learner and then as a classroom teacher. One of the most important findings of this study was the need to encourage the lifelong use of portfolios for all educators, but most critically at the earliest stages of pre-service preparation. Those who are taught to use portfolios to collect, work, and showcase their efforts as learners are better prepared to share that learning strategy with their own students.

The Strength of the Professional Portfolio

Organization is fundamental to the continued utility of the portfolio as a tool for personal development. Whether it is accomplished by using a 3-ring binder or computer hardware is irrelevant. Success lies in its continued and enthusiastic use to foster lifelong learning.

The Impact of Technology

Technology impacts many aspects of classroom teaching and learning. The Intelligent Portfolio's ability to function as a tool in this process is only now being realized. It should be seriously considered by teachers. Fortunately, the decision to move from a hard copy to an electronic environment is one that can be postponed without loss of functionality or utility.

Portfolio Folders, Collection Points, and Technology

The Professional Portfolio provides an opportunity to share ideas with peers and colleagues. Common folders foster a concentration on the essential foundations of Demonstrating, Interacting, Thinking, Writing, and Reading. Artifacts can be shared because they are easily located in similar Collection Points. The process of sharing is aided further by similar software packages and like storage media. While the advantages of like portfolios are numerous, customization serves the individual needs of portfolio users. If customized, the modifications should be limited to changes that enhance the utility of the portfolio for everyday use.

Working: the Purview of the Teacher as Expert

The artifacts of the Working folder are the proper focus for the classroom teacher. However, without an extensive cache of Collecting artifacts gathered during the Teacher-Learner experience, the resources needed for a classroom teacher will be unavailable and very costly to recreate. All aspects of the portfolio play an important role in the successful implementation of this tool for the Teacher as Expert.

Conclusion

Jennifer's encounter with portfolios chronicles many of the outcomes teachers often share when reflecting on their experiences with these professional tools. Many teachers are introduced to the strengths of portfolios early in their academic career, yet find it necessary to all but abandon their use when they become classroom teachers. Lack of on-site support and significant time constraints play heavily on this loss of devotion. To be effective tools for professional development, portfolios must make a tangible contribution to becoming a better teacher without taking valuable time away from the teaching and learning process. By incorporating Jennifer's suggestions into the organizational structure of the Smart and Intelligent Portfolios, teachers have a vehicle they can use with tangible and measurable results—not just for part of their career, but for a lifetime.

PART V

Portfolios for the Teacher as Scholar

Are you focused on research, publications, and grant writing? Do you need accurate records of your scholarship for promotion and tenure? Then, this is the portfolio for you.

Chapters 11, 12, and 13 concentrate on the Smart and Intelligent Portfolios for the Teacher as Scholar. Part V is a unique focus on the use of portfolios to give back something of value to the field of education.

Chapter 11	Chapter 12	Chapter 13
The Smart Portfolio for the Teacher as Scholar	*The Intelligent Portfolio for the Teacher as Scholar*	*Portfolios in Transition: The Teacher as Scholar*
The Smart Portfolio sports the same basic structure as previous implementations. But some new Collection Points are needed to support the Teacher as Scholar.	The electronic version of the Teacher as Scholar portfolio provides some valuable tools to enhance your image as an education professional.	If you want to see how the Smart and Intelligent Portfolios fared as an integral component of a doctoral program, Chapter 13 is recommended reading. After all, practical application is the true measure of the portfolio.

CHAPTER 11

The Smart Portfolio for the Teacher as Scholar

Introduction

For the Teacher as Scholar, the Smart Portfolio emphasizes content-specific expertise, breadth of professional skills, deep understanding of teaching and learning, and pursuit of personal recognition in a particular academic discipline. The portfolio contains artifacts that demonstrate ongoing excellence in teaching and a strong disposition toward research and writing. Public recognition as an educator is important for promotion and tenure. The portfolio serves as an historical record of a professional's knowledge, competence, and contributions to the field.

Together we will create the Smart Portfolio for the Teacher as Scholar by answering 4 familiar questions.

Foley returns to guide the construction of the Smart Portfolio for the Teacher as Scholar. He will address the following four questions:

(1) Where Do I Begin?
(2) How Do I Organize the Portfolio?
(3) What Do I Collect?
(4) Who Will Assess My Work?

Where Do I Begin?

For the Teacher as Scholar, the five essential foundations of the portfolio are organized to serve a different set of professional skills than any previous version of the Smart Portfolio. Examine how Interacting, Reading, Thinking, Demonstrating, and Writing now suit the particular demands of the Teacher-Scholar (see illustration on page 114). Compare them to previous applications.

Where do I begin? Read this section carefully! Your Portfolio won't be Smart without these essential elements.

Thinking remains the pivotal foundation—as in all versions of the portfolio. In this final implementation, however, Interacting steps forward as the most critical of the five foundations.

1. **Interacting** For the Teacher as Scholar, Interacting directly impacts teaching and learning. Research skills and data-gathering methodologies are finely tuned by constant exposure to the educational community. Validated findings are readily communicated to the widest audience possible. Interacting provides a source of artifacts for the Smart Portfolio especially with regard to professional service, teaching, and scholarship.

> **INTERACTING**
> Sharing ideas, discussing and defending, actively constructing artifacts during group inquiry.

> **READING**
> Gathering evidence of new knowledge and information from texts, articles, and similar resources.

> **THINKING**
> Making new meaning, connecting ideas, taking stock, constructing new perspectives.

> **DEMONSTRATING**
> Presenting, critiquing, publishing, enhancing traditional lessons, applying thinking and learning.

> **WRITING**
> Formal and informal writing demonstrating thoughtfulness and integrating new knowledge.

2. **Reading** Reading returns to the forefront of the portfolio, as the Teacher as Scholar continues to accumulate artifacts that generate new thinking. Reading adds to our knowledge base; outdated artifacts must be continually replaced with current research. Continuous examination of artifacts encompassing Content Area Material, Classroom and Library Resources, and the World Wide Web is necessary for personal and professional growth.

3. **Thinking** Thinking serves as the platform from which the Teacher as Scholar explores new dimensions in the science of teaching and the art of learning. The educator is constantly considering new information, forming and re-forming educational concepts and ideas, and designing models for classroom learning. Thinking remains the most powerful foundation for new portfolio artifacts involving Reflection and Self-assessment.

4. **Demonstrating** Presentation overheads, lecture notes, and in-service programs offered by the Teacher-Scholar constitute the majority of Demonstrating artifacts. For this foundation, educators apply new learning to the practical environment of the classroom and the public arena of the auditorium. Learning projects, instructional lessons, classroom research, and applied explorations contribute artifacts to the Smart Portfolio via the foundation of Demonstrating.

5. **Writing** For the mature educator, Writing provides evidence of scholarship. Building written artifacts extends ideas and new knowledge is constructed. Published ideas are integrated into a professional body of literature for others to consider when gathering their own artifacts and formulating their own ideas.

Interacting, Reading, Thinking, Demonstrating, and Writing are the sources for new portfolio artifacts. In fact, all artifacts are gathered from one or more of these five foundations as Teacher-Scholars develop their Smart Portfolios. With so many artifacts in hand, the next logical issue to be addressed involves organizing these items of evidence into folders.

How Do I Organize the Portfolio?

The emphasis for the Teacher as Scholar is on the *Showcase* collection points. Collecting and Working artifacts continue to move the Teacher as Scholar toward recognition as an authority in the field. The following graphic depicts the final version of the Smart Portfolio with additional Collection Points added to the Showcase folder.

How do I organize my portfolio? Collecting, Working, and Showcase folders will help you organize your artifacts for easy retrieval.

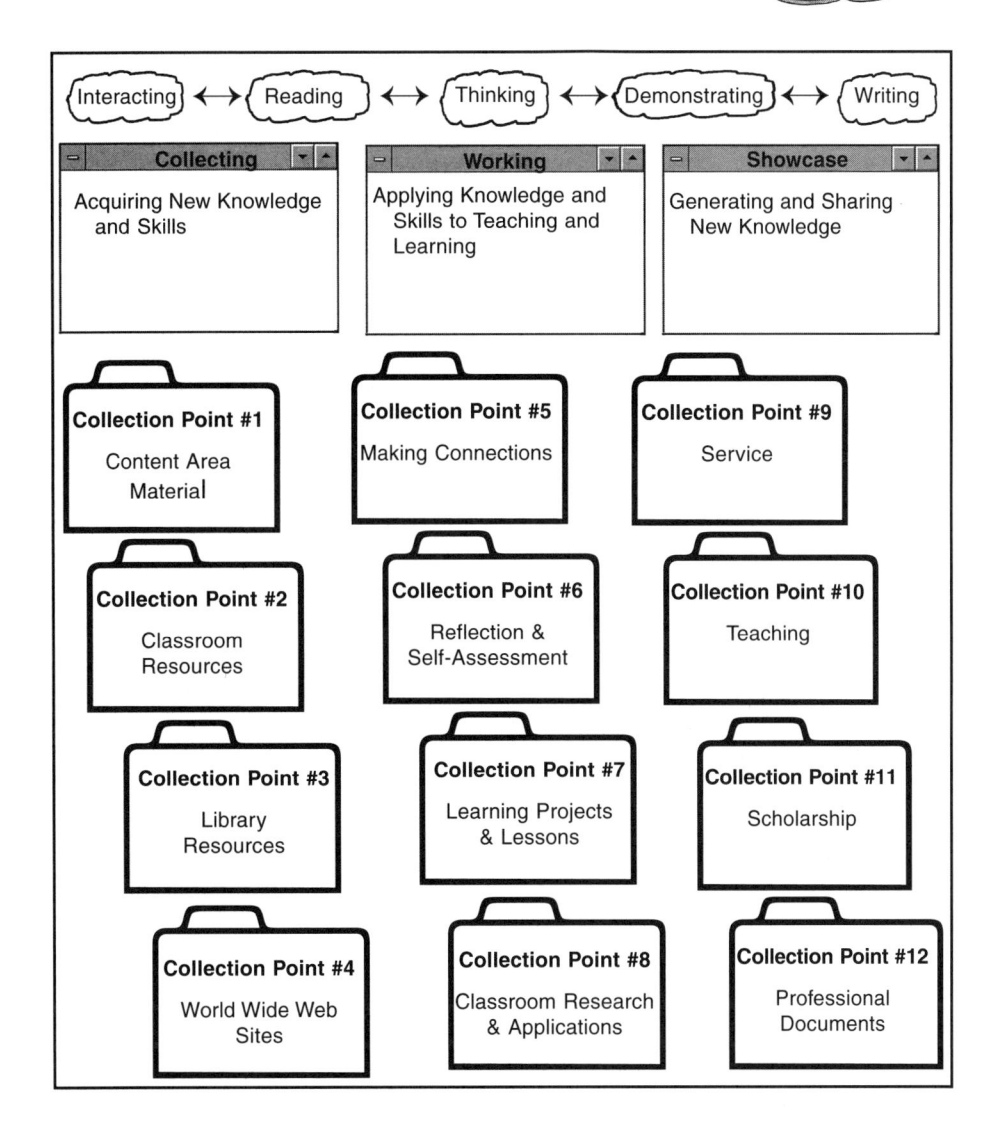

Interacting ↔ Reading ↔ Thinking ↔ Demonstrating ↔ Writing

Collecting	Working	Showcase
Acquiring New Knowledge and Skills	Applying Knowledge and Skills to Teaching and Learning	Generating and Sharing New Knowledge

Collection Point #1 — Content Area Material

Collection Point #2 — Classroom Resources

Collection Point #3 — Library Resources

Collection Point #4 — World Wide Web Sites

Collection Point #5 — Making Connections

Collection Point #6 — Reflection & Self-Assessment

Collection Point #7 — Learning Projects & Lessons

Collection Point #8 — Classroom Research & Applications

Collection Point #9 — Service

Collection Point #10 — Teaching

Collection Point #11 — Scholarship

Collection Point #12 — Professional Documents

Collecting Folder

Artifacts placed in the first four Collection Points are similar to those of the previous portfolios. The major difference is that these *Collecting artifacts* serve a different purpose. Just as Teacher-Learners and Teacher-Experts must be collectors, so must the Teacher as Scholar—but, for a markedly different reason. Previous implementations of the Smart Portfolio collected artifacts as a means to building a concrete knowledge base from which to grow as a teacher. The Teacher as Scholar collects artifacts in order to expand a personal reservoir of working articles to explore pedagogical concepts, develop classroom-appropriate materials, and share successful applications. Collection Points for Content Area Materials, Classroom and Library Resources, and World Wide Web sites continue to serve the collecting needs of the Teacher-Scholar.

Working Folder

Interacting, Demonstrating, and Writing are the principal foundations of the Working folder, producing new artifacts to be shared with the educational community. Learning Projects and Lessons are merged into a single repository while Collection Point #8 combines Applications and Classroom Research. Consolidating these points in no way diminishes the importance of these materials, but rather makes these artifacts more manageable for the Teacher-Scholar. The Smart Portfolio continues to host innovative, unique, and personalized artifacts for the Teacher as Scholar. As the best Working artifacts are evaluated and validated, they are moved into the Showcase section of the portfolio to become permanent artifacts in the portfolio of the Teacher as Scholar.

Showcase Folder

The Showcase folder undergoes a dramatic evolution as the Teacher as Scholar moves to the final phase of an educator's career. Collection Point #9 for Service, Collection Point #10 for Teaching, and Collection Point #11 for Scholarship emphasize the focus of the portfolio on *Showcase artifacts*. Collection Point #12 remains consistent as a repository for Professional Documents.

Service to the community, attention to pedagogy, and a concentration on scholarship become the hallmarks of the professional who returns to the discipline some measure of the treasures received throughout a career in the field of education.

Collection Point #9: Service   As a contributing member of the academic community, the Teacher as Scholar is expected to become actively involved in the community. For many, service is a criterion for tenure consideration. Examples of artifacts for this collection point include evidence of time spent with "Habitat for Humanity," accolades for *pro bono* consulting work, communications with a local school board, and letters of appreciation from a local civic task force. Service is a hallmark of the mature scholar.

Collection Point #10: Teaching   The Teacher as Scholar has practical knowledge of a long list of teaching and learning strategies acquired through years of classroom experience. In this Showcase Collection Point, such artifacts are to be stored until they can be shared with fellow educators. Artifacts for this Collection Point include published lesson plans, curriculum research, teacher in-service programs, innovative teaching techniques, and formal classroom evaluations. Teaching is a hallmark of the mature scholar.

Collection Point #11: Scholarship   The Teacher as Scholar becomes a colleague by engaging in academic literature published in professional journals, scholarly presentations at regional, state, national, and international conventions, and well-grounded research that improves the practice of teaching. Artifacts found in this Collection Point include prominent textbooks and articles, grant applications and awards, noted teaching manuals and instructional materials, and well-scrutinized research reports. Scholarship is a hallmark of the mature scholar.

Collection Point #12: Professional Documents   The Teacher as Scholar continues to pursue professional credentials. The vita must be current, complete, and easily accessible. Personal acknowledgments and kudos are gathered as testimony to a career dedicated to excellence in teaching. These artifacts tell a story about the educator's growth from the perspective of a pre-service learner to the experienced teacher in the classroom to the research-based scholar. Artifacts evidence an historical record of a scholar's professional knowledge base, competence in practice, and contributions to the field.

The Smart Portfolio is a tool for learning, assessment, and professional development. As a learning tool, it holds the evidence of thinking and learning. As an assessment tool, it is evaluated with both summative and formative appraisals. As a professional development tool, it promotes personal interaction and academic sharing. The *Showcase* folders of the Smart Portfolio also contribute to the future for the Teacher as Scholar if used as evidence for promotion and tenure.

What Do I Collect?

What do I collect? For the Teacher as Scholar, an artifact is evidence of knowledge, skill, understanding, and experience.

Foley is poised to offer specific examples of artifacts that might be stored in Collection Points for the Teacher as Scholar. While some of the items are similar to previous implementations, see if you can identify the significant differences in this version of the Smart Portfolio.

Collection Point #1

This folder should already be filled with artifacts. But the Teacher as Scholar has sources for new artifacts beyond other educators.

Content Area Materials
Journal Articles
Subject Matter Books
Textbooks
Raw Lesson Plans taken from the Internet

Classroom Resources
Shared lessons from Colleagues
Classroom Handouts from Seminars/Sessions
Teaching Strategies Applied to New Situations

Collection Point #2

Classroom Resources go in this folder.

Library Resources
Requests for Books, Articles, and Resources
Audiovisual Resources
Library Reference/Reserve Materials

Collection Point #3

Library Resources are much more evident in this version of the Smart Portfolio.

Collection Point #4

URL's for the Teacher as Scholar consist of Sites that promote thinking about teaching and learning.

World Wide Web Sites
Search Engines
Subject Matter Sites
Educational Institutions
Commercial Software Sites
Content Specialties

Making Connections
Points of Contact
Mental Maps
Book notes
Insight into Classroom Issues/ Problems Unresolved Questions

Collection Point #5

New ideas come from reading. Interacting with colleagues and students helps us to get new ideas.

Collection Point #6

Self-Assessment leads to continuous improvement. Ask, "How could I do this better?"

Reflections & Self-Assessment
Self-analysis of Presentation Skills
Personal Philosophy of Teaching and Learning
Session Feedbacks and Critiques

Learning Projects and Lessons
Completed Units of Instruction
In Progress Learning Projects
New Course Designs

Collection Point #7

If you use it in the classroom, develop it here.

Collection Point #8

Explore and take risks in this Collection Point. Try new strategies in the classroom. Evaluate your success.

Applications and Research
New Teaching Strategies
Findings from Journals
Research in the Discipline
Testing Results

Service
Committee Meetings
Advisement
Task Force Member
Professional Organizations

Collection Point #9

Are you sharing your talents with the community and your discipline? Track those efforts here.

Collection Point #10

Still teaching? Keep sharp by adding artifacts that improve your personal in-classroom skills.

Teaching
Teacher Effectiveness Forms
Assessment Tools
Rigorous Methodology Practice
Video

Scholarship
Honors/Awards
Published Works
Successful Grants
Discipline-Specific Scholarly Work

Collection Point #11

Display your published Best Work for all to see. Put any grants you received in this folder too.

Collection Point #12

The last folder is your most stable. Continue to amass professional career artifacts.

Professional Documents
Graduate Transcripts
Professional Awards
Professional Certifications
Teaching Certificates
Curriculum Vitae

Who will assess my work? Assessment will be "High Stakes" for the Teacher as Scholar!

The artifacts placed in the first four Collection Points by the Teacher as Scholar are much like those of the previous professional portfolios. The Working folder as well is similar to earlier versions except that Collection Points #7 and #9 and Collection Points #8 and #10 are combined. Consolidating these Collection Points does not diminish the importance of these materials. Working artifacts continue to represent the most innovative, unique, and personalized products of the portfolio.

Who Will Assess My Work?

The portfolio for the Teacher as Scholar is a high-stakes process. Showcase artifacts play a vital role in decisions where annual performance reviews and tenure decisions are anchored to portfolio demonstrations. Publications stored in portfolio folders provide the evidence of scholarly work integral to promotion and tenure. The lessons, research, and applications it holds furnish the material for new textbooks. Assessment tools, committee minutes, and session critiques offer personal feedback of professional endeavors.

For the Teacher as Scholar, assessment is more often performed by a committee of peers in search of evidence of effective teaching, scholarship, and community service. The Smart Portfolio supports this pursuit with tangible artifacts to strengthen your testimony for continuance, tenure, and advancement.

The Smart Portfolio also contains other authentic assessments. The Teacher as Scholar seeks out these low-stakes assessments from students, colleagues, and editors. When viewed as a whole, the Teacher as Scholar's Smart Portfolio becomes an accurate portrait of performance.

The Portfolio Poster

For the Teacher as Scholar experience, an "Exhibition" is employed to display the results of the Smart Portfolio. As a tool for learning through self-evaluation combined with assessment, the portfolio poster has real impact. The poster should be able to stand on its own merit, but defending and connecting leads the true scholar to new endeavors. A three-panel poster board exhibits the 12 Collection Points of the Collecting, Working, and Showcase folders. The recommended format encourages analysis and synthesis—prerequisites to a successful formal evaluation and self-assessment.

For the Smart Portfolio, a posterboard, complete with file folders and manila envelopes, holds specific artifacts to visually and concretely present the products of your thinking and learning.

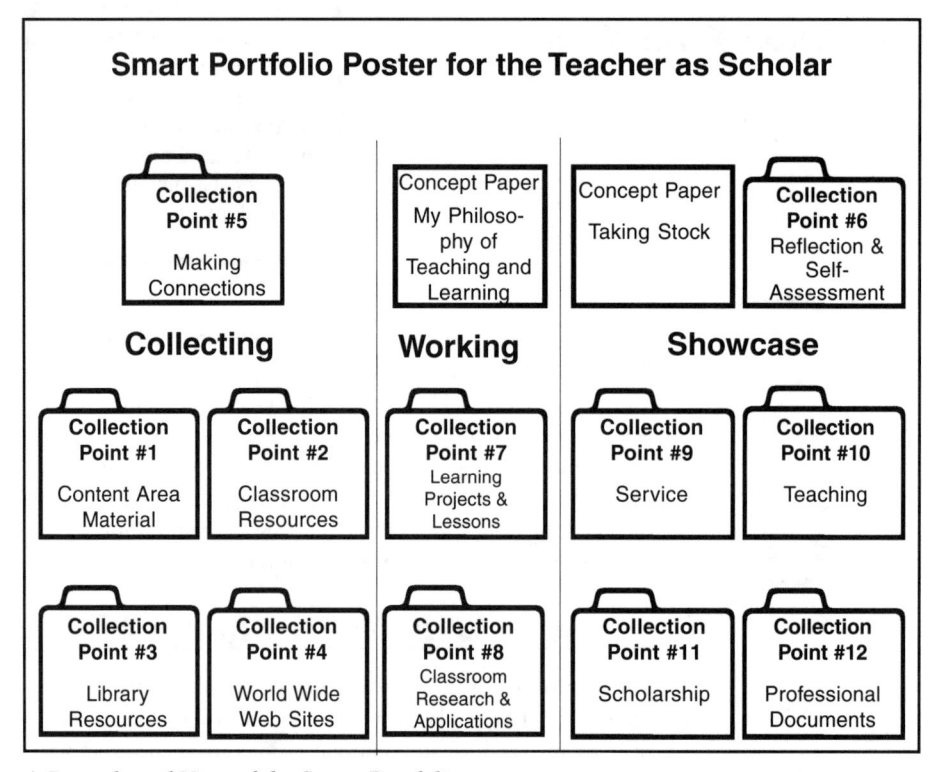

Smart Portfolio Poster for the Teacher as Scholar

Collecting	Working	Showcase
Collection Point #5 — Making Connections	Concept Paper — My Philosophy of Teaching and Learning	Concept Paper — Taking Stock
		Collection Point #6 — Reflection & Self-Assessment
Collection Point #1 — Content Area Material	Collection Point #7 — Learning Projects & Lessons	Collection Point #9 — Service
Collection Point #2 — Classroom Resources		Collection Point #10 — Teaching
Collection Point #3 — Library Resources	Collection Point #8 — Classroom Research & Applications	Collection Point #11 — Scholarship
Collection Point #4 — World Wide Web Sites		Collection Point #12 — Professional Documents

A Posterboard View of the Smart Portfolio

Collection Points #5 and #6 are placed at the top of the poster next to your Philosophy of Teaching and Learning to draw attention to these important artifacts.

Conclusion

The Smart Portfolio's main purpose at this stage of an academic career is to provide an historical record of a professional's knowledge base, competence in practice, and contributions to the discipline. There are many other varieties of portfolios from which to choose. Some are concerned with process, others with products. Many are short-lived with limited scope and purpose. But tracking your life's work is more than a transitory enterprise.

The Smart Portfolio documents the personal activities, interests, and accomplishments of the Teacher as Scholar. It facilitates self-evaluation, external assessment, and professional growth. Think about that! Here is a tool for the professional scholar that houses artifacts important to every aspect of personal development—all in a single location.

In this final version of the Smart Portfolio, Showcase artifacts take on prominence for the Teacher as Scholar. Artifacts representing Service, Teaching, and Scholarship, in addition to an expanded folder of Professional Documents, are the domain of the mature educator.

Foley Tips

Let me offer a final set of tips for the Teacher as Scholar.

Foley has some final tips for users of this version of the Smart Portfolio.

1. **Be a role model and practice what you *teach*.** Demonstrate knowledge, skills, and dispositions which evidence "Best Practice" in the classroom and in the seminar room. The Smart Portfolio can help.

2. **Attend professional seminars, conferences, and conventions.** Volunteer to share what you know, discuss what you think, and listen to new ideas. Argue your side, but be open-minded and take risks.

3. **Enlighten the general public about educational concerns and issues.** Use your portfolio to prepare and present helpful programs to the other key participants in the teaching-learning process—parents and community members.

4. **Help new teachers grow and mature.** Share portfolio artifacts documenting the steps in your journey as an educator.

5. **Review Collection Points #9, #10, and #11.** These three repositories define the Teacher as Scholar. Service, Teaching, and Scholarship are the hallmarks of the mature educator.

6. **Continue to monitor your own learning with the Smart Portfolio.** Write your history a day at a time. Consider the Intelligent Portfolio.

CHAPTER 12
The Intelligent Portfolio for the Teacher as Scholar

Introduction

At this point in an educator's career, serious consideration should be given to converting to the Intelligent Portfolio. Evidence of lifelong learning produces an accumulation of artifacts best managed electronically. Speed of access, portability for demonstration purposes, and specialized educational hardware contribute to the utility of the portfolio for the Teacher as Scholar.

Three simple tasks convert the Smart Portfolio to its computerized counterpart:

Step One: **Creating Portfolio Folders** for Interacting, Reading, Thinking, Demonstrating, and Writing,

Step Two: **Populating Portfolio Folders** with the most efficient and effective combination of software packages and computer hardware required for this phase of your educational career, and

Step Three: **Organizing Folders and Collection Points** to store the electronic artifacts accumulated in the Collecting, Working, and Showcase folders of your portfolio.

Step One: Creating Portfolio Folders

Here's Step One: Creating Your Portfolio Folders.

A knowledge of how the Apple and Windows operating systems generate a computer desktop is sufficient to create portfolio folders that take on the appearance of the graphic shown on page 124 and are described in the following paragraphs. Each folder is used for a specific purpose within the Intelligent Portfolio.

Interacting

One of the primary responsibilities of the Teacher as Scholar is to develop new ideas and advance them among colleagues. The Interacting folder supports this charge with a suite of software and hardware that provides as many and varied communications alternatives as possible: electronic mail, newsgroups, Internet access, and interactive discussions. The folder also holds personal management software including calendars and appointment schedules.

Reading

Reading is essential to new learning and idea sharing. Reading software and hardware options include access to Gopher materials, libraries, and the educational resources of the

124 *Professional Portfolios for Teachers*

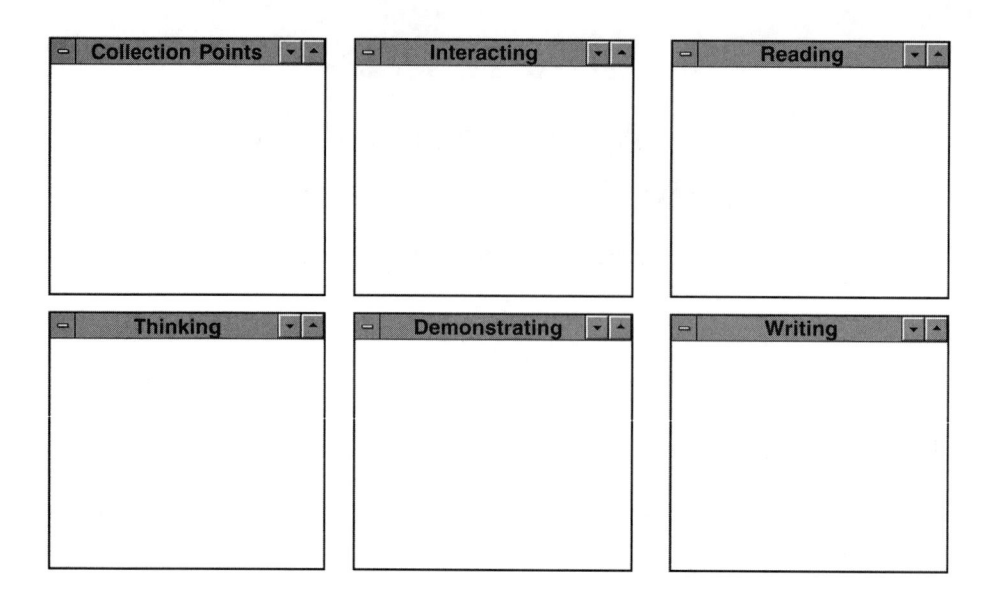

| Collection Points | Interacting | Reading |
| Thinking | Demonstrating | Writing |

World Wide Web. A few new technological additions contribute to a more scholarly reading environment for the Teacher-Scholar.

Thinking

The Thinking folder remains pivotal to the portfolio user. Thinking builds a viable and respectable research base so critical to the Teacher-Scholar. As a result, this folder accommodates software packages that promote the higher order taxonomies of analysis, synthesis, and evaluation. Several automated utilities are incorporated into this folder to address the particular demands for innovation in teaching and learning.

Demonstrating

Instructional and professional materials prepared by manipulating artifacts collected in the Intelligent Portfolio are maintained in the Demonstrating folder. Presentations, lectures, and in-service programs offered by the Teacher-Scholar constitute testimonials as an authority in the field. The folder contains alternative presentation systems, additional software capabilities, and a far more sophisticated suite of hardware. Of particular note is the addition of a Web design software package to aid in the development of Internet-based educational materials.

Writing

Both publications and formal authored presentations are viable media to share new educational concepts and practices. Completed manuscripts and other publication-ready compositions encounter the features of desktop publishing software found in this folder of the Intelligent Portfolio. Course development software combines with color laser printing and the latest CD-ROM technology to take the portfolio user to new levels of document production.

Step Two: Populating Portfolio Folders

Ready for Step Two? Let's place some software and hardware into the folders...

The focus for the Intelligent Portfolio turns to scholarship, publishing, and presentation. The electronic version of the portfolio contains software that supports new thinking. Continuing as our guide, Foley describes the components of the portfolio folders, starting with the Interacting folder.

Interacting Software

For the Teacher as Scholar, sharing ideas takes on a higher level of interaction than previous portfolio implementations. As a result, the most exhaustive suite of communication tools and personal management software is proposed to support the effort of the Teacher-Scholar.

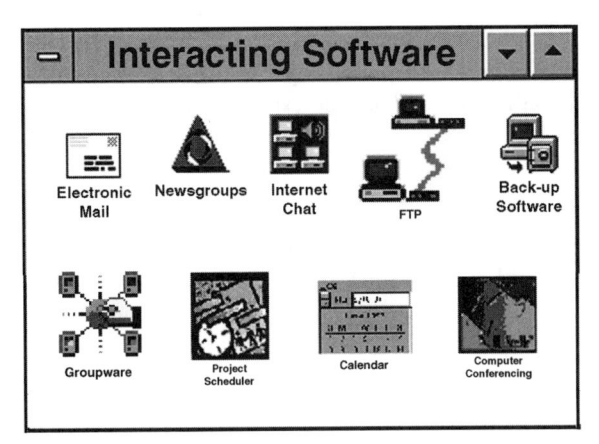

Examine the various utilities that have been added to this folder to support Interacting.

Interacting Software: Electronic Mail, Newsgroups, Internet Chat, FTP, Back-up Software, Groupware, Project Scheduler, Calendar, Computer Conferencing

Electronic Mail Interacting by electronic mail is a prerequisite for the Teacher as Scholar. Sharing ideas electronically speeds outgoing communications while simultaneously managing a growing stack of incoming messages. Interacting via email ensures timely replies and tracks important contacts. Broadcasting important announcements is simplified by email as it instantaneously distributes attachments in the form of computerized data files. Finally, email software adds new features with nearly every release and upgrade. Look for electronic mail to become increasingly important across all versions of the Intelligent Portfolio.

Newsgroup Services Newsgroups provide a forum to share and exchange ideas among professionals with common interests. A news service provides a selection of 5,000–8,000 different subjects covering a wide range of topics—some appropriate for educational purposes, others not. Some of the most respected newsgroup services include: alt (alternative), bionet (medical), news (news services), comp (computer-related groups), rec (recreational), sci (science-related), and K12 (K-12 education). Newsgroups exist for nearly every conceivable content area for classroom instruction. Educators may consider creating their own newsgroups to address a specific area of professional concentration. These groups, called "moderated newsgroups," are as sweeping in their impact on the Interacting responsibilities of the Teacher as Scholar as the publication of a new textbook and provide an excellent avenue for reaching a large audience quickly.

Internet Relay Chat (IRC)   A step beyond email and newsgroups is the feature called Internet Relay Chat, or IRC. IRC was included in the portfolio for the Teacher-Learner and subsequently omitted from the Teacher-Expert version. It returns in this implementation of the Intelligent Portfolio for the Teacher as Scholar because of the renewed importance attached to the foundation of Interacting. Computer users enter a "channel" and broadcast messages to other on-line users much like selecting a channel on a citizen's band radio. Users have "handles," also known as nicknames. Text is transmitted to other users sharing the same channel. Although less private than either email or newsgroups, IRC reaches people interactively. It even comes with its own set of protocol and etiquette. Problems associated with IRC, in addition to the privacy issue, include timing (everyone must be on-line at the same time) and spontaneity (not everyone is at their best when it comes to off-the-cuff communication). But, for the Teacher as Scholar, IRC provides an excellent avenue for generating discussion and obtaining immediate feedback.

File Transfer Protocol (FTP)   FTP servers provide a host of materials from fellow educators willing to share their lessons and instructional materials. Most files are either freeware (no cost) or shareware (minimal payment to the author requested). Oftentimes, these on-line materials include surprisingly excellent resources addressing a particular subject matter area. In previous implementations, the Intelligent Portfolio explored the use of FTP to locate and download math tutors, science projects, and language compositions. It is time to return the favor by providing links to materials produced by the Teacher as Scholar.

Back-up Software   Back-up software is an operating system utility typically provided free of charge. Computer novices often ignore what veteran users have learned the hard way: select a back-up software package early and use it routinely. Pick a day of the week and save a copy of every user file contained on hard disk. A Zip Drive, which we recommend for back-ups, is discussed in detail as a component of the Thinking Hardware. The first time a hard drive goes bad, a directory is corrupted, or a file is inadvertently deleted, portfolio users come to appreciate the discipline of periodic system back-ups.

Groupware   Some of the newest and most powerful cross-platform software packages available are known as "groupware" because they integrate several capabilities into a single, seamless, and consistent format. Currently, one of the most popular groupware packages is "FirstClass." FirstClass combines the power and versatility of local networking with the vast resources of Internet Web sites, so users work in a collaborative on-line environment. For the Interacting folder, FirstClass is recommended primarily for its Advanced Workgroup Conferencing capability. The shared discussion areas allow the Teacher as Scholar to exchange messages and files on topics of interest without filling up private email mailboxes. Conferences appear as folders accessed with a simple mouse click. On-line "conversations" are easily monitored to ensure that learning objectives are met. A powerful system of privileges and permissions assigns different levels of access so users share critical information among authorized personnel only. With all these features in a single package, educators flock to FirstClass both as a medium for sharing ideas and as one of the first tools in a distance learning classroom.

Project Scheduling Software   Several software packages provide the capability to track specific due dates, key milestones, and critical activities. Project schedulers track simultaneous projects and manage multiple projects that share common resources. They identify cross-project interdependencies such as the need to complete one project before manpower resources can be diverted to a subsequent effort. Finally, project schedulers present "what if" models to determine the best fit of tasks which must be performed with the resources available.

Calendar Allied closely to project scheduling software, calendars provide a less comprehensive (but nevertheless critical) function of tracking personal and group meetings, reserving meeting locations, and supporting a "to do" list. Most packages simulate the "look" of a desktop calendar, but offer significantly more options including up-to-date information accessed via key word searches, group scheduling, and personalized reports.

Computer Conferencing Interacting takes on new dimensions with Internet videoconferencing. By adding a video capture card and camera, the Intelligent Portfolio transforms a personal computer into a videophone. Computer conferencing software opens as many as 12 participant windows simultaneously. Scholars in the United States see and talk to educators in Europe. Multiple parties at different locations participate in an exchange of text and slides. Interacting is fostered by face-to-face communications using the same Internet connection that currently sends and receives electronic mail and accesses the World Wide Web.

Based on personal preferences and budgets, participants decide whether to be a sender, a receiver, or both. They share an on-screen environment or participate without being seen. Computer conferencing opens doors to other forms of worldwide video and audio communication. For this reason, we recommend computer conferencing software in the Interacting folder.

Interacting Hardware

Since the Interacting folder is the preeminent foundation for the Teacher as Scholar, it contains the basic hardware system components necessary for the Intelligent Portfolio. Additional hardware is suggested to support the multimedia aspects of the folder.

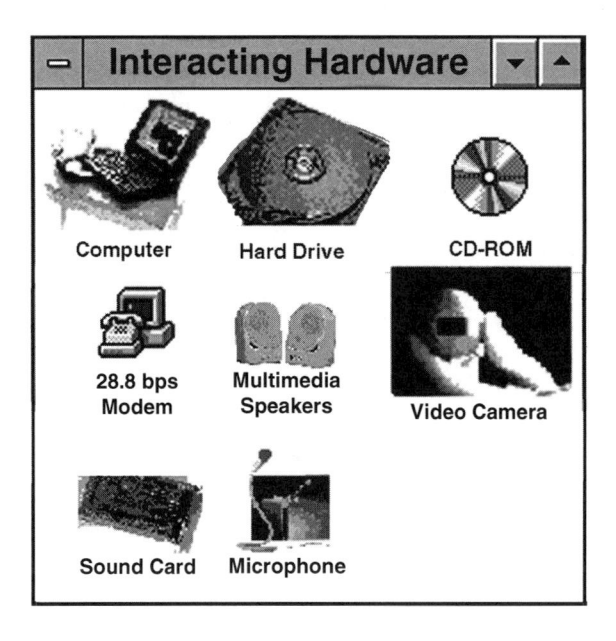

Personal Computer   A laptop computer remains the recommended system for this implementation of the Intelligent Portfolio. Desktop systems provide similar capabilities. For certain scholars, they may even prove more beneficial. Portability and convenience remain the overriding consideration concerning the choice of platforms. For the office or home-bound scholar, a desktop system is the logical choice. A more demanding travel schedule dictates a move toward the laptop. Regardless of which platform is selected, an important list of minimum capabilities includes:

Apple Compatible Systems. Macintosh with a 68060 microprocessor or better, 32 megabytes of random access memory (RAM), a 1 gigabyte hard drive (2 gigabyte recommended), and the Macintosh Operating System 7.5 (Mac 8.0 OS recommended).

Windows Compatible Systems. A personal computer with a Pentium microprocessor, 32 megabytes of random access memory (RAM), a 1 gigabyte hard drive (2 gigabyte recommended), and the Windows 95 Operating System (Windows 98 recommended).

CD-ROM Player   For the Teacher as Scholar, the Intelligent Portfolio employs CD-ROM technology not only to input thousands of applications, but also as the primary storage and retrieval medium for the artifacts that have been accumulated. Since many of these artifacts include ample video, image, and sound files in addition to liberal text files, faster speed CD-ROM players are highly recommended.

High-Speed Modem   A state-of-the-art modem supports high-speed communications with scholars using applications proposed for the Intelligent Portfolio. For both home and office phone lines, you should use the fastest modems affordable.

Multimedia Speakers   Magnetically shielded speakers compliment the presentation capabilities of the Intelligent Portfolio. Multimedia exhibitions enhance the realism of educational materials and aid in computer conferencing. Connected directly to the CD-ROM player, users enjoy audio software and recorded music in true digital sound. Most multimedia speakers operate from the computer's internal power supply with AC adapter power available.

Video Camera   Video cameras digitize and transmit images up to 15 frames per second complete with audio. They typically encompass a field of view of about 65 degrees (the equivalent of a 35mm photo camera) and offer a fixed focus from 18 inches to infinity. The video camera compliments other multimedia hardware to offer full multimedia video transmit and receive functionality.

Multimedia Sound Card   For true multimedia, a sound card is required. Many laptop and desktop systems come with these cards already built into the machine. Most personal computers play sound without a special card using their built-in speaker. However, the quality tends to be less than satisfactory for the teaching and learning experience. Multimedia sound cards add professional CD-quality music and interact with advanced software packages to offer voice-quality input and output.

Microphone   A microphone also digitizes audio. Once converted, the resulting files can be saved or transferred outside the Intelligent Portfolio. Together with a video camera, sound card, and speakers, the microphone completes a suite of multimedia hardware to support any level of interaction desired by the Teacher as Scholar.

Reading Software

This folder contains elements which complement other foundations of the portfolio with automated access to remote computers, documentation servers, library accounts, and Web sites.

Reading Software

Telnet Software   Telnet accesses remote host computers, reading files and using options and features for which privileges have been extended. Telnet serves many of the reading needs of the Teacher as Scholar. Subject matter areas include: Agriculture, Animals, Chemistry, Congress, Current Events, Environment, Geography, Government, Health, History, Religion, Space, Transportation, and Weather. Many sites register new users upon initial entry; some allow anonymous log-ins. Remember to document the method of entry to include user names and passwords created at each site.

Library Resources   Many of the available Telnet sites also access academic, research, and public libraries. These sites include automated card catalogs, electronic books, and digital libraries, along with volumes of periodicals stored on CD-ROM servers. The Teacher as Scholar has access to dozens of free library resources.

Gopher Documentation Management   Gopher is a documentation management system that spread rapidly in the early 1990s. While it has been largely supplanted by the graphic-intensive World Wide Web, there are still thousands of Gopher servers available, and teachers can still locate valuable resources with this simple tool. As a Teacher-Scholar, your responsibility to share your knowledge can be enhanced by contributions to Gopher sites you deem commendable. Any artifacts considered valuable to the academic community should be donated via email to a Gopher publisher. While you may not wish to initiate a site (because of the obsolescence of the technology), you may be able to contribute to the resources that already exist.

Web Browser Software   By this point in your career, you have accumulated a considerable list of Internet resources with application to specific content areas. A directory of these resources becomes an indispensable addition to the Intelligent Portfolio. These addresses are links to exciting locations encompassing literally every subject matter area of concern to the educator. Web Browser software opens the doors to these sites and navigates the portfolio user through the wealth of information that lies within the Web.

Reading Hardware

We've added a desktop scanner to the existing suite of basic computer hardware and peripheral devices. The scanner digitizes hard copy text and images captured from various sources, creating an electronic artifact for your portfolio.

Desktop Scanner Place a document on the scanner, click the mouse button, choose image or text, and the scanner selects the ideal settings to capture the electronic document. Once the document is scanned, it can be copied and pasted into many software applications. Scanners translate color or black-and-white images and text documents for publications and classroom materials.

Thinking Software

Thinking software includes spreadsheets, databases, idea generators, statistics packages, and utilities.

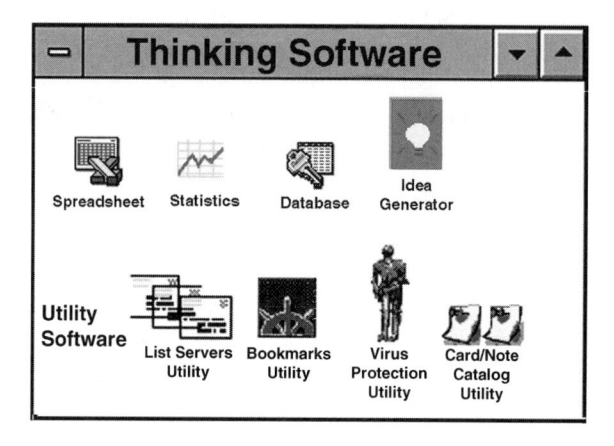

Spreadsheets Spreadsheet software supports "what if" analysis: "What if" a school district decided to increase its technology budget by $150,000—what impact would that decision have on the available funds for the science, math, and language programs? "What if" thematic units were used exclusively in curriculum development—would that increase student achievement scores? The use of spreadsheets to examine data gathered in the Intelligent Portfolio provides a foundation for new thinking.

Statistical Software Research is steeped in statistical analysis. An added tool for the Teacher as Scholar, the desktop statistics package markedly enhances the process of evaluating data, presenting findings, and forming conclusions. In addition to common descriptive statistics such as averages and standard deviations, a robust statistics package features on-line help, introductory tours, on-demand tutorials, and electronic glossaries. Examples run independently from start to finish, or from within a procedure for a more in-depth explanation of certain program operations. "Show me" features move the user quickly to relevant tutorial sections from any point. "What's This" is a context-sensitive feature that provides short cuts to operations, an index of definitions, and rules of thumb for interpreting a particular statistic. A chart advisor selects an appropriate graphic to display the data in an easy-to-understand format. Finally, a solid statistical package incorporates database management to maintain the data sets, perform complex comparative operations, and offer a range of personalized reports.

Database Management Software Lists of professional points of contact, upcoming major conferences, and prospective publishers are maintained using database management software. Telephone numbers of fellow educators, World Wide Web sites, and abstracts of important publications are also primary candidates for database applications. Some of the newer, more powerful packages offer more than 20 custom databases to help users get started. Some can transform a data file into graphically oriented tables, making interpretation a more visual experience. Finally, they convert data to and from a variety of popular data formats making shared files among teachers easy and fast.

Idea Generator Software   Brainstorming software is a creative way to explore new ideas, linking them directly to other topics, expanding subject matter areas, or integrating them into thematic units. Idea-generating packages offer automated planning and diagramming tools that simultaneously express ideas visually and create concrete outlines.

Some brainstorming packages operate on the principle of the "exhaustion of the interaction of words." They expand ideas from research to the classroom using a database of related word chains. And they have several features for directly querying the database for ideas.

Utility Software   Utility software packages provide a host of serviceable features including text editors, undelete routines, card files, phone dialers, calculators, time clocks, and hard disk managers. They offer specific capabilities to edit small text files, recover files that were deleted by mistake, and track personal phone numbers. There are four utilities that are essential: list servers, bookmarks, virus protection, and a card catalog.

List Server   A list server is an automated mailing list and distribution system. It extends electronic mail by serving the mutual interests of many computer users simultaneously. While email is placed in the Interacting Software folder, list servers—with their ability to access specific topics much like a magazine subscription—are so focused that the utility is placed here as one of the key elements of Thinking Software.

With most list servers, users subscribe by sending email to a moderator; they are notified by return email that their subscription was received and processed. List servers also provide an easy method for disseminating information to a target group. However, since an individual's email inbox could easily become inundated with extraneous messages, most computer users restrict their subscriptions to a few, highly selective services. Some subscribe only to moderated list servers managed by individuals who weed out mail that contributes little to the selected topic.

Bookmarks   The Bookmarks pop-down menu in the Web browser categorizes, sorts, and manages Web locations. To use the Bookmark feature of your Web browser, you must first navigate to a site that contains enough valuable information to permanently include the address as a Bookmark. Once added to the list, subsequent access is only a mouse click away. Bookmarks may also be grouped by category to avoid time better spent tapping into a well-designed list of interesting sites.

Virus Protection   Virus protection for the portfolio serves two purposes. First, this utility detects viruses downloaded from the Internet or inadvertently transferred via infected diskettes. Second, it ensures that you are not the source of viruses passed to unsuspecting recipients of your electronic artifacts. Virus protection software is configured to examine the hard disk whenever the system is started and floppy diskettes whenever a file is accessed for the first time. In addition, any file downloaded from the Internet or retrieved via file transfer from another host system is examined immediately before it is accessed. Downloaded files account for the majority of infections. Most trusting users execute software without first scanning them for a virus. It can be a costly mistake.

Card Catalog   A card catalog utility provides an electronic notepad for jotting down sporadic ideas to be considered at a more convenient time. The user of the Intelligent Portfolio is encouraged to always keep a window open to this utility and open a card whenever a new idea surfaces.

Thinking Hardware

The Thinking folder remains a pivotal repository for artifacts of the Teacher as Scholar. The recommended components are primarily upgrades and expansions to basic system hardware.

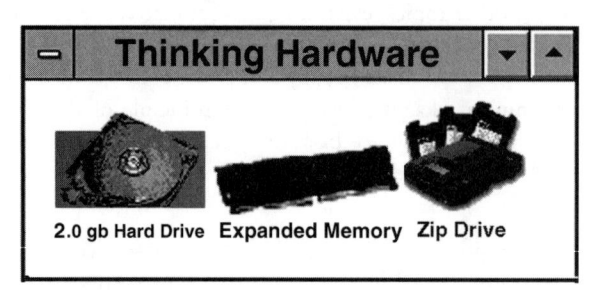

Thinking Hardware

2.0 gb Hard Drive   Expanded Memory   Zip Drive

2-Gigabyte Hard Drive   The addition of so many software packages in the Interacting and Reading folders dictates an upgrade to the features and capabilities of the basic system. For this implementation of the Intelligent Portfolio, a 2-gigabyte hard drive is highly recommended to store the vast number of artifacts for the Teacher as Scholar.

Expanded Memory   Closely associated to a larger hard drive is the need for expanded memory. Excessive delays when launching applications or when moving from one application to another are an indication that upgrades to memory capacity are needed. In addition to the 32 megabytes of Random Access Memory already included in the basic system, additional memory should be considered as soon as your system seems sluggish. This enhancement should be at the top of the list of computer upgrades.

Zip Drive   A zip drive is a high-capacity storage device that operates much like a traditional floppy disk drive. Although the two drives look similar, they are technically different. Floppy and zip drives are similar in shape; however, they are very different with respect to storage capacities. The 3.5-inch floppy stores 1.4 megabytes of data, while the zip disk holds 100 megabytes, giving the zip drive nearly 70 times the storage capacity. The zip drive also serves as the primary back-up medium for critical portfolio software and files.

Demonstrating Software

A graphics presentation package augments Web development software for the Teacher as Scholar. The Demonstrating folder also hosts graphics utilities to manipulate and display multimedia files.

Graphics Presentation Software   Designed to assist with the development of slides, transparencies, and hard-copy handouts, a graphics presentation system combines text, clip art, and drawing tools to construct multimedia presentations. For the Teacher as Scholar, a graphics package provides the following list of features and options:

- Graphics creation, edit, and production
- On-line help including topic searches
- Drawing tools
- Presentation schemes (layouts, backgrounds, and colors)
- Tools (spell checker, thesaurus, grammar)

Demonstrating Software

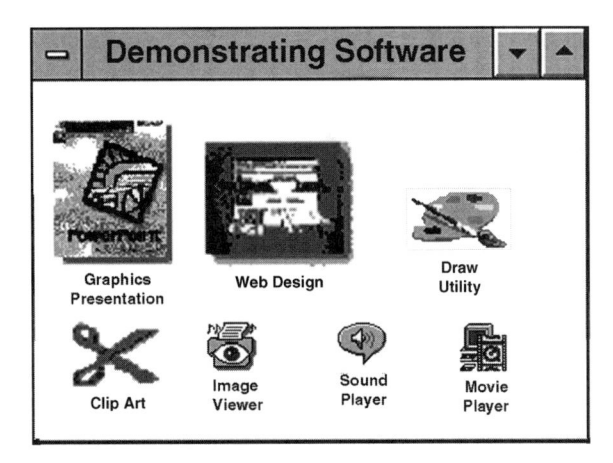

- Graphics Presentation
- Web Design
- Draw Utility
- Clip Art
- Image Viewer
- Sound Player
- Movie Player

- Editing features
- Views (outlines, sorters, and notes)
- Personalized slide setups (templates and master slides)
- Manual and automatic slide shows
- Output and presentation options (speaker notes and multiple slide handouts)

Web Design Software   Web Design software creates Home pages for presenting educational material. Some sites offer entire academic programs via the Web. For the Teacher as Scholar, this package has the potential to reach even more interested individuals than even a textbook published by a well-known author. Web design software provides easy-to-use development tools including customized Home pages, file management, course and student management, on-line chat rooms, bulletin boards, and electronic mail.

Drawing Package   Drawing tools create and manipulate graphics files so important to visual-based lessons. The ability to cut and paste images and textual information and resize graphics to suit the presentation are key features of any drawing utility. A full-featured package also provides color, flip/rotation of images, and an on-screen slide show capability.

Image Viewer and Clip Art Software   Image viewers operate on picture files (.gif, .jpg, and .bmp files) captured by an optical scanner, digitized by cameras or video recorders, or taken directly from the Internet. For example, an Internet-based lesson on the Grand Canyon offers 479 different sites containing images of this national treasure. Most viewers edit the captured image by cropping or capturing only a portion of the graphic appropriate for the lesson. If appropriate images are not available, Clip Art provides cartoon-like images that may support the learning experience. A full-featured viewer adds text, permits cut and paste editing, and offers drawing tools to focus the attention of the student on relevant information. Image viewers and clip art are some of the most used tools in the Intelligent Portfolio.

Sound and Movie Player Software   Several excellent helper applications are available to capture and play visual images and sound files. Sound Players capture audio (as .snd or .wav files) and incorporate them into instructional material. Movie Players allow the user to view, save, edit, and play video clips taken from the World Wide Web (as .mpg or .avi files). Combining motion with sound, these files provide powerful images for the learner. Sound files load faster and require less memory than video clips; they also take much less storage on the hard drive. The use of this medium requires additional hardware such as sound cards, memory upgrades, and a choice of audio reproduction.

Demonstrating Hardware

Images, sounds, video clips, and graphics-based presentations demand more sophisticated hardware to support the large files and processing speeds required to present seamless demonstrations for the Teacher as Scholar.

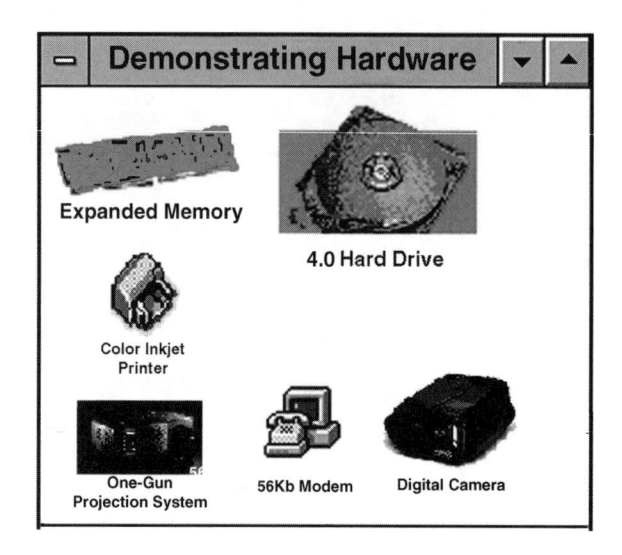

Expanded Memory The basic computer system configuration called for 32 megabytes of memory. Earlier, in the Thinking folder, upgrades to memory were suggested. Now, in the Demonstration folder, we urge you to consider doubling internal memory to 64 megabytes. The increase ensures that all but the very largest video clips will load and play without hesitation. Also, additional memory supports more efficient use of the graphics and course development software packages.

Large-Capacity Hard Drive Large files require higher-capacity drives. Fortunately, the cost of these particular peripherals is falling with each product announcement. For the Demonstrating folder, a 4 gigabyte hard drive is recommended. A smaller drive is acceptable, but expect to migrate files to zip drives more frequently. For most, it will be a trade-off between convenience and cost.

Color Printer The Demonstrating Hardware folder implies the need for color printing capability. Color laser quality is preferred; however, color inkjet printers are acceptable. As with many hardware choices, the trade-off is between speed, quality, and cost. Whichever printer is selected, it must be capable of printing high-quality classroom materials and professional-looking handouts.

One-Gun Projector As a lecturer, the Teacher as Scholar cannot depend on the availability or compatibility of overhead projectors when securing audiovisual facilities for a major presentation. Laptops do not always connect to these systems with standard interface cables. Signals are not always the same between the computer and projector.

Fortunately, inexpensive projection systems are now widely available. A one-gun projector is portable, durable, easy to set up, and most importantly, very effective. Today's laptops are equipped with RGB ports for direct connection to most one-gun projection systems. In only a few minutes, the presenter is ready for the session—from bag to briefing in less than 10 minutes. The flat panel projector recommended in earlier implementations of the Intelligent Portfolio is no longer suitable; the quality of hardware contributes to your reputation as a Teacher-Scholar.

High-Speed (56Kb) Modem   A 56 kilobit per second modem addresses the demand for faster communications via telephone lines. Some Internet providers already offer this service, with more upgraded providers coming on line every month. However, unlike previous technology, these faster speeds require 56 kbs modems on *both* ends of the communications link to operate at the increased speeds. Also, access from home may be unreliable because of the age of telephone lines that may have been installed many years ago when line quality was not as critical to voice communications. Portfolio users should consider these cautions before purchasing upgraded modems.

Digital Camera   Developing effective instructional resources depends on the use of visual material appropriate for the target audience. Students in primary grades need more images. However, even children in upper grades benefit from strong visual course materials. Obtaining images from the Internet is little more than a point and click exercise. The Teacher as Scholar, however, should not be limited to what is available from a particular Web site. A digital camera captures images wherever they can be found, holding as many as 120 image-files which can be downloaded to the Intelligent Portfolio.

Writing Software

The written word is the hallmark of the Teacher as Scholar. The Intelligent Portfolio provides tools ranging from word processors to more sophisticated document publication software.

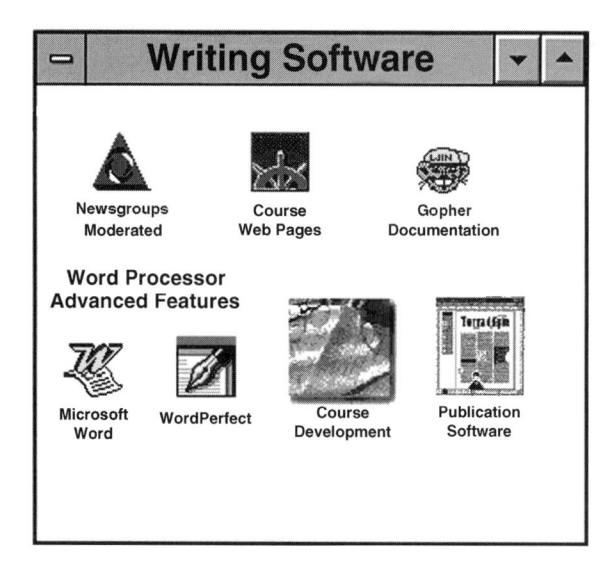

Moderated Newsgroups   Newsgroups were included in earlier implementations of the portfolio for sharing information and communicating with fellow educators. In this version of the Intelligent Portfolio, the Teacher as Scholar is called on to initiate a newsgroup. Typically, they are formed by users sharing common interests. Newsgroup providers gladly include these new offerings because of public demand for these services. Some services submit candidates for a new newsgroup to a community vote; many are added temporarily for a trial period. Those receiving enough positive attention are retained past the trial period. The Teacher as Scholar sponsors newsgroups that solicit ideas, papers, comments, and issues from other learners and experts. Moderating a newsgroup brings credit to your reputation as a leader and authority in the field.

Web Pages   The future of educational technology lies with the Internet. Web pages provide graphical user interface which makes using the Internet easy to use even for the computer novice. The use of Course Web Pages is still in its infancy, however, more and more lesson plans, syllabi, assessment tools, student handout materials, and guides for the classroom teacher are available than ever before. The Teacher as Scholar is expected to prepare these materials; to do so demands that the educator learn how to use certain Web-based tools.

Hypertext markup language (HTML) is the native programming language of tags, codes, and keywords that produces the images, fonts, and formats found on all the best Web pages. Fortunately, user-friendly tools are now available to create HTML without the obtuse programming languages that have limited the development of such material in the past. Many word processors also convert text, insert images, provide tabbed fields, and otherwise translate regular documents into HTML code. Editors, built into the newer Web browsers, edit and save Web pages with personalized changes. With today's most popular browsers, the task of developing course Web pages is much like preparing a typical word processing document.

Gopher Documentation   Although the use of the Gopher network for documentation management is waning, it remains very popular in the academic community. The Gopher system was included in previous implementations of the Intelligent Portfolio as a means of locating education-specific resources. It is now time to contribute to this cache of resources. Forming a Gopher site is probably beyond the scope of most Teacher-Scholars. Adding a category to an existing site, however, is not. Much like the newsgroup, maintaining a Gopher site filled with valuable resources requires patience, professionalism, and some practical experience with computer files and their management. Many Gopher masters provide the technical services, asking instead for new materials in order to keep their site current and attractive to other explorers.

Full-Featured Word Processor   The advanced features of word processing include formatting, grammar tools, and editing features. A spell checker and on-line thesaurus are helpful tools when preparing journal articles, speeches and presentations, and a host of educational literature. Table of Contents writers quickly index publications, while templates provide a standard format for recurring documents. Hyphenators, auto-correction, word counts, mail merging, and drawing features round out a list of capabilities that comprise full-featured word processor.

Desktop Publishing Software   Even with all the options inherent in a full-featured word processor, they often fall short of true publication quality. For professional educators who want to add polish to their publications, desktop publishing software offers such features as multiple fonts, seamless integration of graphics and text, and multi-columnar presentations. Products from this software package include camera-ready manuscripts and other professional looking materials. Perhaps the Teacher as Scholar might even take on the responsibilities of moderating and publishing a newsletter specific to an area of expertise.

Course Development Software   Course development software provides a comprehensive cache of tools to aid in the preparation of classroom materials. The Teacher as Scholar is in an excellent position to design, develop, and distribute course materials. Course development software manages the more mundane aspects of instructional design leaving the teacher with more time to concentrate on the unique features of the curriculum. Such software includes a word processor-like capability sufficient to generate the text of the course material. Spell checkers, grammar checkers, and a thesaurus are usually included in the package. In addition, most course development software provides a template for preparing documents such as a course syllabus, book reviews, and chapter outlines. Test creation modules with item analysis and letter-grading features help the educator develop assessment tools. Bibliographies, indexes, and tables of content can also be created "on the fly." The most successful packages add features such as performance task managers that set and maintain curriculum goals, link student tasks with learning objectives, and provide anecdotal feedback on student work. Some even contain modules that allow students to work at home and integrate their efforts with on-site schoolwork.

Writing Hardware

Writing Hardware includes color laser printing and a CD-ROM Burner for distributing educational materials.

Color Laser Printer   The Teacher as Scholar produces quality materials, including color images, graphs, and charts. Laser printers deliver high-quality black and white text intermingled with color graphics at a fraction of the cost of color printing services. The inkjet printer, recommended earlier, is outpaced by the volume of writing artifacts and the quality expected from the professional Teacher-Scholar.

CD-ROM Burner   Not long ago, access to a CD-ROM burner was unaffordable for the average computer user unless they were producing hundreds of distribution disks. Today, this peripheral is well within the reach of personal budgets. Storing some three quarters of a million characters on a single CD-ROM makes the distribution of educational material easier and more cost effective. A blank compact disk costs only a few dollars, and prices continue to decline. Mailing costs are also significantly reduced. Speed, portability, and convenience are additional reasons to consider the use of the CD-ROM burner for the Writing Hardware folder of the Teacher-Scholar.

138 *Professional Portfolios for Teachers*

(Can you identify the differences between the Teacher as Scholar and previous portfolios?)

Step Three:
Organizing Folders and Collection Points

Many folders in this version of the Intelligent Portfolio contain the same information as previous versions; many even retain the same name. However, please draw your attention to the differences in this portfolio and how the Collection Points evolve. For example, the Collecting folder continues to serve as a repository for 25 percent of the Intelligent Portfolio's artifacts. Another 25 percent are found in the Working folder with the remaining 50 percent of the artifacts stored in the Showcase folder as the best research, professional presentations, and proof of scholarship. The recommended proportions of Collecting-Working-Showcase artifacts for the Teacher as Scholar are represented below.

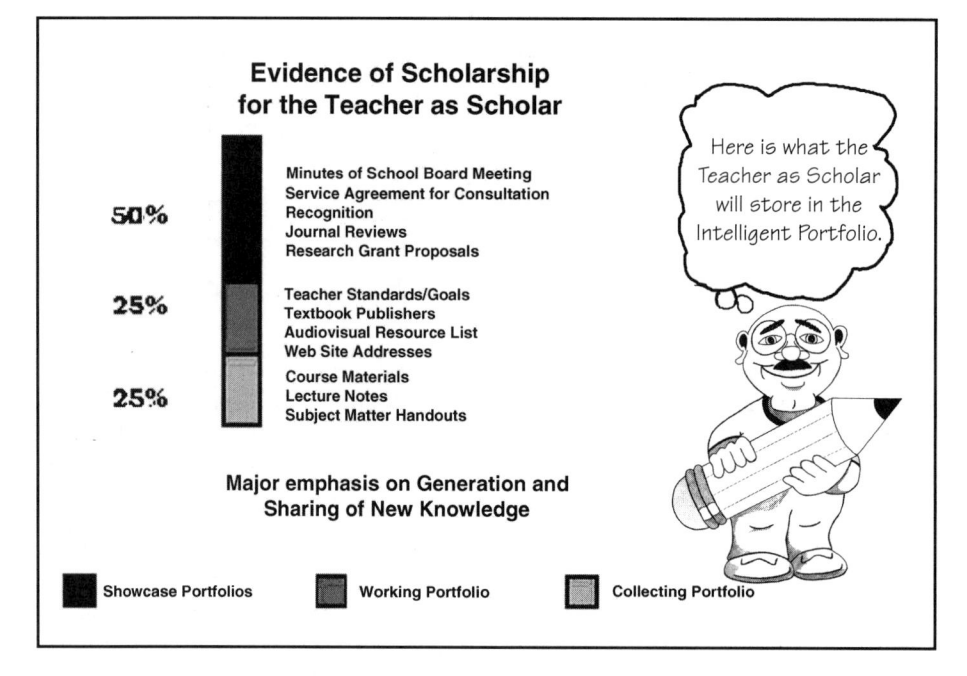

Evidence of Scholarship for the Teacher as Scholar

(Here is what the Teacher as Scholar will store in the Intelligent Portfolio.)

- **50%** — Minutes of School Board Meeting; Service Agreement for Consultation; Recognition; Journal Reviews; Research Grant Proposals
- **25%** — Teacher Standards/Goals; Textbook Publishers; Audiovisual Resource List; Web Site Addresses
- **25%** — Course Materials; Lecture Notes; Subject Matter Handouts

Major emphasis on Generation and Sharing of New Knowledge

■ Showcase Portfolios   ■ Working Portfolio   ■ Collecting Portfolio

Collecting Folder

Artifacts from earlier implementations of the portfolio are not expected to remain in the Collecting folder for very long. The Teacher as Scholar collects materials important enough to make timely contributions to the profession and discards those which do not.

Collection Point #1: Content Area Material   This Collection Point houses countless artifacts accumulated through years of dedication to a particular subject matter area. The entire Collecting folder requires continual attention to ensure inclusion of the latest artifacts and the culling of old, outdated materials. Content Area Material should focus on a few specific disciplines chosen by the educator for her or his research. The **best** handouts, journal articles, lesson notes, and course materials are placed in this folder.

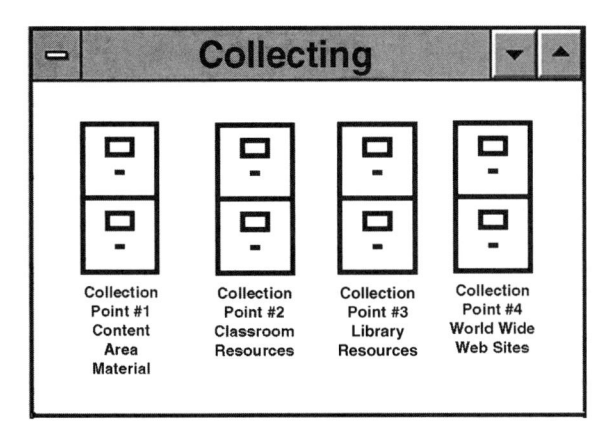

We advised previous users of the Smart and Intelligent Portfolios to "collect, collect, collect" new artifacts related to content material; that advice applies to the Teacher-Scholar as well. More to the point, a scholar's responsibility to identify, incorporate, and disseminate the best in educational materials increases in this phase of a career. Any subject-specific artifacts that might contribute to a deeper understanding of the discipline should be considered.

Collection Point #2: Classroom Resources   Collection Point #2 is the target for newly acquired classroom resources. Textbook publishers, Web site creators, and curriculum designers are sources for innovative lesson ideas. Placing these materials in this Collection Point marks them for future integration with other materials that address a particular learning objective.

Collection Point #3: Library Resources   The purpose and content of this Collection Point changes very little among the three implementations of the Intelligent Portfolio. Library Resources continue to house pertinent information regarding library access to educational materials. For the Teacher as Scholar, the school library adds a wealth of electronic artifacts. In addition to books and journals, some schools' technology budgets provide laser discs, videotapes, audio selections, and cable television programs for the classroom.

Collection Point #4: World Wide Web Sites   New Web site addresses for education-related Internet sites continue to be added to this Collection Point. The emphasis here is on sites that provide resources for research, subject matter publications, professional organizations, libraries, museums, educational news, and more.

Working Folder

The Working folder takes on a somewhat different purpose than previous implementations. It becomes a temporary location for work-in-progress. Twenty-five percent of the artifacts under development are housed in the Working folder.

Collection Point #5: Making Connections   Making Connections takes on the interacting responsibility of the Teacher-Scholar in the electronic version of the professional portfolio. This Collection Point contains mindmaps and drawings where ideas begin to form. Ideas from reading mix with conversations with colleagues to extend thinking and integrate new knowledge.

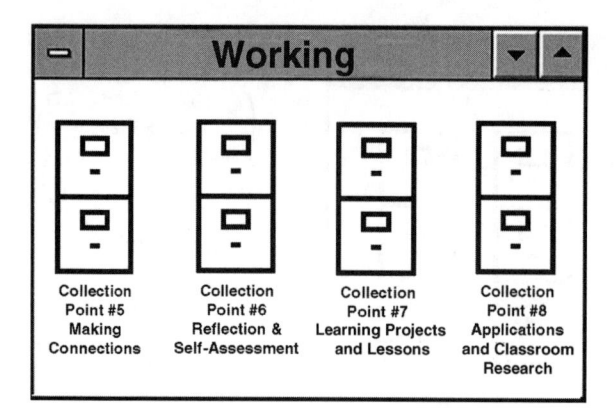

140   *Professional Portfolios for Teachers*

[Working folder diagram: Collection Point #5 Making Connections; Collection Point #6 Reflection & Self-Assessment; Collection Point #7 Learning Projects and Lessons; Collection Point #8 Applications and Classroom Research]

A temporary location for "work in progress," the Working folder combines your best artifacts.

Collection Point #6: Reflection and Self-Assessment Documentation of personal career goals demands a record of individual accomplishments. The professional educator maintains a series of individual goals that span a career of lifelong learning. Evidence of advancement toward these milestones should be maintained in this Collection Point.

Collection Point #7: Learning Projects and Lessons For the Teacher-Expert portfolio, Learning Projects and Lessons had their own collection points to handle the vast quantity of artifacts developed during the teacher's time in the classroom. For the Teacher as Scholar, these artifacts are regrouped into a single folder. They hold classroom projects, bulletin board templates, and class handouts plus the best lesson plans that surface after years of in-class validation.

Collection Point #8: Applications and Classroom Research Applications and Classroom Research are also grouped under a single collection point. The Teacher as Scholar combines principles of educational research with tried and true classroom applications to create new, innovative artifacts.

Showcase Folder

This implementation of the Intelligent Portfolio focuses on the mature educator. Representing nearly half of the Intelligent Portfolio, this folder holds presentations, publications, and course artifacts stored in the Collection Points 9–12.

The expanded Showcase folder reflects the importance of service, teaching, and scholarship.

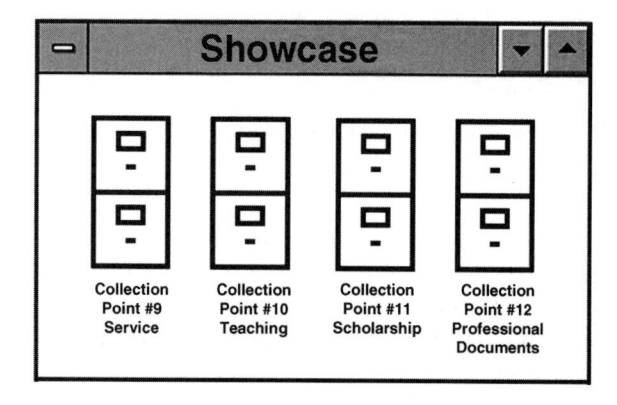

[Showcase folder diagram: Collection Point #9 Service; Collection Point #10 Teaching; Collection Point #11 Scholarship; Collection Point #12 Professional Documents]

Collection Point #9: Service   Teachers are often partnered with other educators to provide personal service to schools, districts, and their own discipline. Collection Point #9 holds the artifacts of that service and includes items such as letters of appointment, minutes of important meetings, publications of policy and procedures, and calendars of pending appointments and upcoming seminars. Some of the more popular commitments that an educator might undertake include serving as an officer in a national education association, a member of an accreditation team or school board (publicly elected or private), a consultant to a school district on issues of law, facilities, or technology, or a program chairman for a national conference.

Collection Point #10: Teaching   Scholars focus their practical classroom experience on the identification, development, and dissemination of the best instructional materials to practicing teachers who may not have the time or expertise to develop this material themselves. Artifacts stored in this folder begin their journey in the Working folder where the Teacher-Learner's primary responsibility is to collect artifacts. Once collected, the Teacher-Expert places the material into motion by incorporating the artifacts into actual classroom lessons. The Teacher as Scholar fine tunes the artifacts and distributes them as validated course material—literally, the best of the best.

Collection Point #11: Scholarship   Artifacts of scholarly work not placed in the previous Service and Teaching collection points are stored in this folder. For example, a seventh grade science lesson on the human heart might garner an award from the National Science Foundation. That award, along with any accompanying citation, is placed in this folder. Or, perhaps the educator presented a lesson on science pedagogy as an in-service program. If the lesson explored new science course work, that, too, is placed in this Collection Point. Publications, editorials, or reviews from journal committees are stored here as well. Finally, any research grant applications, correspondence, and award letters are evidence of scholarly work and should be placed in this folder.

Collection Point #12: Professional Documents   The final Collection Point holds "official" documents for the Intelligent Portfolio. The desktop scanner, provided in the Writing Hardware folder, is used to input these artifacts. An education vitae, validated teaching certificate, and undergraduate and graduate transcripts are maintained in this folder and updated at least semiannually to ensure they remain current.

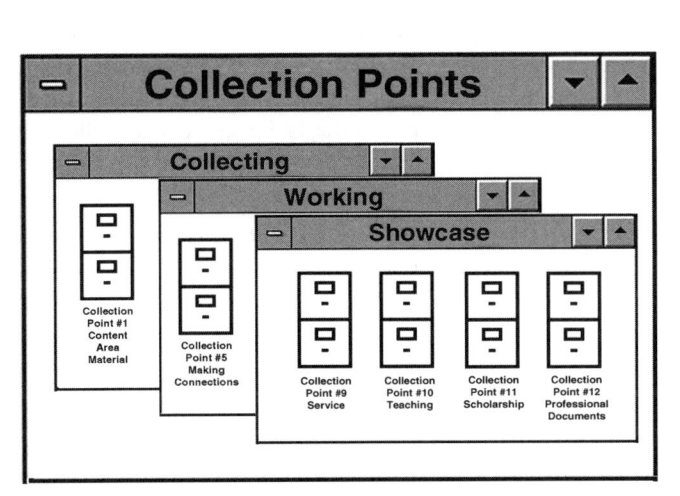

Conclusion

The focus for the Teacher as Scholar culminates in the Showcase folder of the Intelligent Portfolio. Electronic artifacts continue to be collected, new thinking produces new artifacts, but the emphasis is now on showcasing those artifacts.

Foley Tips

A few final tips for using the Intelligent Portfolio as a Teacher-Scholar.

1. **Showcase your best.** This version of the Intelligent Portfolio contains additional items of both hardware and software to support development efforts that make the Teacher as Scholar unique. Depend on past artifacts as a source of innovative new presentations, publications, and course materials.

2. **Revisit Collection Points as artifacts are added to the portfolio.** Unlike previous versions which suggested weekly or semester review of artifacts, new additions and deletions should trigger the reexamination of Collection Points. Ensure that new materials deserve to remain in your portfolio.

3. **Continue to upgrade your Intelligent Portfolio.** The only Tip which remains consistent throughout all implementations of the Intelligent Portfolio is to continually upgrade hardware and software. New operating systems, software versions, and hardware peripherals should be evaluated in light of how each can benefit the Intelligent Portfolio. Consider only those changes that enhance the utility of your Intelligent Portfolio to serve as a lifelong tool for learning and development.

4. **Survey previous implementations of the Intelligent Portfolio.** Important artifacts which once served only as collecting or working items are now the basis of new thinking for the Teacher-Scholar.

5. **Enroll in technical classes which support the Intelligent Portfolio.** Each recommended package has features beyond those basics applicable to the Intelligent Portfolio. Most colleges and universities have a wealth of computer courses. Take advantage of these opportunities.

6. **Add Collection Points to the Intelligent Portfolio.** The Teacher as Scholar will undoubtedly identify many more Collection Points than those offered in this chapter. New points should be added if they provide a valuable repository for your artifacts. It is advisable that you do not delete any of the 12 recommended Collection Points: They have proven themselves in study and practical application. Folders without artifacts are an indication that a substantial aspect of your portfolio may be deficient.

7. **The future is on the Internet.** Many of the folders and Collection Points identified in this chapter depend upon the Internet as a source of information. The scholar should expect to use the Internet for research and exhibition.

CHAPTER 13

Portfolios in Transition: The Teacher as Scholar Perspective

Introduction

In a small conference room, 36 candidates shook hands with one another, greeted the cadre of faculty assigned to their doctoral program, and listened as speakers introduced a barrage of administrative details. The doctoral candidates were embarking upon a journey which, at that stage, must have appeared to have no destination: three years of classes lie ahead followed by the impending dissertation and a formidable oral defense. What did begin immediately was a professional portfolio agenda that would serve the doctoral candidates throughout their program.

Introducing the Portfolio

The doctoral candidates represented a wide range of occupations and an even wider range of classroom teaching experiences. A bag of tools would aid them in their journey through the course work, learning groups, and mentoring experiences that had been integrated into the program. They were about to be introduced to the tool that would be put in use immediately and become a constant companion over the next several years. That tool was the "professional portfolio."

To introduce the portfolio and its component elements, the authors of this book provided a three-hour workshop to cohort members and interested faculty. It began with an introduction and a brief history of the portfolio as an assessment tool. As the latest evolution of the transition from learner to expert to scholar, the professional portfolio emerged as a teacher's tool for lifelong learning.

The Prototype Study of the Smart and Intelligent Portfolio for Teacher as Scholar begins...

Example Artifacts
- Book Notes/Bibliography
- Personal Teaching Philosophy
- Writing Assessment and Holistic Scoring Guide
- Curriculum Guide
- Unit Plan of Instruction
- Annotated Shakespeare Bibliography
- Personal Goals for the Year
- Teaching Certificate
- NCTE Web Site Home Page
- Grade Reports
- Course Syllabus

An in-class exercise was employed to bring home the benefits of the portfolio as an organizational tool. Cohort members were divided into teams of three and provided with a packet of materials (artifacts) representing possible items of value in a portfolio. Each team was asked to identify where selected items should be stored—in which of the Collection Points simulated by loose leaf reproductions and manila envelopes.

The Questions

The exercise provided some unexpected results. The teams concurred on nearly every artifact, as a rationale was offered for each item regardless of its final disposition. The exercise brought to light six key questions from team members that deserved attention. Foley will introduce those inquiries.

- Who will be using the portfolio and do the characteristics of that individual change over time?
- What kinds of artifacts are important? Will it depend on whether you are a learner, teacher, or scholar?
- How will artifacts be stored and will all users store them in the same location?
- Where should artifacts be stored for easy retrieval?
- When is the electronic format a better choice than hard copy?
- And, finally, the easy question: Why are portfolios so important? The answer will run the gamut of your educational career.

And Now, Some Answers...

The questions proposed by members of the group had already been asked many times during the planning sessions that led to the design of the new doctoral program. The very nature of the Smart Portfolio and the Intelligent Portfolio depended on resolving these questions. As the concepts of the portfolio were reinforced from the outset of the program, students were quick to recognize that the professional portfolio addressed many of the answers they were seeking. We will look at the questions—and their respective answers—one at a time.

Question: Who will be using the portfolio? Answer: The Teacher as Learner, Teacher as Expert, and Teacher as Scholar.

Who will be using the portfolio?

From the outset, it was apparent that different implementations of the portfolio would be required if it were to prove useful to the lifelong learner. The concept of Teacher as Learner, Teacher as Expert, and Teacher as Scholar was immediately appealing to the cohort. It answered the question of "Who" would be using the portfolio. The realization that educators display characteristics of three different natures over the span of a 30-year career was both perplexing and comforting. Group members began to consider where in their academic career they found themselves at this particular moment in time. Reflective self-assessment would become second nature by the end of their first academic year.

What kinds of artifacts are important?

Question: What artifacts are important? The answer depends on whether you are a Teacher-Learner, Teacher-Expert, or Teacher-Scholar.

The key components of both the Smart and Intelligent Portfolios brought closure to the question of **"What"** artifacts will be gathered and stored. For the teacher, the five foundations identified in the professional portfolio: Reading, Writing, Thinking, Interacting, and Demonstrating dictate what artifacts are to be gathered. Since artifacts are usually created or constructed by the portfolio keeper, it was easy to anticipate a Teacher as Learner focus on Reading (e.g. book notes and bibliographies), a Teacher as Expert focus on Demonstrating (e.g. lesson plans, assessments, and classroom activities), and a Teacher as Scholar focus on Interacting (e.g. publications and professional service).

How will the artifacts be stored?

Collecting, Working, and Showcase folders provide yet another answer to the novice portfolio user. By matching these folders with a particular phase of a teacher's career, the **"How"** question met with simple resolve. As proposed in the professional portfolio, Collecting artifacts are the major concern of the Teacher-Learner (as teachers build their knowledge base), Working artifacts are most often used by the Teacher-Expert (as teachers hone their classroom skills), and Showcase artifacts determine the success of the Teacher-Scholar (as teachers contribute to their discipline).

Question: How will the artifacts be stored? Answer: In Collecting, Working, and Showcase folders.

Question: Where will these artifacts be stored? Answer: in one of the many proposed Collection Points.

Where should artifacts be stored for easy retrieval?

Collection Points answer the **"Where"** question. Each Collection Point is a repository for storing artifacts. They expand to whatever size is required to host a career's worth of educational resources, and ensure that students will find common locations for similar artifacts.

When is the electronic format the best choice?

Question: When is the Electronic format preferred? Answer: It's your choice based on technical competence and experience.

The question of "**When**" to use the Smart versus the Intelligent Portfolio was addressed. The cohort coined a new term for many of its members: "the *technologically challenged.*" Those unfamiliar with technology expressed apprehension with the demands of the Intelligent Portfolio. Their fears were somewhat allayed when it was explained that the **Intelligent Portfolio** is merely an electronic extension of the **Smart Portfolio,** and using a computer made particular sense for those who were already conversant in the use of technology. However, either format ensures similar assessments at the conclusion of the semester: Content of materials was all-important. Evidence of thinking was critical. Form was incidental.

Why are portfolios so important?

The answer to this question would evolve throughout the semester. When the structure and objectives of the cohort study were being developed, it was predicted that doctoral students were far too advanced in their formal education and on-the-job experience to be considered for any but the Teacher as Scholar version of the Smart or Intelligent Portfolio. The authors presupposed that postgraduate students would come to the program already masters of the Teacher-Learner experience and successful participants in the Teacher-Expert role.

Question: Why are Portfolios so important to the teacher? Answer: Teaching, Learning, and Assessment.

Surprisingly, vastly different levels of experience were discovered. A cautiously prepared survey revealed that few cohort members employed portfolios in their own classrooms, several vaguely recalled the use of portfolios during their undergraduate education, and others had yet to experience portfolios in any form. It became apparent well before the end of the first semester, that regardless of the level of formal education or professional tenure, novice portfolio users are best served by starting with the Teacher as Learner implementation and its emphasis on Collecting artifacts. Moving directly to the use of the Teacher as Expert or Teacher as Scholar portfolios without previous portfolio experience is a prelude to confusion and failure.

Conclusion

Questions afforded a constant challenge during the study, as the professional portfolio was adjusted and adapted to the needs of students. One of the most successful portfolio experiences was the Final Exhibition conducted during the last week of the semester. The exhibition integrated the combination of learning opportunities provided by courses, several research papers, and ongoing mentoring projects. The time spent sharing, demonstrating, and interacting during this public display of learning offered further testimony to the lasting contributions made by the Professional Portfolio. Other findings included:

- **The need to increase the research base for portfolios.** Precious little research is available to either confirm or deny the value of portfolios. "You are part of the ongoing research effort that will produce significant findings in the years ahead" was difficult for the cohort members to accept at first. Later, the idea that they were making history became an exciting impetus to complete their portfolios.
- **The value of creating a portfolio by collecting and later evaluating artifacts.** Gathering your best artifacts into a single document contributes to your professional development.
- **The importance of constantly assessing your portfolio.** Informal self-assessments and peer assessments are equally important as formal instructor assessments when it comes to portfolios.
- **An awareness that not all portfolios will look the same.** While all professional portfolios include many common artifacts, folders, and collection points, they will necessarily differ to reflect the personality of the user.
- **An appreciation that not every portfolio must become Intelligent.** The Smart Portfolio works equally as well.
- **The realization that Reading, Writing, Thinking, Interacting, and Demonstrating are integral to the portfolio.** These foundations extend to the very core of learning. Neglecting any one of them will be at the peril of a comprehensive portfolio.
- **The significance of Collection Points both as a repository for artifacts and as a construct for their retrieval.** Store artifacts in collection points so you can find them.
- **The fact that the Intelligent Portfolio best serves your needs when it is equipped with the tools suited for the task at hand.** Do not become enthralled with the more elaborate hardware and software packages.

It is exciting to participate in a new and revolutionary campaign. Teachers who animate the concepts and principles of the Professional Portfolio, we believe, can honestly claim participation in just such an experience. From beginning teachers to their classroom counterparts to scholarly peers in the field, we extend our gratitude for your lasting contributions to the expanding research base on portfolios. For us, the value of the Professional Portfolio was evidenced by members of the doctoral cohort each time they expressed a heartfelt "thank you" for a learning experience they will always remember: an experience based on sharing, interacting, and discovery—an experience based on the Professional Portfolio.

PART VI
Assessing Teacher Portfolios

Assessing portfolios can be fast and efficient with a comprehensive assessment tool and an exhibition rubric.

Chapter 14 will guide you through a comprehenisve assessment process using our Portfolio Assessment Tool and a formal Portfolio Exhibition.

Chapter 14

Assessing the Professional Portfolio

Chapter 14 describes the Portfolio Assessment Tool for the Professional Portfolio. Examples are shown for teachers as learners, experts, and scholars. The chapter includes suggestions for the final portfolio exhibition.

CHAPTER 14

Assessing the Professional Portfolio

*"The good thinker in virtually any
field is intellectually self-watching,
self-guiding, and self-assessing."*

(Tishman, Perkins & Jay, 1995, p. 65)

Introduction

From the beginning we have established that learning is the purpose and intent of the portfolio. Evidence of learning is gathered in accordance with the framework and goals of the professional portfolio. Artifacts are assessed in a variety of ways and by a variety of assessors, resulting in a multidimensional appraisal. As individuals build a unique knowledge base, they move toward deeper understanding and create an historical record of learning as they journey through their career. The professional portfolio has evolved from a container holding best works to a documented chronicle of a professional career. Still the larger question remains: "How do we assess a portfolio with validity and reliability?"

Validity stems from numerous and varied assessments—contained within the portfolio itself. Reliability is realized when different assessors reach a common consensus. Such an approach ensures that the portfolio remains multidimensional. Portfolios begin with artifacts as tangible evidence that learning has occurred. What one knows (content knowledge), what one can do (performance), and what one understands and articulates (application) are all part of the holistic assessment. Each artifact is assessed at the time it is created and presented, often accompanied by a written rationale for its inclusion in the portfolio. Then artifacts are modified and stored in the portfolio at designated Collection Points.

Assessment balanced with constructive criticism is called Formative Assessment: Teacher-Learners, Teacher-Experts, and Teacher-Scholars are offered feedback, given meaningful comments, and offered time to improve the artifact. During the Formative Assessment phase, the assessor returns a paper with comments and suggestions rather than with a grade to encourage the Teacher-as-Learner to rethink; Teachers-as-Experts receive immediate feedback following a lesson presentation; and Teachers-as-Scholars receive feedback from editors after submitting a piece for publication.

The use of the Professional Portfolio often includes a Summative Assessment at the end of a particular learning experience. For example, Teachers-as-Learners are required to take the National Teacher Examination. This battery of tests determines whether or not the teacher will be certified. Teachers-as-Experts are assessed by their principals a few times each academic year as a measure of their overall teaching competence. Teachers-as-Scholars receive assessments via an evaluation questionnaire. This assessment tool is a factor in promotion and tenure decisions.

Portfolio assessments are typically performed over long periods of time after many artifacts of Collecting, Working, and Showcase have been gathered. To add dimension to the learning process, the professional portfolio should be formally presented. The "Portfolio Exhibition" is as much another learning experience as it is an assessment. In fact, an exhibition provides the ultimate self-evaluation.

It is appropriate that a book about professional portfolios ends with assessment. Considering the research and literature on portfolios, the greatest concern remains with evaluation. First, there are the more traditional questions about summative learning:

- *How is the learner's knowledge base to be measured?*
- *How will the teacher's performance be rated?*
- *How can a scholar's contribution to the knowledge base be determined?*

To these questions we will add the often overlooked questions about formative evaluation:

- *Has the learner been encouraged to expand that knowledge base?*
- *Has the teacher's classroom practice shown continuous improvement?*
- *Has the scholar's research base been extended beyond minimum expectations?*

Only when all of these questions are addressed and answered can we begin to see the power of the portfolio as a balance between its roles as a tool for assessment and a tool for learning.

The Portfolio Assessment Tool

To prepare for the defense of the portfolio, we recommend using the Portfolio Assessment Tool (PAT). Grounded in research and validated by actual classroom application, the PAT is equally appropriate as a reflective personal critique or an instructive feedback instrument. Figure 14-1 shows the PAT and its three primary components: the Formative Assessment (Part I), the Summative Assessment (Part II), and Final Comments (Part III). Let's take a closer look at the PAT.

Part I: The Formative Assessment

A formative evaluation provides ongoing feedback regarding the application of the portfolio in the classroom (as a learner or teacher) or the seminar room (for the scholar). Formative Assessments are always conducted as the process is underway. They include an understanding of the actual portfolio process and an attempt to remedy any problems that might surface during its use. The Formative Assessment requires the educator to review the portfolio regularly to resolve discrepancies and act upon the artifacts that have been captured. The Formative Assessment is based on the five Foundations of the Smart and Intelligent Portfolios: Reading, Writing, Thinking, Interacting, and Demonstrating.

1. **Did you use the Smart or Intelligent Portfolio?** Which did you choose? Did you opt for the Smart Portfolio or migrate to the computer-based Intelligent Portfolio? Although the user may select the Smart or Intelligent Portfolio exclusively, it was found that combining the two portfolio approaches also has considerable merit. Some users decided to base their portfolios on the Smart format using binders and hard copy artifacts —items that made them most comfortable. However, these individuals also captured artifacts in electronic format as computer files. It made little sense to reproduce the artifacts in printed form, when their Smart Portfolio could simply be augmented with a "Table of Contents" that would document the exact location of

these electronic artifacts. Such an approach made sense, and the eclectic methodology was adopted as a viable alternative to a hard and fast use of either the Smart or Intelligent Portfolios.

2. **How many Collection Points did your portfolio contain?** The number of Collection Points in your portfolio depends on several factors. First, of course, is the format of the portfolio itself. While the Teacher-Learner has 10 Collection Points, the Teacher-Expert and Teacher-Scholar have 12. Many of the initial cadre of portfolio users satisfied their organizational needs with less than the recommended number; a few exceeded the number. The PAT includes this question as a gentle reminder that the number of Collection Points was determined from significant research in an effort to cover the range of artifacts that educators commonly experience in the course of their professional growth. If fewer Collection Points are used, the portfolio should be carefully examined to make sure that none of the sources for new thinking are inadvertently omitted.

3. **The Foundations.** For each of the five Foundations, the Portfolio Assessment Tool offers a look at the formative aspects of Collecting, Working, and Showcase artifacts. The PAT offers several questions for consideration—specifically, which are your most important artifacts—with a rationale of why these items were selected. Space is provided to match the evidence with the best four artifacts described. Research found that many subjects readily identified the three or four most important artifacts; however, they were at a loss to explain the importance of others. The result was oftentimes the elimination of these items as unnecessary or excessive. Next, artifacts in each Foundation are identified as Collecting, Working, or Showcase. Each category is tallied and the number is transferred to the Summative Assessment.

Part II: The Summative Assessment

At the end of the evaluation period, the Summative Assessment provides a determination of how well the portfolio aided the teacher in attaining individual personal goals and professional development objectives. The PAT provides a four-step process:

Step A. Confirm Your Status The Summative Assessment of your portfolio results depends on your status as a Teacher-Learner, Teacher-Expert, or Teacher-Scholar. Check the proper box indicating your current status.

Step B. Total Number of Artifacts Throughout the Formative Assessment, the number of artifacts collected were tracked as Collecting, Working, or Showcase. Now it is time to add all the artifacts collected and reported in each of the five Foundations of Reading, Writing, Thinking, Interacting, and Demonstrating. Put the totals in Step B of the Summative Assessment.

Step C. Graphical Display The Smart and Intelligent Portfolios are based on the assumption that the status of an educator dictates the focus of the artifacts. By completing this graphic and calculating the percentage of artifacts in each of three elements (Collecting, Working, Showcase), the power of the portfolio is revealed. Transfer the numbers provided in Step B to one of the graphics in the Step C box. If you are a Teacher-Learner, fill in the first graphic and calculate the percent of artifacts in each element. The same will hold true for the Teacher-Expert and the Teacher-Scholar. Complete **only one graphic.** The percentages should fall in line with the recommended ratios to the right of each graphic. Next, determine whether these numbers reflect your use of the portfolio.

Step D. Final Analysis of Your Portfolio Effort If your status as a learner, expert, or scholar correctly matches the accumulated artifacts, the portfolio has served you well. Now answer Questions (1) through (4):

Question (1). *Did the percentage of artifacts in the Collecting, Working, and Showcase sections of your portfolio agree with the recommended percentages?* Each part of the book focused on a particular aspect of the educator's career, and each version of both the Smart and Intelligent Portfolios was modified slightly to accommodate those variances. If you are a Teacher as Learner, the majority of your artifacts should be located in one of the four *Collecting* folders of Content Area Materials, Classroom Resources, Library Resources, or World Wide Web Sites. The portfolio for the Teacher as Expert has most of its artifacts in the *Working* folders of Making Connections, Reflection & Self-Assessment, Learning Projects, Applications, Lessons, and Classroom Research. Finally, the portfolio of the Teacher as Scholar predominantly utilizes the *Showcase* folders of Service, Teaching, Scholarship, and Professional Documents as its primary Collection Points. Check the box to the right of the question indicating whether the percentage of artifacts in your portfolio agrees with the recommended percentages. This assessment will lead to Question 2 in the Summative Assessment.

Question (2). *Does the analysis of your portfolio artifacts support your status as a learner, expert, or scholar? Why or why not?* If the numbers reported did not match the recommended percentages, perhaps there was a logical reason. Question (2) is designed to make you think about the use of portfolios to support your status as an educator. Complete the question by considering the artifacts collected and whether they are of a quantity and quality consistent with your own lifelong learning and professional development objectives.

Question (3). *Indicate the portfolio Foundation (Reading, Writing, Thinking, Interacting, or Demonstrating) that contributed most to your personal growth and professional development.* Throughout this book we discussed how *Reading* was paramount for the Teacher as Learner, *Demonstrating* was most important to the Teacher as Expert, and *Interacting* was critical to the Teacher as Scholar. Question (3) allows you to take another look at whether the application of your portfolio was consistent with your status. Check the box representing your strongest Foundation. If it was not the recommended element, use the Justification area to explain the variance. This process is an excellent self-assessment and thinking effort. When considering this question, you may choose to define "contributed most" as: "most useful in reaching personal goals," "aided most with new thinking skills and applications," or "resulted in most (qualitatively or quantitatively) personal and professional growth."

Question (4). *Indicate your Weakest Foundation for learning.* Thinking about the weakest of your Foundations also produces new ideas about the use of portfolios. Perhaps you will choose the Foundation that had the least number of artifacts or the one that contributed least to new thinking and innovative ideas about education. Perhaps your assessment may indicate a weakness in more than one of the Foundations. Either way, use the space provided to show how you will address this weakness. How can the portfolio help you resolve this deficiency? A self-assessment that answers this question accurately constitutes an extremely valuable learning exercise.

Part III: Final Comments

The two components of the "Final Comments" section of the Portfolio Assessment Tool provide for free-form observations about the use of your Smart or Intelligent Portfolio. If the PAT is to be used by an external evaluator (e.g. instructor or supervisor), Part III can be extremely useful in elaborating on the Formative and Summative aspects of your portfolio assessment. It provides the final opportunity for additional thinking about your portfolio application.

Figure 14-1

Page 1 of 6

Portfolio Assessment Tool

Your Name: _____

Date of the Assessment/Exhibition: _____

Instructor/Assessor: _____   Personal Assessment ☐

Part I. Formative Assessment

1. Did you use the Smart or Intelligent Portfolio? Or, was your portfolio a combination?
Rationale: _____
_____
_____

Smart ☐
Intelligent ☐
Combination ☐

2. How many Collection Points does your portfolio contain?   __ 6 ☐ 7 ☐ 8 ☐ 9 ☐ 10 ☐ __

3. The five Foundations

3a. READING. READERS gather evidence of new knowledge in the form of journals, booknotes, summaries, outlines, and drawings. Patterns and connections begin to form. READING builds an individual's knowledge base. Do your reading artifacts show evidence of any or all of the following? Enter Yes or No in the spaces provided.

- *Collected a significant amount of new knowledge* ___
- *Strengthened a position with documentation* ___
- *Initiated new ideas for teaching and learning* ___
- *Demonstrated an open-minded attitude* ___
- *Critiqued a resource for publication* ___
- *Suggested and shared new applications of knowledge* ___

Enter the Total Number of READING artifacts captured in your portfolio, categorized as Collecting, Working, or Showcase evidence.

Collecting ____   Working ____   Showcase ____

Identify your best artifacts which evidence your learning through the foundation of READING and give a short rationale.

Artifact 1: _____   Rationale: _____
_____

Artifact 2: _____   Rationale: _____
_____

Artifact 3: _____   Rationale: _____
_____

Artifact 4: _____   Rationale: _____
_____

Figure 14-1

3b. WRITING. Formal WRITING illustrates what we know and understand. Informal WRITING extends our thinking and understanding. Making meaning through WRITING involves formal papers, book reports, thematic units, poems and letters, publication-ready articles, and written classroom lesson plans. Do the WRITING artifacts you prepared demonstrate the following? Enter Yes or No in the spaces provided.

- Documented thinking and learning experiences ___
- Analyzed in-depth educational concepts ___
- Designed new curriculum or course of study ___
- Prepared papers for conference presentation ___
- Self-assessed teaching experiences ___
- Submitted journal articles for publication ___

Enter the Total Number of WRITING artifacts captured in your portfolio, categorized as Collecting, Working, or Showcase evidence.

Collecting **Working** **Showcase**
___   ___   ___

Illustrate professional development in the foundation of WRITING. Cite specific artifacts of your best works along with rationale.

Artifact 1: _____ Rationale: _____

Artifact 2: _____ Rationale: _____

Artifact 3: _____ Rationale: _____

Artifact 4: _____ Rationale: _____

3c. THINKING. Thinking lies at the heart of the portfolio and animates thoughts and ideas, giving them momentum and bringing them to life. A Thinking Journal is a place where we toss around ideas, consider other viewpoints, make connections, and judge our own learning. Do your thinking artifacts provide evidence of any or all of the following? Enter Yes or No in the spaces provided.

- Advanced your Personal Philosophy of Teaching and Learning ___
- Recorded thinking and learning processes in a Journal ___
- Constructed graphic organizers to show patterns of thinking ___
- Initiated problem-solving efforts to address educational issues ___
- Integrated thinking into existing teaching and learning strategies ___
- Generated concepts/ideas that contribute to the knowledge base ___

Enter the Total Number of THINKING artifacts captured in your portfolio, categorized as Collecting, Working, or Showcase evidence.

Collecting **Working** **Showcase**
___   ___   ___

THINKING may be the most important foundation of your Portfolio. List your best artifacts which generated new THINKING.

Artifact 1: _____ Rationale: _____

Artifact 2: _____ Rationale: _____

Artifact 3: _____ Rationale: _____

Artifact 4: _____ Rationale: _____

Figure 14-1

3d. INTERACTING. Interacting addresses the responsibility of educators to argue, defend, and share their ideas. INTERACTING involves peer assessments, memos from group activities, brainstorming sessions, arguments, problems and solutions, and position papers defending different points of view. Do your INTERACTING artifacts show evidence of the following?

- Considered ideas and arguments contrary to your own _3_
- Attended lectures, seminars, or conferences _1_
- Articulated and defended ideas for teaching and learning ___
- Shared ideas with colleagues in formal and informal situations _2_
- Established leadership role in professional organization _4_
- Created an environment that fosters the interaction of educators ___

Page 3 of 6

Enter the Total Number of INTERACTING artifacts captured in your portfolio, categorized as Collecting, Working, or Showcase evidence.

Collecting	Working	Showcase
2	1	1

INTERACTING plays upon your obligation to give something back to the discipline of Education. Can you document any specific occasions of interaction in your Portfolio?

Artifact 1: *Conference materials/resources* — Rationale: *Attended conference to learn about Inclusion*

Artifact 2: *Handouts on Inclusion to share with Faculty* — Rationale: *Prepared handouts to share with colleagues*

Artifact 3: *Records of Inclusion discussions and meetings* — Rationale: *Trace thinking on Inclusion and identify changes in personal understanding about the subject*

Artifact 4: *Voted Vice-President of State Reading Org.* — Rationale: *Meet twice a year and help the President with organizational objectives*

3e. DEMONSTRATING represents the portion of a portfolio rich in the application and transfer of learning. Demonstrations include the text of classroom presentations, speeches, oral interpretations, audiovisual materials, and completed projects using multisensory exhibits. Do your artifacts evidence your growing expertise in demonstrating your knowledge and skills?

- Designed a presentation for peer assessment _2_
- Demonstrated knowledge, skills, and a disposition for teaching ___
- Created a forum to articulate and share best classroom practices 3
- Prepared, delivered, and validated a unit of instruction _1_
- Presented workshops for national audience ___
- Published scholarly resources _4_

Enter the Total Number of DEMONSTRATING artifacts captured in your Portfolio, categorized as Collecting, Working, or Showcase evidence.

Collecting	Working	Showcase
1	2	1

DEMONSTRATING is critical to the well-rounded educator. Learning, of course, takes place in our head. However, you should be able to display tangible evidence of your best DEMONSTRATING artifacts along with an explanation of why these were selected.

Artifact 1: *Unit on Black History* — Rationale: *Did a very successful unit study on Black History*

Artifact 2: *Presentaion for Classroom* — Rationale: *Shared the unit with peers/colleagues and entered it in a contest.*

Artifact 3: *Photo of Shelf in Library for Teacher-Made Materials* — Rationale: *Principal told librarians to find an area for teacher-made materials*

Artifact 4: *Publication of unit acceptance letters* — Rationale: *Submitted and accepted unit on Black History in Social Studies*

158 *Professional Portfolios for Teachers*

Figure 14-1

Part II. Summative Assessment

Step A. Confirm Your Status. Are you a Teacher-

          Learner   Expert   Scholar
           ☐   ☐   ☒

Identify Your Status as an Educator . . .

Step B. Number of Artifacts: Collecting   Working   Showcase
                                           2   7   11

Add the total artifacts collected and reported in the Formative review of the Reading, Writing, Thinking, Interacting, and Demonstrating Foundations . . .

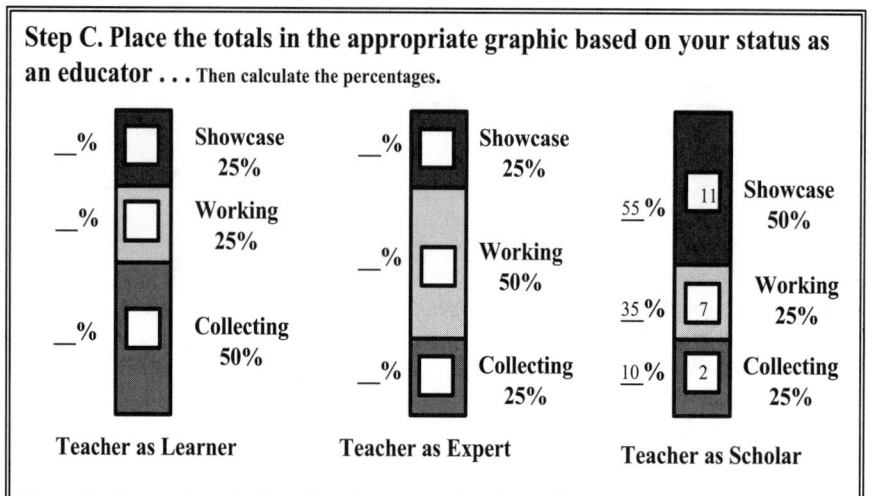

Step C. Place the totals in the appropriate graphic based on your status as an educator . . . Then calculate the percentages.

Teacher as Learner
- __% Showcase 25%
- __% Working 25%
- __% Collecting 50%

Teacher as Expert
- __% Showcase 25%
- __% Working 50%
- __% Collecting 25%

Teacher as Scholar
- 55% [11] Showcase 50%
- 35% [7] Working 25%
- 10% [2] Collecting 25%

Transfer the numbers in Step B to the appropriate boxes in the graphic above depicting your status as an educator . . . Remember, fill the boxes of only ONE graphic. Your Portfolio was for either a LEARNER, EXPERT, or SCHOLAR.

Figure 14-1

Step D. Final Analysis of Your Portfolio Effort

(1). Did the percentage of artifacts in the Collecting, Working, and Showcase sections of your Portfolio agree with the recommended percentages?

[X] Yes [ ] No

If you are a Teacher as Learner, most of your artifacts should be found in the Collecting folders of your portfolio.

If you are a Teacher as Expert, your artifacts should be primarily found in the Working folders of your portfolio.

If you are a Teacher as Scholar, the Showcase folders of your portfolio should hold most of your artifacts.

(2). Does the analysis of the portfolio artifacts support your status as a Learner, Expert, or Scholar? Why or Why not?

[X] Yes [ ] No

Justification: Yes, the majority of my artifacts were the result of showcasing my thinking and learning. The portfolio was a success in terms of providing the avenue for organizing and displaying the results of my efforts.

(3). Indicate the portfolio Foundation that contributed most to your personal growth and professional development.

[ ] R [ ] W [X] T [ ] I [ ] D

Justification: Generating new ideas in my Thinking Journal was by far the strongest aspect of my portfolio. I have used it to record my ongoing efforts in building a strong knowledge base that I can share with my colleagues.

(4). Indicate your weakest Foundation for learning.

[ ] R [ ] W [ ] T [ ] I [X] D

What steps will you take to address this weakness? *Demonstrating should be the strongest Foundation in the portfolio of the teacher-scholar. I feel I still have a long way to go before my demonstrations are the key aspects of my portfolio. Writing is still stronger than demonstrating.*

Figure 14-1

Part III. Final Comments

Use this section to annotate any additional Artifacts or Rationale that support your portfolio.

Even though I did not use the fully functioning Intelligent Portfolio, I was able to accumulate artifacts that were presented in their electronic format. As recommended in the book, since I was using a combination of the portfolios, I used the Smart Portfolio format and created an inventory of my electronic items so that they could be easily retrieved when needed. This combination worked especially well for me during this assessment period and I would strongly recommend the format to those who are still not 100 percent computer literate. I feel I can migrate to the full Intelligent Portfolio whenever I am more comfortable with computer technology.

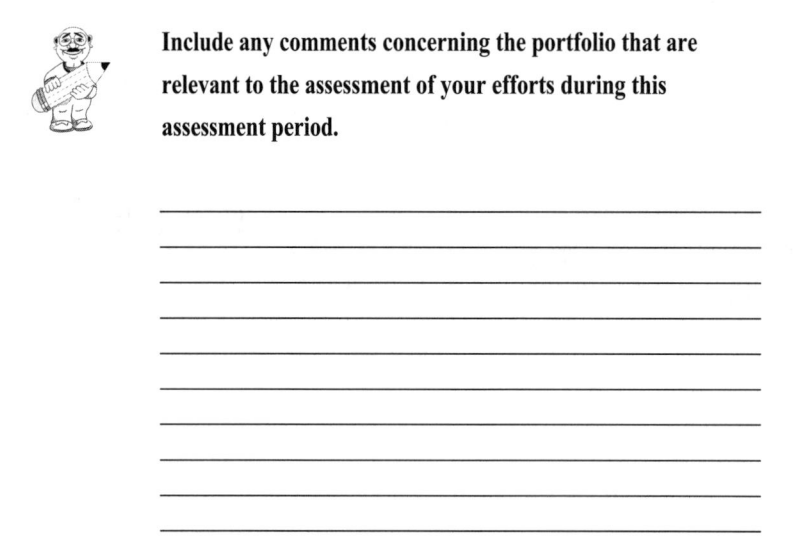

Include any comments concerning the portfolio that are relevant to the assessment of your efforts during this assessment period.

_____
_____
_____
_____
_____
_____
_____
_____
_____
_____

A Look At the Portfolio Assessment Tool In Action

Assessment is pivotal to understanding how the Smart or Intelligent Portfolio can help you attain your goal of professional development. In an effort to make you more comfortable with the PAT, three sample forms are discussed below: one for the Teacher as Learner, Teacher as Expert, and Teacher as Scholar. Example PATs use the Smart Portfolio, the Intelligent Portfolio, or a combination of both. In one example PAT, the use of the portfolio was "right on the money." In other words, the use of the Collection Points and Foundations was appropriate for the educator who completed the PAT. In another example, these indicators were not so precise. The third example fell somewhere in the middle.

PAT for the Teacher as Learner

(Figure 14-2). It was probably not a coincidence that the one educator who chose the Intelligent Portfolio was also a Teacher-Learner. Jonathan Lee already uses a computer in his undergraduate course work. He writes papers with the word processor. He tracks his schedule using a calendar program. He has a comprehensive bibliography on a database management system. Jonathan is typically in one of the many computer labs across campus where he checks his email and researches papers by finding resources on the Internet. His computer at home is no doubt more powerful than any one of the machines at school.

For Jonathan, a laptop computer is the perfect host for his portfolio—one that will grow with him from learner to expert to scholar. Collecting is his forte, and in his Intelligent Portfolio he amassed more than 40 items worthy of future consideration. His Working folders evidence attempts to apply new thinking to these items.

On the other side of the ledger, the PAT indicates that Jonathan did not develop enough Showcase artifacts; he realized this deficiency as he completed the form. Reading is Jonathan's strongest Foundation, and Interacting and Demonstrating his weakest —characteristics to be expected from the Teacher-Learner. But it is possible that Jonathan is not as weak in Interacting as it seems. He may have forgotten to document in his Interacting folder how many emails he sent. Perhaps the instructor will alert Jonathan to his Interacting contributions during her assessment of Jonathan's portfolio. It is highly likely that email provided a significant number of Interacting artifacts that Jonathan overlooked.

162 *Professional Portfolios for Teachers*

Figure 14-2

Example Portfolio Assessment Tool for the Teacher as Learner

Page 1 of 6

Your Name: *Jonathan Lee (Teacher as Learner)*

Date of the Assessment/Exhibition: *May 7, 1998*

Instructor/Assessor: _____   **Personal Assessment** [X]

Part I. Formative Assessment

1. Did you use the Smart or Intelligent Portfolio? Or, was your portfolio a combination? Rationale: *The Smart Portfolio afforded me the opportunity to begin my use of portfolios with a new laptop computer I purchased specifically for my undergraduate studies.*

Smart [ ]
Intelligent [X]
Combination [ ]

2. How many Collection Points does your portfolio contain?   ___ 6 [ ] 7 [ ] 8 [ ] 9 [ ] 10 [X] ___

---

3. The five Foundations

3a. READING. READERS gather evidence of new knowledge in the form of journals, booknotes, summaries, outlines, and drawings. Patterns and connections begin to form. READING builds an individual's knowledge base. Do your reading artifacts show evidence of any or all of the following?

- Collected a significant amount of new knowledge _1_
- Strengthened a position with documentation ___
- Initiated new ideas for teaching and learning ___
- Demonstrated an open-minded attitude _2_
- Critiqued a resource for publication _4_
- Suggested and shared new applications of knowledge _3_

Enter the Total Number of READING artifacts captured in your portfolio, categorized as Collecting, Working, or Showcase evidence.

Collecting: 21
Working: 4
Showcase: 1

Identify your best artifacts which evidence your learning through the foundation of READING and give a short rationale.

Artifact 1: *Bibliographies from Spring 1998 Courses*	Rationale:	*Most of my reading so far has been assigned in one of my Ed courses. The bib lists all these books.*
Artifact 2: *Paper on Children of the 1990's*	Rationale:	*Many new ideas not considered before. Resulted in changing my assumptions about teaching K–4.*
Artifact 3: *Freedom to Learn*	Rationale:	*This was Carl Rogers' book on keeping the classroom free from threats, etc. to learning.*
Artifact 4: *Criticism of Cognitive Psychology*	Rationale:	*This reading critiqued cognitive psychology and its limitations as a classroom teaching strategy.*

Assessing the Professional Portfolio   163

Figure 14-2

Page 2 of 6

3b. WRITING. Formal WRITING illustrates what we know and understand. Informal WRITING extends our thinking and understanding. Making meaning through WRITING involves formal papers, book reports, thematic units, poems and letters, publication-ready articles, and written classroom lesson plans. Do the WRITING artifacts you prepared demonstrate the following?

- *Documented thinking and learning experiences* ___
- *Analyzed in-depth educational concepts* _2_
- *Designed new curriculum or course of study* _1_
- *Prepared papers for conference presentation* ___
- *Self-assessed teaching experiences* _3_
- *Submitted journal articles for publication* ___

Enter the Total Number of WRITING artifacts captured in your portfolio, categorized as Collecting, Working, or Showcase evidence.

Collecting	Working	Showcase
6	6	1

Illustrate professional development in the foundation of WRITING. Cite specific artifacts of your best works along with rationale.

Artifact 1: *Lesson Plan on the Holocaust*   Rationale: *Prepared a thematic unit on the Holocaust which included a study guide objectives, and a quiz.*

Artifact 2: *Paper on Open Education*   Rationale: *This assigned paper reviewed Open Education and its strengths and weaknesses for classroom teachers.*

Artifact 3: *My Philosophy of Learning*   Rationale: *Required journal entries that chart my growth as a teacher and changes to my understanding of learning.*

Artifact 4: _____   Rationale: *The above three artifacts were the best items in my portfolio at this time. I hope to add many more.*

3c. THINKING. Thinking lies at the heart of the portfolio and animates thoughts and ideas, giving them momentum and bringing them to life. A Thinking Journal is a place where we toss around ideas, consider other viewpoints, make connections, and judge our own learning. Do your thinking artifacts provide evidence of any or all of the following?

- *Advanced your Personal Philosophy of Teaching and Learning* _2_
- *Recorded thinking and learning processes in a Journal* _3_
- *Constructed graphic organizers to show patterns of thinking* ___
- *Initiated problem-solving efforts to address educational issues* _4_
- *Integrated thinking into existing teaching and learning strategies 1*
- *Generated concepts/ideas that contribute to the knowledge base* ___

Enter the Total Number of THINKING artifacts captured in your portfolio, categorized as Collecting, Working, or Showcase evidence.

Collecting	Working	Showcase
12	4	0

THINKING may be the most important foundation of your Portfolio. List your best artifacts which generated new THINKING.

Artifact 1: *Lesson Planning Ideas*   Rationale: *Prepared a checklist for developing lesson plans that can be used by a new classroom teacher.*

Artifact 2: *My Philosophy of Learning*   Rationale: *I added this artifact again in Thinking because it generated most of my new ideas about learning.*

Artifact 3: *Operant Conditioning and Programmed Instruction*   Rationale: *Behaviorism and programmed instruction was a new area for me; made sense for classroom mgt.*

Artifact 4: *Discovery Learning*   Rationale: *Discussed strategies for teaching problem-solving with my students.*

Figure 14-2

3d. INTERACTING. Interacting addresses the responsibility of educators to argue, defend, and share their ideas. INTERACTING involves peer assessments, memos from group activities, brainstorming sessions, arguments, problems and solutions, and position papers defending different points of view. Do your INTERACTING artifacts show evidence of the following?

- *Considered ideas and arguments contrary to your own* _1_
- *Attended lectures, seminars, or conferences* _2_
- *Articulated and defended ideas for teaching and learning* ___
- *Shared ideas with colleagues in formal and informal situations* ___
- *Established leadership role in professional organization* ___
- *Created an environment that fosters the interaction of educators* ___

Page 3 of 6

Enter the Total Number of INTERACTING artifacts captured in your portfolio, categorized as Collecting, Working, or Showcase evidence.

Collecting: 2 Working: 1 Showcase: 1

INTERACTING plays upon your obligation to give something back to the discipline of Education. Can you document any specific occasions of interaction in your Portfolio?

Artifact 1: *Group Class Discussions*	Rationale:	*Traded arguments about teaching and learning in Ed Psych 201 and Teaching Math 212*
Artifact 2: *Attended lecture on The 1st Year of Teaching*	Rationale:	*Prepared comments and questions*
Artifact 3: *Attended a distance ed satellite downlink*	Rationale:	*Satellite course on educational technology for the classroom. Prepared questions for lecturer.*
Artifact 4: *Email List-serve for class*	Rationale:	*Communicated with instructor and peers using the list-server provided for class.*

3e. DEMONSTRATING represents the portion of a portfolio rich in the application and transfer of learning. Demonstrations include the text of classroom presentations, speeches, oral interpretations, audiovisual materials, and completed projects using multisensory exhibits. Do your artifacts evidence your growing expertise in demonstrating your knowledge and skills?

- *Designed a presentation for peer assessment* _1_
- *Demonstrated knowledge, skills, and a disposition for teaching* _2_
- *Created a forum to articulate and share best classroom practices* 3
- *Prepared, delivered, and validated a unit of instruction* _4_
- *Presented workshops for national audience* ___
- *Published scholarly resources* ___

Enter the Total Number of DEMONSTRATING artifacts captured in your Portfolio, categorized as Collecting, Working, or Showcase evidence.

Collecting: 1 Working: 2 Showcase: 1

DEMONSTRATING is critical to the well-rounded educator. Learning, of course, takes place in our head. However, you should be able to display tangible evidence of your best DEMONSTRATING artifacts along with an explanation of why these were selected.

Artifact 1: *Teaching Math Using the Slide Rule*	Rationale:	*Prepared lesson on the slide rule and its use and applications prior to the electronic calculator.*
Artifact 2: *Class Exams*	Rationale:	*Added class exams to the portfolio under Demonstrating to keep track of grades/scores.*
Artifact 3: *Learning Assignment #3*	Rationale:	*This assignment demonstrated our best classroom practice for our internship in Grade 3.*
Artifact 4: *Internship Lesson Plan*	Rationale:	*My Junior Achievement lesson plan on taxes is included in this folder.*

Figure 14-2

Page 4 of 6

Part II. Summative Assessment

Step A. Confirm Your Status. Are you a Teacher-

        Learner   Expert   Scholar
         [X]   [ ]   [ ]

Identify Your Status as an Educator . . .

Step B. Number of Artifacts: Collecting   Working   Showcase
                                        42   17   4

Add the total artifacts collected and reported in the Formative review of the Reading, Writing, Thinking, Interacting, and Demonstrating Foundations . . .

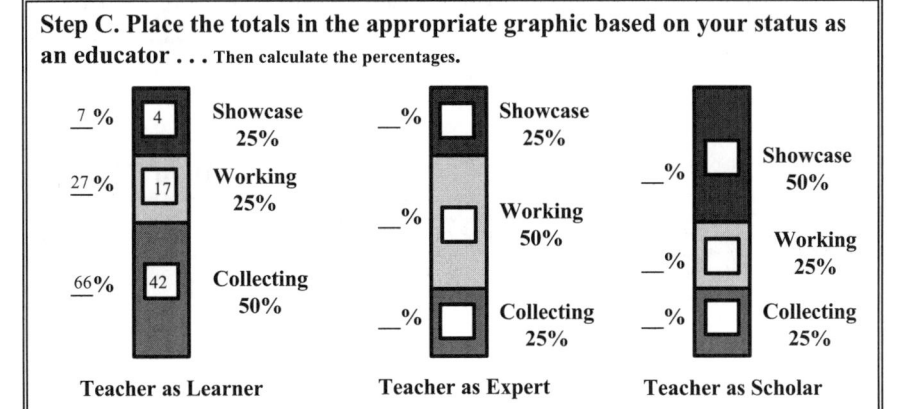

Step C. Place the totals in the appropriate graphic based on your status as an educator . . . Then calculate the percentages.

Teacher as Learner
- 7 % | 4 | Showcase 25%
- 27 % | 17 | Working 25%
- 66 % | 42 | Collecting 50%

Teacher as Expert
- ___% | [ ] | Showcase 25%
- ___% | [ ] | Working 50%
- ___% | [ ] | Collecting 25%

Teacher as Scholar
- ___% | [ ] | Showcase 50%
- ___% | [ ] | Working 25%
- ___% | [ ] | Collecting 25%

Transfer the numbers in Step B to the appropriate boxes in the graphic above depicting your status as an educator . . . Remember, fill the boxes of only ONE graphic. Your Portfolio was for either a LEARNER, EXPERT, or SCHOLAR.

Figure 14-2

Step D. Final Analysis of Your Portfolio Effort

(1). Did the percentage of artifacts in the Collecting, Working, and Showcase sections of your Portfolio agree with the recommended percentages?

[X] Yes   [ ] No

If you are a Teacher as Learner, most of your artifacts should be found in the Collecting folders of your portfolio.

If you are a Teacher as Expert, your artifacts should be primarily found in the Working folders of your portfolio.

If you are a Teacher as Scholar, the Showcase folders of your portfolio should hold most of your artifacts.

(2). Does the analysis of the portfolio artifacts support your status as a Learner, Expert, or Scholar? Why or Why not?

[X] Yes   [ ] No

Justification: Yes, I was very pleased with the number of Collecting artifacts and the number of Working items. I can see from this assessment that I will need to devote a little more attention to the aspect of demonstrating artifacts. Actually, I think I do have more in that area if I were to recognize some of the outside work that turned out better than I originally thought.

(3). Indicate the portfolio Foundation that contributed most to your personal growth and professional development.

[X] [ ] [ ] [ ] [ ]
R   W   T   I   D

Justification: Reading by far provided the largest number of artifacts in my portfolio and for this stage of my professional development provided the highest degree of support for my own personal growth.

(4). Indicate your weakest Foundation for learning.

[ ] [ ] [ ] [X] [X]
R   W   T   I   D

What steps will you take to address this weakness? Interacting and Demonstrating were both weak areas of my portfolio. Demonstrating can be helped by spending more quality time with the assignments and papers that are course requirements. Interacting will take longer since it demands emphasis on communications and that requires time that is not always available to the teacher-learner.

Figure 14-2

Part III. Final Comments

Use this section to annotate any additional Artifacts or Rationale that support your portfolio.

_____
_____
_____
_____
_____
_____
_____
_____

Include any comments concerning the portfolio that are relevant to the assessment of your efforts during this assessment period.

The Smart Portfolio took much longer to set up than originally expected. The instructor provided us with a diskette containing the empty folders for the Teacher-Learner. That significantly reduced setup time and made the organization of the portfolio more straightforward. Now that I am using the Smart Portfolio almost exclusively, I am certain that it will bear fruit throughout my career as an educator.

PAT for the Teacher as Expert

(Figure 14-3). For Jennifer Realdi, the Smart Portfolio brought home the realization that, although she is a classroom teacher, an equal share of her efforts in professional development went to Working and Collecting. The PAT exhibited the strengths of Jennifer's Demonstrating Foundation and the weakness of her Writing efforts. For Jennifer, it was easy to identify appropriate artifacts in each of the Foundations along with an accompanying rationale as to why these were selected as most important.

Reading took on a more vital role as the Teacher-Expert explained that she considers herself still "very much a learner." Certainly, this admission does not discredit either the teacher or the use of portfolios. On the contrary, it shows the value of the portfolio to promote professional growth and personal learning. Thanks in some measure to the assessment tool, Jennifer is addressing the self-proclaimed shortcomings in her Writing artifacts.

This scenario might be characteristic of her status as a novice teacher: one who is concentrating on the development of her classroom techniques at the expense of her communication skills. As Jennifer matures as a teacher with lesson plans, instructional materials, and self-confidence intact, she may feel more obligated to pursue these other areas. Still, she has the strength of Demonstrating as a building block to personal growth. For teachers in the classroom, this is perhaps a key to success.

Jennifer chose the Smart Portfolio format with the rationale that hard copies are "easier to collect for later organizing." As stated several times throughout the book, the use of the Smart Portfolio is not a decision that requires apologies. The construction of Collection Points, Foundations, and folders is identical to the electronic format and just as powerful and comprehensive as its Intelligent Portfolio counterpart. Jennifer will do well to continue its use as long as her responsibilities as a teacher are at the forefront of her current goals. She may find, however, that advancing the Demonstrating skills she finds so exciting may be made easier by automating her portfolio. Computers, and the software applications recommended in this book, are valuable to teachers who develop their own instructional materials.

Figure 14-3

Page 1 of 6

Example Portfolio Assessment Tool for the Teacher as Expert

Your Name: *Jennifer Realdi (Teacher as Expert)*

Date of the Assessment/Exhibition: *May 5, 1998*

Instructor/Assessor: _____   **Personal Assessment** [X]

Part I. Formative Assessment

1. Did you use the Smart or Intelligent Portfolio? Or, was your portfolio a combination? *Rationale: It was easier for me to just collect things for later organization. And, my journal is always hand-written at school.*

Smart [X]
Intelligent ☐
Combination ☐

2. How many Collection Points does your portfolio contain?   __ 6 7 8 9 10 __
☐ [X] ☐ ☐ ☐ ☐ ☐

3. The five Foundations

3a. READING. READERS gather evidence of new knowledge in the form of journals, booknotes, summaries, outlines, and drawings. Patterns and connections begin to form. READING builds an individual's knowledge base. Do your reading artifacts show evidence of any or all of the following?

- *Collected a significant amount of new knowledge* _1_
- *Strengthened a position with documentation* ___
- *Initiated new ideas for teaching and learning* _2_
- *Demonstrated an open-minded attitude* _3_
- *Critiqued a resource for publication* ___
- *Suggested and shared new applications of knowledge* _4_

Enter the Total Number of READING artifacts captured in your portfolio, categorized as Collecting, Working, or Showcase evidence.

Collecting	Working	Showcase
1	2	1

Identify your best artifacts which evidence your learning through the foundation of READING and give a short rationale.

Artifact 1: *Journal notes from a seminar attended readings*   Rationale: *Collected new information from suggested and took journal notes for artifacts.*

Artifact 2: *Lesson idea demonstrated at the seminar*   Rationale: *Did some classroom research to test informal writing strategies.*

Artifact 3: *Summary of my inquiry*   Rationale: *Typed the student responses to see how well the lesson worked in the classroom.*

Artifact 4: *Shared results with other teachers*   Rationale: *Together, we improved the lesson exercise to increase student learning in our classes.*

Figure 14-3

3b. WRITING. Formal WRITING illustrates what we know and understand. Informal WRITING extends our thinking and understanding. Making meaning through WRITING involves formal papers, book reports, thematic units, poems and letters, publication-ready articles, and written classroom lesson plans. Do the WRITING artifacts you prepared demonstrate the following?

- *Documented thinking and learning experiences* _3_
- *Analyzed in-depth educational concepts* _2_
- *Designed new curriculum or course of study* ___
- *Prepared papers for conference presentation* _4_
- *Self-assessed teaching experiences* ___
- *Submitted journal articles for publication* _1_

Enter the Total Number of WRITING artifacts captured in your portfolio, categorized as Collecting, Working, or Showcase evidence.

Collecting	Working	Showcase
2	1	1

Illustrate professional development in the foundation of WRITING. Cite specific artifacts of your best works along with rationale.

Artifact 1: *Wrote a Book Review*	Rationale:	*Submitted book review for publication.*
Artifact 2: *Research Background for Review*	Rationale:	*Looked at what/how the "experts" write reviews.*
Artifact 3: *Example from Personal Experience*	Rationale:	*Composed a paragraph about my classroom to show application in Book Review.*
Artifact 4: *Proposal for Conference*	Rationale:	*Prepared a poster from my Bulletin Board on "Steps to Good Book Reports."*

3c. THINKING. Thinking lies at the heart of the portfolio and animates thoughts and ideas, giving them momentum and bringing them to life. A Thinking Journal is a place where we toss around ideas, consider other viewpoints, make connections, and judge our own learning. Do your thinking artifacts provide evidence of any or all of the following?

- *Advanced your Personal Philosophy of Teaching and Learning* _4_
- *Recorded thinking and learning processes in a Journal* _3_
- *Constructed graphic organizers to show patterns of thinking* _2_
- *Initiated problem-solving efforts to address educational issues* _1_
- *Integrated thinking into existing teaching and learning strategies* ___
- *Generated concepts/ideas that contribute to the knowledge base* ___

Enter the Total Number of THINKING artifacts captured in your portfolio, categorized as Collecting, Working, or Showcase evidence.

Collecting	Working	Showcase
2	2	0

THINKING may be the most important foundation of your Portfolio. List your best artifacts which generated new THINKING.

Artifact 1: *Report to Principal*	Rationale:	*Wrote an explanation of teacher concerns about unsupervised students in the building at night.*
Artifact 2: *Team Illustrations of Possible Solutions*	Rationale:	*Diagrams of 3 solutions to supervising students.*
Artifact 3: *Journal Entries*	Rationale:	*Thought about this problem in my journal.*
Artifact 4: *New Problem-Solving Strategies Learned*	Rationale:	*Tried some new strategies on problem-solving with my students.*

Figure 14-3

3d. INTERACTING. Interacting addresses the responsibility of educators to argue, defend, and share their ideas. INTERACTING involves peer assessments, memos from group activities, brainstorming sessions, arguments, problems and solutions, and position papers defending different points of view. Do your INTERACTING artifacts show evidence of the following?

- *Considered ideas and arguments contrary to your own* _3_
- *Attended lectures, seminars, or conferences* _1_
- *Articulated and defended ideas for teaching and learning* ___
- *Shared ideas with colleagues in formal and informal situations* _2_
- *Established leadership role in professional organization* _4_
- *Created an environment that fosters the interaction of educators* ___

Page 3 of 6

Enter the Total Number of INTERACTING artifacts captured in your portfolio, categorized as Collecting, Working, or Showcase evidence.

Collecting	Working	Showcase
2	1	1

INTERACTING plays upon your obligation to give something back to the discipline of Education. Can you document any specific occasions of interaction in your Portfolio?

Artifact 1: *Conference materials/resources*   Rationale: *Attended conference to learn about Inclusion*

Artifact 2: *Handouts on Inclusion to share with Faculty*   Rationale: *Prepared handouts to share with colleagues*

Artifact 3: *Records of Inclusion discussions and meetings*   Rationale: *Trace thinking on Inclusion and identify changes in personal understanding about the subject*

Artifact 4: *Voted Vice-President of State Reading Org.*   Rationale: *Meet twice a year and help the President with organizational objectives*

3e. DEMONSTRATING represents the portion of a portfolio rich in the application and transfer of learning. Demonstrations include the text of classroom presentations, speeches, oral interpretations, audiovisual materials, and completed projects using multisensory exhibits. Do your artifacts evidence your growing expertise in demonstrating your knowledge and skills?

- *Designed a presentation for peer assessment* _2_
- *Demonstrated knowledge, skills, and a disposition for teaching* ___
- *Created a forum to articulate and share best classroom practices* 3
- *Prepared, delivered, and validated a unit of instruction* _1_
- *Presented workshops for national audience* ___
- *Published scholarly resources* _4_

Enter the Total Number of DEMONSTRATING artifacts captured in your Portfolio, categorized as Collecting, Working, or Showcase evidence.

Collecting	Working	Showcase
1	2	1

DEMONSTRATING is critical to the well-rounded educator. Learning, of course, takes place in our head. However, you should be able to display tangible evidence of your best DEMONSTRATING artifacts along with an explanation of why these were selected.

Artifact 1: *Unit on Black History*   Rationale: *Did a very successful unit study on Black History*

Artifact 2: *Presentaion for Classroom*   Rationale: *Shared the unit with peers/colleagues and entered it in a contest.*

Artifact 3: *Photo of Shelf in Library for Teacher-Made Materials*   Rationale: *Principal told librarians to find an area for teacher-made materials*

Artifact 4: *Publication of unit acceptance letters*   Rationale: *Submitted and accepted unit on Black History in Social Studies*

Figure 14-3

Part II. Summative Assessment

Step A. Confirm Your Status. Are you a Teacher-

　　　　　　　Learner　　Expert　　Scholar
　　　　　　　☐　　　　　☒　　　　☐

Identify Your Status as an Educator . . .

Step B. Number of Artifacts:　　Collecting　　Working　　Showcase
　　　　　　　　　　　　　　　　　　　　8　　　　　　　8　　　　　　4

Add the total artifacts collected and reported in the Formative review of the Reading, Writing, Thinking, Interacting, and Demonstrating Foundations . . .

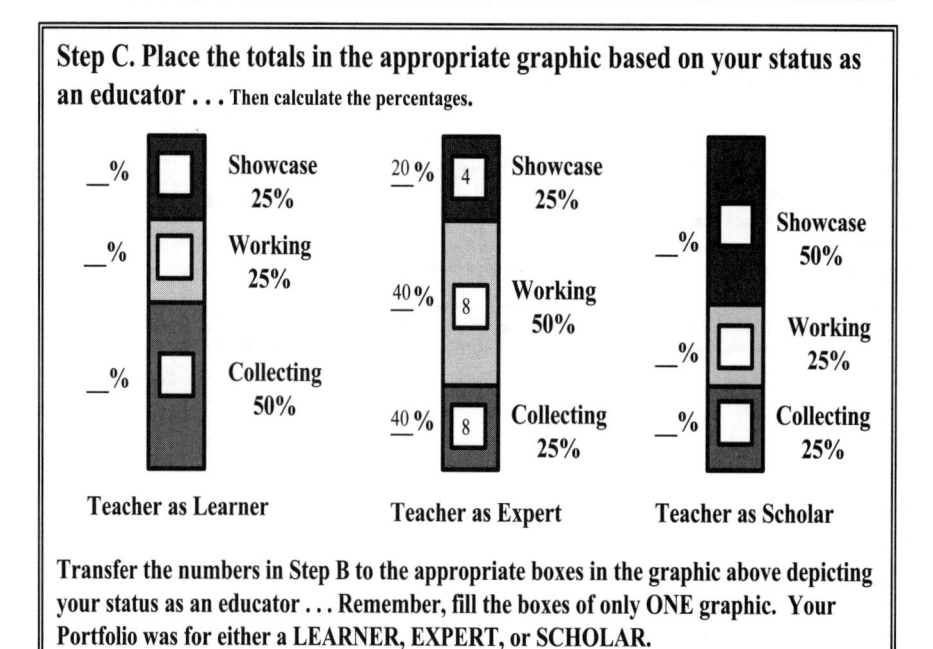

Step C. Place the totals in the appropriate graphic based on your status as an educator . . . Then calculate the percentages.

Teacher as Learner	Teacher as Expert	Teacher as Scholar
__% Showcase 25%	20% [4] Showcase 25%	__% Showcase 50%
__% Working 25%	40% [8] Working 50%	__% Working 25%
__% Collecting 50%	40% [8] Collecting 25%	__% Collecting 25%

Transfer the numbers in Step B to the appropriate boxes in the graphic above depicting your status as an educator . . . Remember, fill the boxes of only ONE graphic. Your Portfolio was for either a LEARNER, EXPERT, or SCHOLAR.

Figure 14-3

Step D. Final Analysis of Your Portfolio Effort

(1). Did the percentage of artifacts in the Collecting, Working, and Showcase sections of your Portfolio agree with the recommended percentages? ☐ Yes ☒ No

> If you are a Teacher as Learner, most of your artifacts should be found in the Collecting folders of your portfolio.
>
> If you are a Teacher as Expert, your artifacts should be primarily found in the Working folders of your portfolio.
>
> If you are a Teacher as Scholar, the Showcase folders of your portfolio should hold most of your artifacts.

(2). Does the analysis of the portfolio artifacts support your status as a Learner, Expert, or Scholar? Why or Why not? ☒ Yes ☐ No

> Justification: *Yes, I am a beginning teacher still testing the waters and honing my skills. I am reaching toward scholarship but I am still very much a learner.*

(3). Indicate the portfolio Foundation that contributed most to your personal growth and professional development. ☐ ☐ ☐ ☐ ☒

> Justification: *Demonstrating—that's why I became a teacher. I am good at it and practice it every day. The portfolio has helped me immeasurably in the development of demonstrating lessons.*

R W T I D

(4). Indicate your weakest Foundation for learning. ☐ ☒ ☐ ☐ ☐

> What steps will you take to address this weakness? *Writing. I am going to take a Writing Workshop this summer and try to write the same time and place every day. The portfolio can help me by increasing my quantity of artifacts that will contribute to my new writing efforts.*

R W T I D

Figure 14-3

Part III. Final Comments

Use this section to annotate any additional Artifacts or Rationale that support your portfolio.

While the Portfolio Assessment Tool pointed out several areas of consideration, I feel that it also helped me think about how I use the portfolio in my responsibilities as a classroom teacher. There were many, many artifacts that I have included in my portfolio that were not mentioned in the PAT. These, as well as others that never made it to the portfolio, were invaluable in furthering my professional development and personal growth during this assessment period.

Include any comments concerning the portfolio that are relevant to the assessment of your efforts during this assessment period.

I felt intimidated about the use of technology for portfolios. In this PAT, I mentioned that I chose the Smart Portfolio because it was easier for me to collect the artifacts and organize them later. Truth is, the Intelligent Portfolio provides better organization for my lifelong objectives as an educator and I will attempt to convert my portfolio to the Intelligent format in the coming months.

PAT for the Teacher as Scholar

(Figure 14-4). Rebecca Slater represented the Teacher-Scholar for this assessment. Grounded in scholarly pursuits, for Rebecca the portfolio became a source of new ideas and an aid to thinking that quickly bore fruit. It is important to note that at no time did this educator abandon her responsibilities to Reading as a Foundation and Collecting as an integral element of the portfolio. Indeed, if you closely examine her development of artifacts from Collecting to Working to Showcase, you will see that nearly all of her Showcase artifacts began as articles read and solutions explored from the research. For the Teacher as Scholar, this progression lies at the heart of continued professional development.

Rebecca also discovered that Demonstrating was her weakest link in the portfolio when in fact, it should be one of, if not *the*, strongest element. She has some work to do to address this weakness. Also obvious are the insufficient steps she has identified in the PAT to address this area. Her assessor would be expected to identify this shortcoming and assist her in further defining the steps she will take toward improvement. For example, Rebecca could be asked to prepare a conference proposal or enroll in a Speaker's Bureau, either of which would increase the opportunity to demonstrate the excellence of her thinking to colleagues and peers.

It should be noted that Rebecca decided to employ a combination of the Smart and Intelligent Portfolios. She stated that her level of "computer literacy is not sufficient to take on the Intelligent Portfolio task." While this might be true, she should be encouraged to use a combination of portfolio formats. If both formats are to be employed, the Smart Portfolio should serve as the primary portfolio. An inventory of electronic artifacts printed periodically and stored in a Smart Portfolio Collection Point will serve as a table of contents to ensure that artifacts can be readily retrieved.

Summary

Jonathan, Jennifer, and Rebecca provided excellent illustrations of portfolio assessments and confirmed our beliefs that the portfolio is a boon to teachers from the first uncertain days of undergraduate courses to the final stages of scholarly pursuits.

One final aspect of portfolio assessment is proposed now. The portfolio is more than a Tool for Learning. It is more than a chronicle of personal development. ***The portfolio is a Celebration of Learning!***

176 *Professional Portfolios for Teachers*

Figure 14-4

Example Portfolio Assessment Tool for the Teacher as Scholar

Page 1 of 6

Your Name: *Rebecca Slater (Teacher as Scholar)*

Date of the Assessment/Exhibition: *May 12, 1998*

Instructor/Assessor: _____   **Personal Assessment** [X]

Part I. Formative Assessment

1. Did you use the Smart or Intelligent Portfolio? Or, was your portfolio a combination? *Computer literacy level is below what is needed to fully implement the Intelligent Portfolio; however, many of my artifacts are electronic.*

Smart ☐
Intelligent ☐
Combination [X]

2. How many Collection Points does your portfolio contain? ___ 6 [X] 7 ☐ 8 ☐ 9 ☐ 10 ☐ ___

3. The five Foundations

3a. READING. READERS gather evidence of new knowledge in the form of journals, booknotes, summaries, outlines, and drawings. Patterns and connections begin to form. READING builds an individual's knowledge base. Do your reading artifacts show evidence of any or all of the following?

- Collected a significant amount of new knowledge ___
- Strengthened a position with documentation _4_
- Initiated new ideas for teaching and learning _1_
- Demonstrated an open-minded attitude ___
- Critiqued a resource for publication _3_
- Suggested and shared new applications of knowledge _2_

Enter the Total Number of READING artifacts captured in your portfolio, categorized as Collecting, Working, or Showcase evidence.

Collecting: 1
Working: 1
Showcase: 2

Identify your best artifacts which evidence your learning through the foundation of READING and give a short rationale.

Artifact 1: *Teaching Idea*
Rationale: *Read "Creative Reading" text and developed a "book writing" project for class.*

Artifact 2: *Presentation: Research-based*
Rationale: *Portfolio posters: low stakes assessment of higher order learning.*

Artifact 3: *Critiqued article for publication*
Rationale: *Read and made suggestions for article under review in refereed journal.*

Artifact 4: *Submitted a Grant Proposal*
Rationale: *Researched need/proposed solution on topic outside of my personal field of study.*

Figure 14-4

> **3b. WRITING.** Formal WRITING illustrates what we know and understand. Informal WRITING extends our thinking and understanding. Making meaning through WRITING involves formal papers, book reports, thematic units, poems and letters, publication-ready articles, and written classroom lesson plans. Do the WRITING artifacts you prepared demonstrate the following?
> - Documented thinking and learning experiences __
> - Analyzed in-depth educational concepts __
> - Designed new curriculum or course of study _2_
> - Prepared papers for conference presentation _3_
> - Self-assessed teaching experiences _1_
> - Submitted journal articles for publication _4_

Page 2 of 6

Enter the Total Number of WRITING artifacts captured in your portfolio, categorized as Collecting, Working, or Showcase evidence.

Collecting	Working	Showcase
0	2	2

Illustrate professional development in the foundation of WRITING. Cite specific artifacts of your best works along with rationale.

Artifact 1: *Promotion and Tenure Application* — Rationale: *Prepared necessary documents and overview/reflective self-assessment.*

Artifact 2: *Designed New Online Course* — Rationale: *Wrote a grant for this online course and offered a presentation for its adoption.*

Artifact 3: *Prepared paper: Low Stakes Assessment of High Order Thinking* — Rationale: *Submitted to educational journal.*

Artifact 4: *Portfolio Article Submitted* — Rationale: *Transitional Portfolios were a topic of interest during this assessment; article prepared.*

3c. THINKING. Thinking lies at the heart of the portfolio and animates thoughts and ideas, giving them momentum and bringing them to life. A Thinking Journal is a place where we toss around ideas, consider other viewpoints, make connections, and judge our own learning. Do your thinking artifacts provide evidence of any or all of the following?

- Advanced your Personal Philosophy of Teaching and Learning _4_
- Recorded thinking and learning processes in a Journal __
- Constructed graphic organizers to show patterns of thinking _1_
- Initiated problem-solving efforts to address educational issues __
- Integrated thinking into existing teaching and learning strategies _2_
- Generated concepts/ideas that contribute to the knowledge base _3_

Enter the Total Number of THINKING artifacts captured in your portfolio, categorized as Collecting, Working, or Showcase evidence.

Collecting	Working	Showcase
1	1	2

THINKING may be the most important foundation of your Portfolio. List your best artifacts which generated new THINKING.

Artifact 1: *Construction of two graphics* — Rationale: *Organized and shared my "big picture" of learning.*

Artifact 2: *Handout on the "Thinking Journal"* — Rationale: *Application of best journal thinking—action research project.*

Artifact 3: *Created cover design* — Rationale: *Used "post-its" (yellow stickies) to design an online course on portfolio tri-folds.*

Artifact 4: *Revised "My Philosophy of Teaching"* — Rationale: *Used my philosophy to model for students; did updates to my portfolio to show revised thinking.*

Figure 14-4

3d. INTERACTING. Interacting addresses the responsibility of educators to argue, defend, and share their ideas. INTERACTING involves peer assessments, memos from group activities, brainstorming sessions, arguments, problems and solutions, and position papers defending different points of view. Do your INTERACTING artifacts show evidence of the following?

- Considered ideas and arguments contrary to your own __
- Attended lectures, seminars, or conferences __
- Articulated and defended ideas for teaching and learning _1_
- Shared ideas with colleagues in formal and informal situations _2_
- Established leadership role in professional organization _3_
- Created an environment that fosters the interaction of educators _4_

Enter the Total Number of INTERACTING artifacts captured in your portfolio, categorized as Collecting, Working, or Showcase evidence.

Collecting	Working	Showcase
0	2	2

INTERACTING plays upon your obligation to give something back to the discipline of Education. Can you document any specific occasions of interaction in your Portfolio?

Artifact 1: *Book writing defense* — Rationale: *Defended my thinking and new ideas before a committee of teacher-educators.*

Artifact 2: *Committee minutes* — Rationale: *Served on University committee and School of Education committees.*

Artifact 3: *Membership on the Board of Examiners* — Rationale: *Nominated, invited, trained, and attended for NCATE Board of Examiners (Review Committee).*

Artifact 4: *Writing with Teachers Seminar* — Rationale: *Worked with teachers to join in professional conversations.*

3e. DEMONSTRATING represents the portion of a portfolio rich in the application and transfer of learning. Demonstrations include the text of classroom presentations, speeches, oral interpretations, audiovisual materials, and completed projects using multisensory exhibits. Do your artifacts evidence your growing expertise in demonstrating your knowledge and skills?

- Designed a presentation for peer assessment __
- Demonstrated knowledge, skills, and a disposition for teaching __
- Created a forum to articulate and share best classroom practices __
- Prepared, delivered, and validated a unit of instruction _1_
- Presented workshops for national audience _3_
- Published scholarly resources _2 and 4_

Enter the Total Number of DEMONSTRATING artifacts captured in your Portfolio, categorized as Collecting, Working, or Showcase evidence.

Collecting	Working	Showcase
0	1	3

DEMONSTRATING is critical to the well-rounded educator. Learning, of course, takes place in our head. However, you should be able to display tangible evidence of your best DEMONSTRATING artifacts along with an explanation of why these were selected.

Artifact 1: *Work on Portfolio* — Rationale: *Designed and implemented portfolio assessment rubric and presentation.*

Artifact 2: *Article: Action vs. Reaction* — Rationale: *Wrote article for The English Journal.*

Artifact 3: *Keynote Speaker for Reading Teacher* — Rationale: *Provided the keynote address at the national IRA Conference in Dallas.*

Artifact 4: *Article for Reporter* — Rationale: *NCATE publication article on reflections on classroom training.*

Figure 14-4

Part II. Summative Assessment

Step A. Confirm Your Status. Are you a Teacher-

Learner	Expert	Scholar
☐	☐	☒

Identify Your Status as an Educator . . .

Step B. Number of Artifacts: Collecting Working Showcase
                                      2   7   11

Add the total artifacts collected and reported in the Formative review of the Reading, Writing, Thinking, Interacting, and Demonstrating Foundations . . .

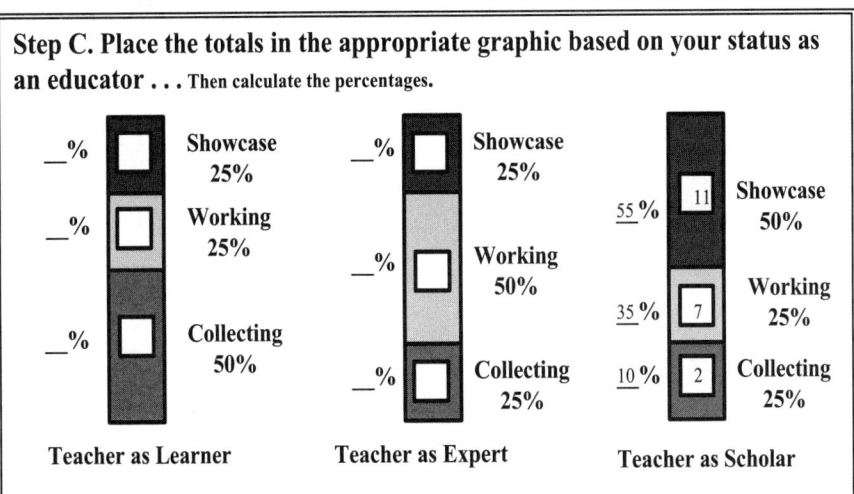

Step C. Place the totals in the appropriate graphic based on your status as an educator . . . Then calculate the percentages.

Teacher as Learner
- ___% Showcase 25%
- ___% Working 25%
- ___% Collecting 50%

Teacher as Expert
- ___% Showcase 25%
- ___% Working 50%
- ___% Collecting 25%

Teacher as Scholar
- 55% [11] Showcase 50%
- 35% [7] Working 25%
- 10% [2] Collecting 25%

Transfer the numbers in Step B to the appropriate boxes in the graphic above depicting your status as an educator . . . Remember, fill the boxes of only ONE graphic. Your Portfolio was for either a LEARNER, EXPERT, or SCHOLAR.

Figure 14-4

Step D. Final Analysis of Your Portfolio Effort

(1). Did the percentage of artifacts in the Collecting, Working, and Showcase sections of your Portfolio agree with the recommended percentages?

[X] Yes [ ] No

If you are a Teacher as Learner, most of your artifacts should be found in the Collecting folders of your portfolio.

If you are a Teacher as Expert, your artifacts should be primarily found in the Working folders of your portfolio.

If you are a Teacher as Scholar, the Showcase folders of your portfolio should hold most of your artifacts.

(2). Does the analysis of the portfolio artifacts support your status as a Learner, Expert, or Scholar? Why or Why not?

[X] Yes [ ] No

Justification: Yes, the majority of my artifacts were the result of showcasing my thinking and learning. The portfolio was a success in terms of providing the avenue for organizing and displaying the results of my efforts.

(3). Indicate the portfolio Foundation that contributed most to your personal growth and professional development.

[ ] R [ ] W [X] T [ ] I [ ] D

Justification: Generating new ideas in my Thinking Journal was by far the strongest aspect of my portfolio. I have used it to record my ongoing efforts in building a strong knowledge base that I can share with my colleagues.

(4). Indicate your weakest Foundation for learning.

[ ] R [ ] W [ ] T [ ] I [X] D

What steps will you take to address this weakness? *Demonstrating should be the strongest Foundation in the portfolio of the teacher-scholar. I feel I still have a long way to go before my demonstrations are the key aspects of my portfolio. Writing is still stronger than demonstrating.*

Figure 14-4

Part III. Final Comments

Use this section to annotate any additional Artifacts or Rationale that support your portfolio.

Even though I did not use the fully functioning Intelligent Portfolio, I was able to accumulate artifacts that were presented in their electronic format. As recommended in the book, since I was using a combination of the portfolios, I used the Smart Portfolio format and created an inventory of my electronic items so that they could be easily retrieved when needed. This combination worked especially well for me during this assessment period and I would strongly recommend the format to those who are still not 100 percent computer literate. I feel I can migrate to the full Intelligent Portfolio whenever I am more comfortable with computer technology.

Include any comments concerning the portfolio that are relevant to the assessment of your efforts during this assessment period.

_____
_____
_____
_____
_____
_____
_____
_____
_____
_____

The Portfolio Exhibition

The idea of a portfolio exhibition to show mastery of content and deep understanding was suggested by Ted Sizer in his trilogy of works: *Horace's Compromise, Horace's School,* and in *Horace's Hope.* Sizer proposes, then explains, and finally, argues for the exhibition process as a comprehensive "reading of what a student can do." We include the Portfolio Exhibition in this text to foster a formal celebration of learning.

The most important works of portfolio users are highlighted on an aesthetically pleasing poster that accompanies the professional portfolio into the exhibition. A 12-minute presentation provides an overview of the learning experience followed by questions from peers and assessors. The discussion of portfolio artifacts should be limited to a specific learning period and include only those items that the individual created. A poster display is organized around a central theme and gives evidence of overall teaching and learning. The goal of the exhibition is to share, explain, and defend the chosen artifacts and articulate how each contributes to professional growth as a teacher.

At the exhibition, peers assess peers, presenters assess themselves, and guests (e.g., instructors and mentors) assess the presenter. The following rubric (Figure 14-5) is proposed to conduct this assessment reliably.

The rubric emphasizes oral communications skills, content knowledge, attitude, and a disposition toward teaching and learning. It also includes a measure of higher-order thinking, engagement, and creative spirit. You may use our rubric or develop one of your own. However, the characteristics you choose to assess the professional portfolio should embody Sizer's (1996) invitation for "students to exhibit their work and to earn their [distinctions] by means of demanding public Exhibitions."

In preparation for the portfolio exhibition, participants should be advised to consider these components:

- **Products**. The amount of work that is visible during the exhibition.
- **Progress**. The selected artifacts must demonstrate evidence of professional growth.
- **Relevancy**. The selected artifacts must illustrate meaningful connections and applications to teaching and learning.
- **Habits of Mind**. The exhibition must showcase a positive attitude toward learning in general and the active engagement in portfolios specifically.
- **Assessment**. The portfolio must serve as a vehicle for redirection and goal-setting toward continuous improvement.
- **Thinking about Thinking**. The portfolio must address the impact of learning on the teacher. In other words, it must answer the question, "So What?"

Specific questions can be provided to facilitate the exhibition process.

- Can you show progress (**growth**) through your artifacts?
- Can you demonstrate **thoughtfulness** and **reflection**?
- Did you include a variety of **quality** artifacts to display?
- Will your artifacts be **useful** in "real life"?
- Did you include evidence of **new learning**?
- Have you changed your **habits of mind** or **ways of knowing**?

Figure 14-5. Sample Rubric

PORTFOLIO EXHIBITION RUBRIC

4 *The contents of the portfolio and the selected poster artifacts reflect superior competence*

- Presented with confidence, well-organized and informative
- Demonstrated deep understanding of content and documented progress toward goals
- Indicated a strong disposition toward application and transfer of learning
- Articulated and defended thoughtful, logical connections and intentions
- Showed a portfolio "Spirit" through significant engagement, interaction, and reflection

3 *The contents of the portfolio and the selected poster artifacts reflect competence*

- Presented with confidence, well-organized and interesting
- Demonstrated a basic understanding of content and spoke of progress toward goals
- Indicated a positive disposition toward application and transfer of learning
- Articulated and defended thinking patterns, connections, and goals
- Showed a portfolio "Spirit" through engagement, interaction, and reflection

2 *The contents of the portfolio and the selected poster artifacts reflect minimal competence*

- Presented an aesthetically appealing poster with relatively few artifacts
- Demonstrated little understanding of content and no mention of progress toward goals
- Indicated a tendency toward application and transfer of learning
- Articulated and defended goals
- Showed a portfolio "Spirit" with little engagement, interaction, and reflection

1 *The contents of the portfolio and the selected poster artifacts reflect incompetence*

- Presented uninteresting, unrelated artifacts of poor quality
- Demonstrated a lack of understanding of content and progress toward goals
- Indicated a poor attitude toward application and transfer of learning
- Articulated goals but found it difficult to discuss their importance
- Showed a lack of the portfolio "Spirit"

- Have your goals helped to focus or **redirect** your learning?
- Has the exhibition increased your **thinking and learning**?

Conclusion

A final caveat provided by Sizer (1996) holds true for the Portfolio Exhibition, "If [portfolio users] are to understand deeply, less is more." Exhibitors tend to volunteer too much information and display too many artifacts. A significant aspect of the learning experience is to find those artifacts that speak to the learning that has occurred and incorporate them into a cogent presentation. Assessors should not become enthralled with quantity; quality should be the hallmark of the professional portfolio.

References

Sizer, T. R. (1996). *Horace's hope.* New York: Houghton Mifflin.
Tishman, S., Perkins, D., & Jay E. (1995). *The thinking classroom.* Boston: Allyn & Bacon.

Postscript

Few have the opportunity to say they were there at the beginning of something new and revolutionary. Members of the ILEAD cohort, the first doctoral program in Instructional Leadership at Duquesne University, can claim participation in just such an experience. From their first introduction to portfolios in June 1997, cohort members sought every opportunity to contribute to our expanding knowledge of portfolios. We would like to applaud their pioneering spirit.

Hopefully, the ideas and concepts presented in this text along with the reflections shared will encourage teachers to adopt the portfolio for their own professional development. Since sharing is the hallmark of teaching and learning, you might be inclined to submit your own experiences and lessons for future revisions of this publication. Please send any communications to the authors.

Attention: Dr. Wilcox/Dr. Tomei
Duquesne University
School of Education
600 Forbes Avenue
Pittsburgh, PA 15282

APPENDIX

This appendix is the hard copy text of the accompanying CD-ROM exercises. Find the instructions for the CD-ROM exercise in Chapter 4, starting on page 25.

Portf_1.htm

Professional Portfolios for Teachers

A Portfolio Exercise

A 4-Step Process for Understanding, Selecting, and Designing Your Own Portfolio

Introduction. This CD-ROM-based exercise introduces **Professional Portfolios for Teachers**. It begins with a Table of Contents followed by the concepts and procedures for collecting artifacts. A checklist is offered to help identify your own personal characteristics as a teacher. The exercise aids in selecting, designing, and building the portfolio most appropriate for your situation. It concludes with a set of Frequently Asked Questions answering the most common inquiries about the practical use of portfolios.

Table of Contents
A comprehensive Table of Contents which permits you to link directly to any subject related to Professional Portfolios.

Step 1. Artifacts Exercise
A short exercise to introduce the concept and principles of collecting, producing, and demonstrating artifacts. *Highly Recommended*.

Step 2. Learner, Expert, or Scholar
Where are you in your academic career? Let's determine your status in academe before going any further.

Step 3. Smart or Intelligent Portfolio
Take a closer look at each portfolio format . . . then let this exercise help you choose which is best for you.

Step 4. Build Your Portfolio
OK, Let's put the portfolio together.

Frequently Asked Questions
Some of the most common questions about portfolios

Table of Contents

You may select a link to access this portion of the Portfolio Exercise directly.

Step 1. Artifacts Exercise

Introduction
Artifacts Described
Who Will Be Using the Portfolio?
What Kinds of Artifacts are Important?
How Will Artifacts Be Stored?
Where Should Artifacts Be Stored?
When Is the Electronic Format a Better Choice?
Why Are Portfolios So Important?

Step 2. Learner, Expert, or Scholar

Introduction
Teacher as Learner
Teacher as Expert
Teacher as Scholar

Step 3. Smart or Intelligent Portfolio

Introduction
Selecting Your Format
The Smart Portfolio
    Foundations of the Smart Portfolio
    Artifacts of the Smart Portfolio
    Collecting Artifacts
    Working Artifacts
    Showcase Artifacts
    Assessing Your Portfolio
The Intelligent Portfolio
    Foundations of the Intelligent Portfolio
    Artifacts of the Intelligent Portfolio
    Collection Points of the Intelligent Portfolio
    Assessing Your Portfolio

Step 4. Build Your Portfolio

For Windows Users
    The Smart Portfolio for the Teacher as Learner

      Building Your Smart Portfolio
      Exhibiting Your Smart Portfolio
    The Smart Portfolio for the Teacher as Expert
      Building Your Smart Portfolio
      Exhibiting Your Smart Portfolio
    The Smart Portfolio for the Teacher as Scholar
      Building Your Smart Portfolio
      Exhibiting Your Smart Portfolio
    The Intelligent Portfolio for the Teacher as Learner
      Building Your Intelligent Portfolio
      Tips for Using the Intelligent Portfolio
    The Intelligent Portfolio for the Teacher as Expert
      Building Your Intelligent Portfolio
      Tips for Using the Intelligent Portfolio
    The Intelligent Portfolio for the Teacher as Scholar
      Building Your Intelligent Portfolio
      Tips for Using the Intelligent Portfolio
  For Macintosh Users
    The Smart Portfolio for the Teacher as Learner
      Building Your Smart Portfolio
      Exhibiting Your Smart Portfolio
    The Smart Portfolio for the Teacher as Expert
      Building Your Smart Portfolio
      Exhibiting Your Smart Portfolio
    The Smart Portfolio for the Teacher as Scholar
      Building Your Smart Portfolio
      Exhibiting Your Smart Portfolio
    The Intelligent Portfolio for the Teacher as Learner
      Building Your Intelligent Portfolio
      Tips for Using the Intelligent Portfolio
    The Intelligent Portfolio for the Teacher as Expert
      Building Your Intelligent Portfolio
      Tips for Using the Intelligent Portfolio
    The Intelligent Portfolio for the Teacher as Scholar
      Building Your Intelligent Portfolio
      Tips for Using the Intelligent Portfolio

Frequently Asked Questions

Question 1: Why should I want a Smart or Intelligent Portfolio?
Question 2: Must I decide to go completely with one format or the other?
Question 3: Must the Portfolio consist of all the Collection Points described?
Question 4: How long will it take to create a Portfolio?
Question 5: Who will evaluate my Portfolio?

Return to the Portfolio Exercise Home Page Click Here .

pf_exer.htm

Professional Portfolios for Teachers

Step 1. Artifacts Exercise

Introduction. Teacher-educators represent a wide range of skills, interests, and experiences. Each of us begins our academic career as a student of Education. Typically, a four-year teacher pre-service program is followed by a lifetime of in-classroom teaching and scholarly pursuits. Learner, expert, and scholar—the roles may change but the need for continuous professional development remains constant. Portfolios have evolved to take center stage in the field of education from their earliest beginnings as assessment tools for the Arts and Music. Today, they are taking on more comprehensive roles in lifelong teacher learning.

Artifacts. For the avid portfolio user, *artifacts* are the evidence of portfolios. Each artifact represents an element of personal intellectual value, a tool to be thoughtfully considered for its potential application in some future academic endeavor. To grasp the fundamental organizational aspects of the portfolio and its component artifacts, the following exercise has been developed. **Click on each of the artifact examples below. How would you categorize the item?** You will be shown several "containers" into which you may place the artifact. Keep in mind that someday you may need to find it again, so make your choice wisely.

Teaching Certificate. Here is your original teaching certificate obtained from the state following completion of your undergraduate program, national teacher examination, and student teaching. You know that you will be expected to produce this artifact on several occasions throughout your career. So, into which of the following folders would you store this artifact? Click on your choice.

- <u>Professional Documents</u>
- <u>Classroom Resources</u>
- <u>Service</u>

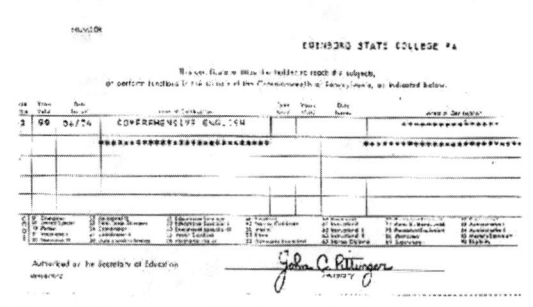

[Image of a Pennsylvania Department of Education Professional Certificate]

Professional Periodicals and Resources. Check out this list of journals and magazines for the professional educator. Which folder seems the most appropriate receptacle for this artifact? Click on your choice.

- <u>Learning Projects and Lessons</u>
- <u>Reflections and Self-Assessment</u>
- <u>Library Resources</u>

[Image showing section "E. PROFESSIONAL PERIODICALS AND RESOURCES" with a sample listing of professional journals by subject area including Art, Bilingual Education, Business Education, Computer Periodicals, English, Industrial Arts, Mathematics, Music, and Physical Education]

Assessment Tool for First Grade. Teachers often share assessment instruments for thematic units which they design. This artifact helps teachers evaluate the success of their lesson. Click on the folder which should house this item.

- <u>Content Area Material</u>
- <u>Learning Projects and Lessons</u>
- <u>Teaching</u>

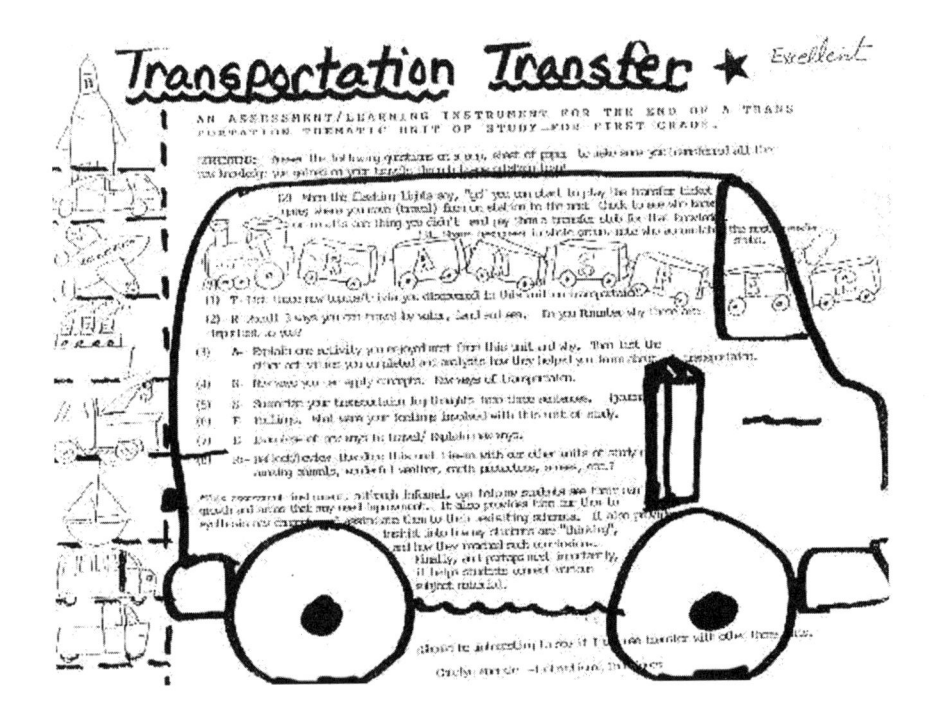

Electronic NCTE Site. This last artifact is relatively easy, so no hints. Click on your choice.

- Making Connections
- Classroom Research and Applications
- World Wide Web Sites

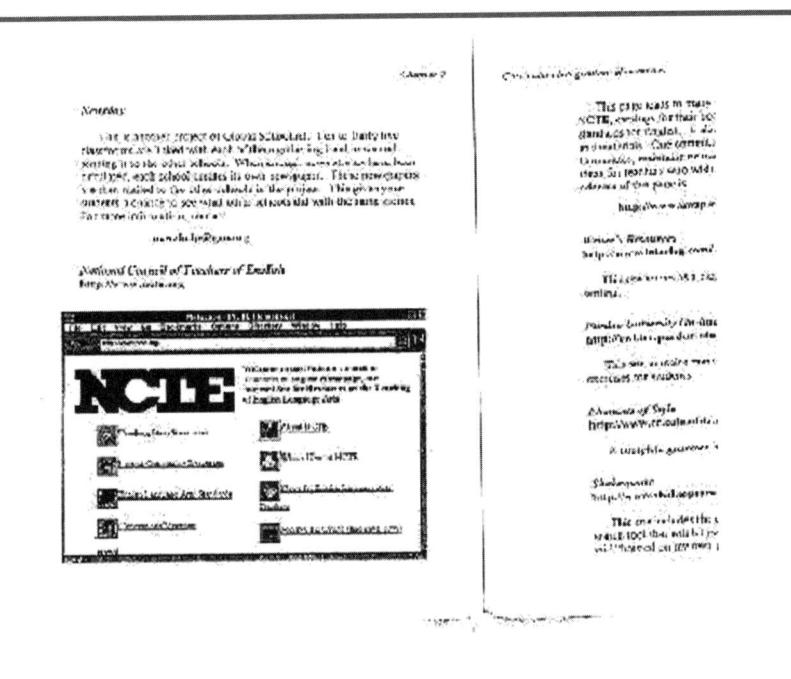

Interim Summary. OK, how did you do? There are no right or wrong answers when it comes to artifacts. But you probably did come away from the exercise with several questions, such as who, what, how, where, and when. Perhaps we can supply an answer to these common questions about the use of portfolios. **We will ask Foley to help us.**

Who will be using the portfolio and do the characteristics of that individual change over time?

- Different implementations of the portfolio are required if it is to prove useful to the lifelong learner. The concept of **Teacher as Learner, Teacher as Expert, and Teacher as Scholar** answers the question of WHO would be using the portfolio. Educators display characteristics of three different natures over the span of a 30-year career in education. An internal assessment of where the portfolio user is in an academic career must be considered before the correct format of the portfolio can be selected. If you are not yet certain which "Teacher" you are, the next exercise will assist you in making this important determination. For now, let's continue with the questions...

What KINDS of artifacts are important? It will depend on whether you are a learner, teacher, or scholar.

- For the educator, the five overarching Foundations — **Reading, Writing, Thinking, Interacting, and Demonstrating** — dictate WHAT artifacts are to be gathered. With Thinking as the focal point for all implementations, artifacts can be scrutinized for their value to the educator as they read, write, interact, and demonstrate their knowledge. The focus of your collections will depend on whether you consider yourself to be a Learner, Expert, or Scholar.

- **Collecting, Working, and Showcase folders** provide the answer to HOW artifacts will be stored in the portfolio by matching these folders with a particular phase of a teacher's career. Collecting artifacts are the major concern of the Teacher-Learner, Working artifacts are most often used by the Teacher-Expert, and Showcase artifacts determine the success of the Teacher-Scholar.

How will artifacts be stored and will all users store them in the same locations?

- **Collection Points** serve as repositories for storing artifacts; that's your answer to the WHERE question. Each Collection Point expands to whatever size is required to hold a career's-worth of educational resources, all but assuring that students will find common locations for similar artifacts.

Where should artifacts be stored for easy retrieval?

- The question of WHEN to use the **Smart or Intelligent Portfolio** is perhaps the most common question raised when selecting a portfolio format. Hard copy or electronic is a choice many feel must be made exclusively and permanently. Neither is correct. Let's go ahead and complete this review, because in just a few minutes, we provide an entire exercise devoted to this question. We will help you decide which is best for you.

When is the electronic format a better choice than hard copy?

And, finally, the easy question: Why are portfolios so important? The answer will run the gamut of your educational career.

- The final question may indeed be the easiest to answer. WHY portfolios are important to the educator can be answered in four words: **Learning, Teaching, Assessment, and Growth**. The collection of artifacts is pointless unless it contributes to your learning and, later, to the way you convey that learning to those under your charge. Portfolios have always placed personal and professional evaluation at the forefront of their intent; they will continue to be viewed in this light for many years to come. Finally, our portfolio will take aim on professional growth and personal development. The Smart and Intelligent Portfolios have your maturity as an educator as its primary focus.

Conclusion. Congratulations for completing Step 1 of the Portfolio Exercise. Hopefully, you found some answers to those initial first questions you might have had about portfolios. Let's return to the Portfolio Exercise Home Page and continue our exploration. Click Here

les_exer.htm

Professional Portfolios for Teachers

Step 2. Learner, Expert, or Scholar

Introduction. One of the most important questions asked during the previous exercise had to do with *Who* would be using the portfolio. Remember this question from Foley?

Who will be using the portfolio and do the characteristics of that individual change over time?

What "flavor" of portfolio you will adopt depends in large measure on where you are in your academic career. We have designed a checklist to help you identify your own characteristics as an educator. Check the boxes that apply to you, then click on the icon at the bottom of the list containing the most number of checked boxes.

Portfolio User A	Portfolio User B	Portfolio User C
☐ First Time Portfolio User	☐ Requires Student Use of Portfolios	☐ Uses Portfolios for Professional Development
☐ Undergraduate Student	☐ Classroom Teacher	☐ Teacher of Teachers
☐ Student Teaching	☐ Curriculum Designer	☐ Featured Speaker
☐ Awaiting Certification	☐ Holds Master's Degree	☐ Attends Conferences
☐ Awaiting Graduation	☐ Attends In-Service Training	☐ Publishes Journals
☐ Other	☐ Other	☐ Publishes Books
☐ Other	☐ Other	☐ Other

Si_exer.htm

Step 3. Smart or Intelligent Portfolio

Introduction. The question of whether to use the *Smart* or *Intelligent* Portfolio strikes at the heart of the utility of these learning assessment tools. Not every portfolio must evolve into its electronic counterpart. The Smart Portfolio is always acceptable. Your selection of format should be considered a matter of preference and not a matter of technology. Remember what Foley says...

> Chossing between the Smart and Intelligent Portfolio depends on your mastery of technology not the utility of your portflio.

- Both are based on the Foundations of **Reading, Writing, Thinking, Interacting, and Demonstrating**.
- As you have already seen, the emphasis on **Collecting, Working, and Showcase** artifacts depends on who is using the portfolio.
- The portfolio is best designed to serve the needs of the **Teacher-Learner, Teacher-Expert, and Teacher-Scholar.**

Manila envelopes, held in a binder, provide an acceptable venue for sharing artifacts. The Intelligent Portfolio should be considered an extension of the hard-copy format. The computer makes sense for those who are already conversant in the use of technology. However, either format can provide similar value for its user. Content of material is all-important. Evidence of thinking is critical. Form is incidental.

Foley will aid in the selection, construction, and integration of the portfolio most appropriate for your station. He will graphically illustrate the proper blend of Collecting, Working, and Showcase artifacts that will support the use of a portfolio in your professional development as an educator.

Selecting Your Format. The following table provides guidelines to assist you in selecting the correct format for your portfolio: either Smart or Intelligent. It is provided as a guide only and is not meant to produce a black or white, yes or no selection. Use it to help you decide whether to continue this review with the Smart or Intelligent Portfolio. **Click on the appropriate icon at the bottom of the list to continue our journey into portfolios.**

Use the Smart Portfolio if You...	Use the Intelligent Portfolio if You...
☐ Have relatively little experience with portfolios	☐ Are a competent computer user
☐ Are just starting an academic career	☐ Accumulate a large number of artifacts
☐ Accumulate relatively few artifacts	☐ Take your portfolio on the road
☐ Use the portfolio for "internal" use	☐ Capture artifacts of multimedia content
☐ Use the portfolio as an instructional tool	☐ Continually update your portfolio
☐ Prefer hard-copy materials	☐ Use the portfolio for presentations
☐ Prefer non-technology tools	☐ Could benefit from electronic storage/retrieval
	☐ Have time to learn computer applications
	☐ Share artifacts electronically with colleagues
▼ Explore the Smart Portfolio	▼ Explore the Intelligent Portfolio

Portbld.htm

Step 4. Build Your Portfolio

You should have satisfactorily completed the previous three exercises before arriving at this point where you are ready to begin building your own portfolio. The previous exercises were designed to prepare you for this step by helping you define three fundamental characteristics of yourself as a possible portfolio user:

First, do you understand the nature and purpose of artifacts? The first exercise gave you some hands-on experience critically analyzing materials that you will be **collecting, working, and showcasing** in your portfolio. You must understand these three primary categories of artifacts. If you skipped this important foundation exercise or would like a refresher, please click on Portfolio Exercise.

Second, have you identified yourself as a **Learner, Expert, or Scholar**? This question is fundamental to choosing the correct version of the portfolio for the particular stage in your academic career. If you assume that you might be one or the other — and assume wrong — you could go a long way in developing aspects of your portfolio that will be inappropriate or confusing. If you would like to look at the criteria discussed in the second exercise again to ensure you correctly defined your academic position, please click on Learner, Expert, or Scholar.

Third, did you decide whether the **Smart or Intelligent Portfolio** is better suited to your personal needs? Remember, either format provides the structure you will need to use the portfolio as a tool for lifelong learning. The only factor in deciding which one to use is .... **wait a minute!!** If you reviewed the third exercise, you already know the answer to that! If you don't, you may wish to take the time to compare and contrast the two formats. Please click on Smart or Intelligent Portfolio.

Pick the Format that is Best Suited to Your Portfolio Needs, then Click to Download the File.

For Windows 95 Users....

Smart Portfolio			Intelligent Portfolio
Teacher as Learner			File Download
Teacher as Learner			File Download
Teacher as Expert	File Download	Teacher as Expert	File Download
Teacher as Scholar	File Download	Teacher as Scholar	File Download

For Macintosh Users....

Smart Portfolio			Intelligent Portfolio
Teacher as Learner			File Download
Teacher as Learner			File Download
Teacher as Expert	File Download	Teacher as Expert	File Download
Teacher as Scholar	File Download	Teacher as Scholar	File Download

Conclusion. Congratulations on completing the Final Step of the Portfolio Exercise. By now, you should be comfortable with artifacts. You should know whether you are a Learner, Expert, or Scholar. And, you should have decided whether to use the Smart or Intelligent Portfolio. If any of these questions are still unanswered, you may wish to review one of the exercises. To return to the Portfolio Exercise Home Page and revisit the areas as many times as you wish, click here.

Faq_port.htm

Frequently Asked Questions

Question 1: Why should I want a Smart or Intelligent Portfolio? What's in this for me?

Answer: The portfolio contains a record of your work. It exhibits what you have read, thought, and discussed. But, what is more important, it is evidence of your personal progress — how your thinking has changed, how new input has improved your attitude, how new knowledge mixes with prior knowledge — and how this progress enables you to transfer and apply what you have learned. There is great value in thinking about how you think and learn, in setting goals and evaluating how well you have met them. Learning to assess yourself strengthens your ability to assess others more accurately. And that is a major responsibility of an educator.

Question 2: The Smart Portfolio or the Intelligent Portfolio…must I decide to go completely with one format or the other?

Answer: Many people combine the two formats. Some things, especially Internet-based resources, they keep in their Intelligent Portfolio. Others, such as handouts from classes taken, they place in the envelopes of the Smart Portfolio. You can use both. The Smart Portfolio should then become the "staging area" for your artifacts. Keep an inventory listing of everything that is on your computer in the appropriate Collection Point on the Smart Portfolio. That way, you have a single focal point for retrieving artifacts in the future. Don't forget — if you begin with the Smart Portfolio, you can always transfer your artifacts to an electronic medium.

Question 3: Must the portfolio consist of all of the Collection Points described or can I develop a similar but more individualized format?

Answer: The Collection Points were proposed for a basic application. You may indeed determine that some you need, others you may not, while still others (not proposed) are more important. Use the concept of the Collection Points to help you identify those which are suited to your particular professional development needs. Feel free to adapt the portfolio structure.

Question 4: How long will it take to create a portfolio?

Answer: Maintaining a portfolio becomes second nature once you establish a viable organizational pattern. Many people fail with portfolios because they are unable to identify and use a pattern that works for them. Begin with what you have and where you are now. Artists have pictures; builders have blueprints; writers have manuscripts. Students have papers and classroom handouts. Teachers have exercises, tests, and lesson plans. Scholars have publication abstracts. Organize what you have and add new artifacts as they are acquired. Most of your time will be needed to think about what those artifacts actually mean to you as a learner. The portfolio must show this evidence of personal learning. Regular journal entries are helpful and take relatively little time if you keep your journal handy. Creating a portfolio to support lifelong learning and professional development should take a long time — it should take your entire career.

Question 5: Who will evaluate my portfolio?

Answer: Portfolios can involve three different evaluators with three different purposes. First, a portfolio might be evaluated by your instructor. Instructors are usually interested in the quality and quantity of artifacts and how well they demonstrate what students know. Second, your portfolio might be evaluated by your peers. Although peers can offer insight and new perspectives, their evaluative benefit is best acknowledged when they use what they learn from viewing other portfolios. Finally, your portfolio must be evaluated by you. Self-evaluation is the most difficult, but perhaps the most valuable form of assessment. In the end, you must monitor and manage your own learning and professional development. The portfolio is there to help.

Return to the Portfolio Exercise Home Page Click Here

les1.htm

Teacher as Learner

So...You are a Teacher-Learner! Congratulations.

If your selections were predominantly from the "Portfolio User A" list, chances are good that you are a Teacher-Learner.

The portfolio for the Teacher as Learner emphasizes Collecting artifacts; Working and Showcase artifacts play a secondary role. **Reading** is stressed as the key element of the portfolio and along with it, access to libraries, Web sites, classroom resources, and content area materials.

If you decide to use technology to support your efforts, a suite of hardware, software, and support that will facilitate the gathering of materials will be added to your portfolio.

Your role as a Teacher-Learner will lay the foundation for your academic career. The portfolio can become a lifelong tool for professional development and it can begin immediately to house the artifacts that will become part of your teaching tools and, later, for the creation of new knowledge.

Portfolio Exercise Main Menu. So far, you have successfully reviewed the various categories of artifacts and identified yourself as a Teacher-Learner. Let's return to the Main Menu of this exercise so we can examine next the differences between the Smart and Intelligent Portfolios.

Teacher as Expert

So...You are a Classroom Teacher! Then you should be looking at the Teacher as Expert Portfolio.

Selections from the "Portfolio User B" list indicate that you are most likely a Teacher-Expert.

Practicing teachers, whether they use portfolios themselves or require them from their students (or both), find that most of their artifacts emphasize the Working aspects of the portfolio. Collecting had been paramount in the Teacher-Learner version of the portfolio. But it, along with Showcase items, plays a secondary role for the teacher in the classroom.

Demonstrating is the key element for the Teacher as Expert portfolio, and computer hardware and software are included to facilitate the presentation of materials in a classroom environment.

Your role as a teacher demands a focus on thinking and the development of new knowledge that will make your classrooms special. New lessons, course materials, and student handouts will be created from the artifacts gathered in the previous version of the portfolio.

Portfolio Exercise Main Menu. The review began with a look at the various categories of artifacts and moved on to an exercise that helped you identify yourself as a Teacher-Expert. Let's return to the Main Menu of this exercise so we can examine the differences between the Smart and Intelligent Portfolios next.

Les3.htm

Teacher as Scholar

So...You are a Scholar! The Teacher as Scholar Portfolio is your domain.

The characteristics listed under "Portfolio User C" are most indicative of the Teacher-Scholar — the professional educator whose forum is the journal and whose domain is public presentation.

Spanning the boundaries of publication, presentation, and interactions, the Teacher-Scholar has the most comprehensive suite of portfolio artifacts. **Showcase** takes precedence over either Collecting or Working as this educator attempts to share ideas spanning a career in the field of education.

Interacting is key, and the use of technology by the Teacher as Scholar encompasses the most extensive suite of computer hardware and applications. Discussions with colleagues, demonstration of artifacts in a professional forum, and the pursuit of thinking and learning describe the Teacher-Scholar.

The Teacher-Scholar has the responsibility to give back to the discipline some of the expertise, knowledge, and dedication that has been received over the years. Sharing is paramount.

<u>Portfolio Exercise Main Menu</u>. Artifacts began this exploration. Now that you know you are a Teacher-Scholar, we will wrap up this exercise with an examination of the differences between the Smart and Intelligent Portfolios. Let's do that next.

Appendix 207

spspsp.htm

Professional Portfolios for Teachers

The Smart Portfolio

The following graphic depicts the portfolio with all its components. We will examine each of them individually before showing you how to construct your own version of the Smart Portfolio.

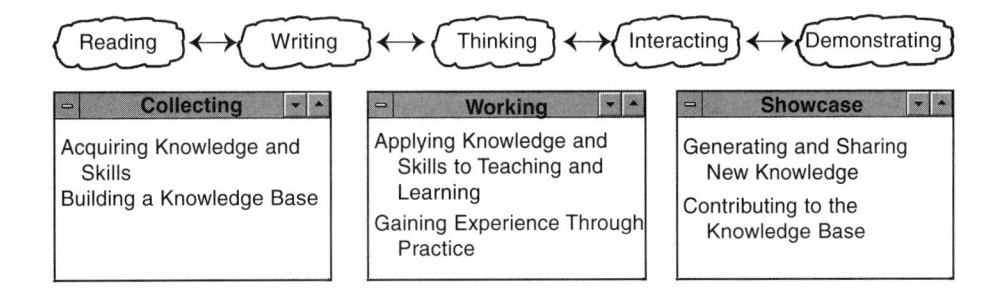

(Reading) ⟷ (Writing) ⟷ (Thinking) ⟷ (Interacting) ⟷ (Demonstrating)

Collecting	Working	Showcase
Acquiring Knowledge and Skills Building a Knowledge Base	Applying Knowledge and Skills to Teaching and Learning Gaining Experience Through Practice	Generating and Sharing New Knowledge Contributing to the Knowledge Base

The Foundations of the Smart Portfolio

(Reading) ⟷ (Writing) ⟷ (Thinking) ⟷ (Interacting) ⟷ (Demonstrating)

We will begin our examination with a look at the portfolio's essential elements. The Smart Portfolio is always introduced with its five essential Foundations: Reading, Writing, Thinking, Interacting, and Demonstrating. Understanding that these elements are totally integrated when we teach and learn is essential to proper construction of the Smart Portfolio. Teaching and learning require active engagement. Consider the following:

- **Reading** begins the process of gathering evidence of knowledge in the forms of artifacts. Diagrams, booklists, booknotes, summaries, outlines, sketches, and drawings show the evidence that new knowledge has been accumulated. Patterns begin to form.

- **Writing** connects what we are learning with what we already know, offering the opportunity to transfer and apply new information and ideas. Formal papers, book reports, thematic units, poems and letters, publication-ready articles, and written classroom lesson plans are good examples.

- **Thinking** lies at the heart of the portfolio, which infuses personal feelings into thoughts and ideas. Often referred to as the "Thinking Journal," this foundation provides "a place where our thinking can become visible, a place where we toss around ideas, consider what others think, make connections between new and prior knowledge, examine our own thinking strategies, and judge our own learning" (Wilcox, 1997). Some of the most common Thinking processes in the Smart Portfolio include responses to electronic mail, process memos, mind maps, records of personal dialogs and interviews, thinking charts, and problem-solving exercises.

- **Interacting** addresses the responsibility of an educator to share. Whether the individual is involved in group projects as a requirement of a pre-service course or has already launched his or her student teaching role, the cooperative partnering of ideas with fellow educators is an obligation that can be furthered by the Smart Portfolio. Peer assessments, memos from group activities, brainstorming sessions, arguments, problems and solutions, and position papers defending different points of view are examples.

- **Demonstrating** is the second constructive process in the Smart Portfolio. Combined with Writing, Demonstrating represents the portion of a portfolio rich in the application and transfer of learning. Demonstrations include the text of classroom presentations, speeches, oral interpretations, audiovisual materials, and completed projects using multisensory exhibits.

Organizing the Artifacts of the Smart Portfolio

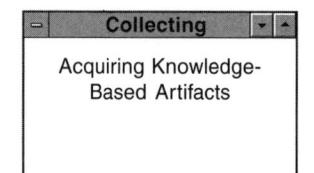

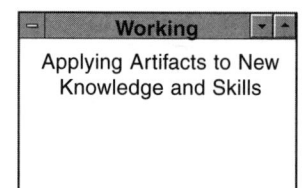

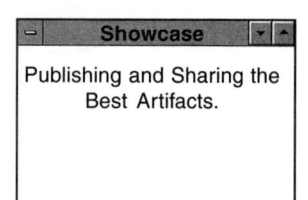

Collecting	Working	Showcase
Acquiring Knowledge-Based Artifacts	Applying Artifacts to New Knowledge and Skills	Publishing and Sharing the Best Artifacts.

Collecting, Working, and Showcase represent the artifact folders of the Smart Portfolio. By considering these repositories, a pattern emerges for easy storage and retrieval of artifacts.

- The **Collecting Folder** focuses on acquiring knowledge and skills. Most of the evidence of learning will be housed in the Collecting folders of the Smart Portfolio.

- The **Working Folder** holds artifacts created as knowledge is applied and new skills are acquired.

- The **Showcase Folder** contains artifacts that are moved into this folder when they are ready to be published and shared with your colleagues. Published artifacts are maintained in the Showcase Folder.

Collecting Artifacts

Each of the following graphics provides a few examples of the specific types of items that comprise Collecting artifacts. Artifacts that you collect will be placed initially into this folder.

Content Area Materials
Units of Study
Model Lessons
Professional Journal Articles
Teaching Videos
Booknotes

Classroom Resources
Monographs on Classroom Discipline and Learning
Sample Teaching Lessons
Higher Order Thinking Strategies for Children
Multiple Intelligence Exercises

Library Resources
Pamphlet "How to Access the Card Catalog"
Personal Research Searches
Requests for Books, Articles, and Resources
Materials for Review

World Wide Web Sites
Search Engines
Quick Retrieval Instructions
Subject Matter Sites
Lesson Plan Sites
Collaborative Sites

Working Artifacts

As knowledge is applied and new skills acquired, artifacts will be created and placed in Working folders created for work in progress. A few more examples will help clarify the kinds of artifacts most appropriate for this folder.

Making Connections
Responses and Reactions to Readings
Journal Prompts
Recording Class Discussions
Lecture Interpretations

Reflections & Self-Assessment
List of Personal Goals
Self-Assessing Questions and Answers
Reflections on Progress
Tracking Standards

Learning Projects
Plans for Instruction, Content and Assessments
Learning Center
Special Projects/Reports
Topics and Ideas for the Classroom

Applications and Lessons
Ready to Teach Units
Student Teaching Lessons
Exercises for the Classroom
Assessments (Tests, Quizzes, Rubrics)

Showcase Artifacts

Artifacts assessed for their value might be moved to the Showcase folder and retained there permanently. In addition, documents attesting to your professional development, such as teacher certification credentials, will be captured in here as well.

Service
Committee Meetings
Advisement
Taks Force Member
Professional Organizations
Publication-ready Review

Teaching
Teacher Effectiveness Forms
Assessment Tools
Rigorous Methodology Practce
Video

Scholarship
Honors/Awards
Published Works
Successful Grants
Discipline specific scholarly work

Professional Documents
Graduate Transcripts
Professional Awards
Professional Certifications
Teaching Certificates
Education Vita

Assessing Your Portfolio. One of the benefits of the Smart Portfolio is the way learning is fostered through the assessment process. Assessment must be constant and continuous, just as learning is constant and continuous. With a comprehensive portfolio, you will be the most important evaluator of your own learning. You will learn to determine its value and worth by analyzing your own portfolio using checklists, rubrics, and questions. These exercises will sharpen critical skills and aid in recognizing "best practice" and research. You will set goals and decide whether they were met and what you learned in the attempt. Assessment will give you insight into the process itself and how it connects to instruction.

Conclusion. That concludes our review of the Smart Portfolio. You now have two options:

Portfolio Exercise Main Menu. You can determine, now, that the Smart Portfolio is the way to go for you. If so, go ahead and click on the icon and we will return to the Portfolio Exercise Main Menu so you can move directly to the final section: **Build Your Portfolio.**

Intelligent Portfolio Review . Or, you can choose to take a look at the **Intelligent Portfolio** now — even though it may not be the best portfolio format for you at this time. If you would like to review the Intelligent Portfolio, click on this icon.

Ipipip.htm

The Intelligent Portfolio

It has been mentioned several times already — but bears repeating again — that the Intelligent Portfolio is a matter of personal preference on the format of the Professional Portfolio for Teachers. The all-important issue is one of the utility of these learning assessment tools. Not every portfolio must evolve into its electronic counterpart. Your selection of format should be considered a matter of preference and not a matter of technology.

However, if you are viewing this page, you probably have some interest in making your portfolio electronic. The advantages are significant:

- A suite of computer software supports the Reading, Writing, Thinking, Interacting, and Demonstrating demands of the portfolio.
- The computer hardware that comprises the Intelligent Portfolio provides opportunities for gathering, storing, and retrieving the artifacts that greatly enhance the utility of your portfolio.
- The Intelligent Portfolio serves not only as a repository of your thinking, but also as a showcase for demonstrating your expertise as an educator.
- Electronic artifacts are becoming more common in education. Finding important instructional-based materials on the World Wide Web, for example, is aided by the addition of hundreds of new Web sites each month. Downloading this material to a computer significantly simplifies artifact collection.

The following graphic depicts the Intelligent Portfolio with all its components. We will examine each of them individually before showing you how to construct your own version.

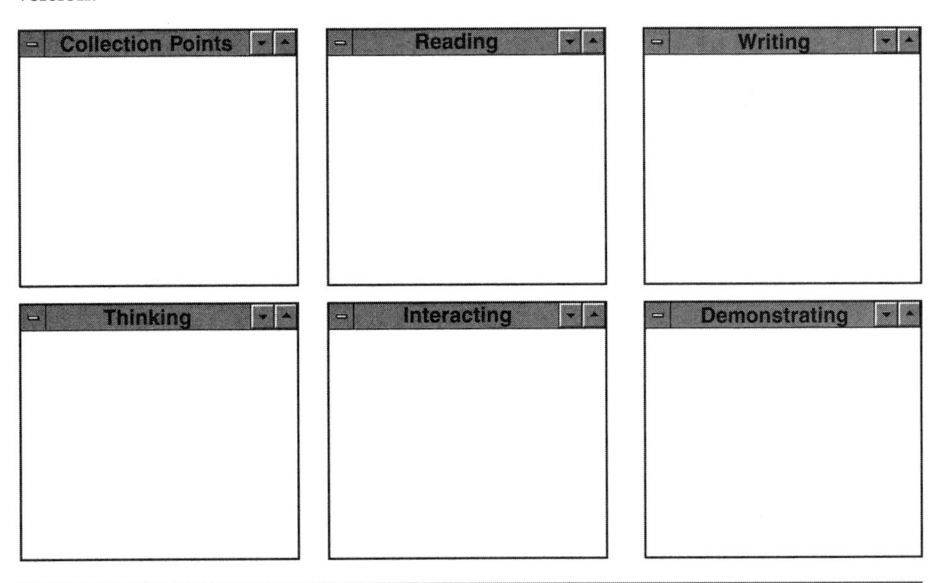

Collection Points	Reading	Writing

Thinking	Interacting	Demonstrating

The Foundations of the Intelligent Portfolio

We will begin our examination with a look at Foundations of the Intelligent Portfolio which are, of course, exactly the same as the Smart Portfolio: Reading, Writing, Thinking, Interacting, and Demonstrating. The major difference is that the Intelligent Portfolio provides for **computer software and hardware** to assist in the exploration and use of these foundations.

- **Reading** will start the process of gathering evidence of knowledge in the forms of artifacts. Diagrams, booklists, booknotes, summaries, outlines, sketches, and drawing mix with previous learning. Patterns and connections begin to form. This is how an individual's knowledge base is built; this is how we construct new knowledge. The Intelligent Portfolio recommends the following suite of software and hardware components:

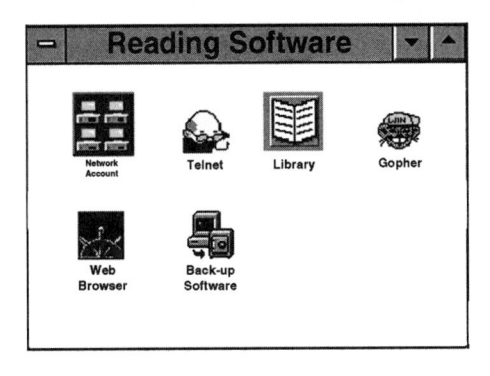

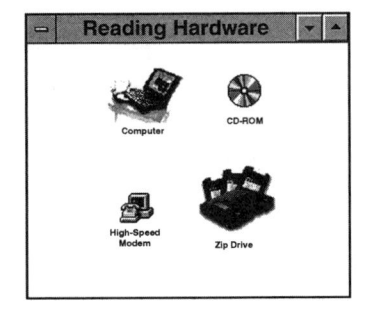

Reading Software
Network Account, Telnet, Library, Gopher, Web Browser, Back-up Software

Reading Hardware
Computer, CD-ROM, High-Speed Modem, Zip Drive

214   *Professional Portfolios for Teachers*

- **Writing** goes hand-in-hand with Reading when constructing new knowledge. Making meaning through writing involves formal papers, book reports, thematic units, poems and letters, publication-ready articles, and written classroom lesson plans. The Intelligent Portfolio suggests software and hardware that supports the composing process:

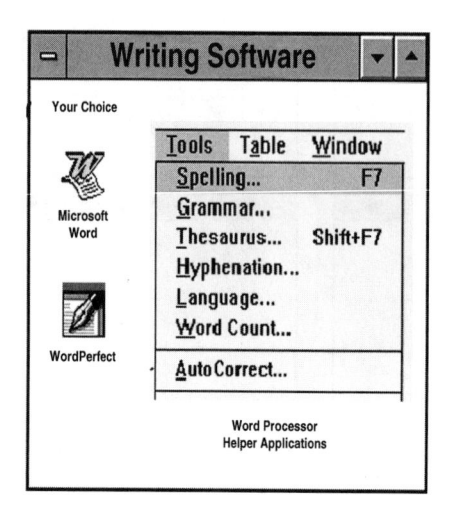

Writing Software

Your Choice

Microsoft Word

WordPerfect

Tools | Table | Window
Spelling... F7
Grammar...
Thesaurus... Shift+F7
Hyphenation...
Language...
Word Count...
AutoCorrect...

Word Processor Helper Applications

Writing Hardware

InkJet Printer   Laser Printer

- **Thinking** lies at the heart of the portfolio and infuses personal feelings into thoughts and ideas. The Thinking journal in the Smart Portfolio is "a place where our thinking can become visible, a place where we toss around ideas, consider what others think, make connections between new and prior knowledge, examine our own thinking strategies, and judge our own learning" (Wilcox, 1997). Some of the most common Thinking processes in the Intelligent Portfolio include responses to electronic mail inquiries, process memos, mind maps, records of personal dialogs and interviews, thinking charts, and problem-solving exercises. Thinking software and hardware offer a variety of automated tools to advance new ideas and educational thought:

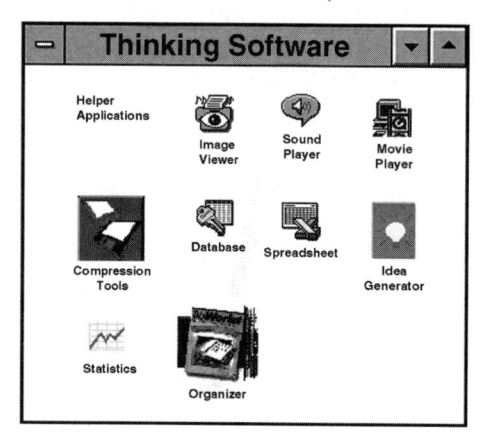

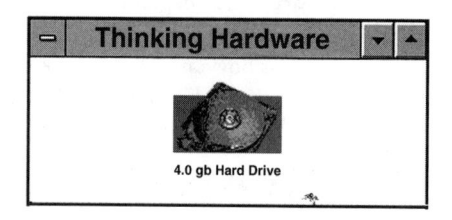

Thinking Software

Helper Applications

Image Viewer   Sound Player   Movie Player

Compression Tools   Database   Spreadsheet   Idea Generator

Statistics   Organizer

Thinking Hardware

4.0 gb Hard Drive

- **Interacting** addresses the sharing responsibilities. Whether the individual is involved in group projects as a requirement of a pre-service course or has already launched out in their student teaching role, the cooperative partnering of ideas with fellow educators is an obligation that can be furthered by the Intelligent Portfolio. Peer assessments, memos from group activities, brainstorming sessions, arguments, problems and solutions, and position papers defending different points of view are examples. And, the Intelligent Portfolio has a few hardware and software components to offer:

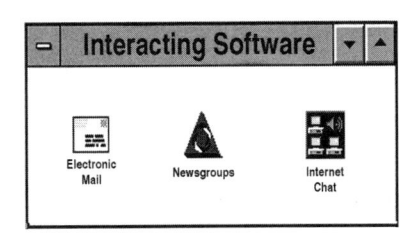

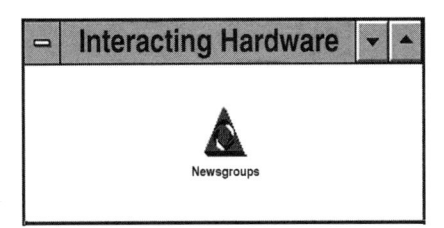

Interacting Software	Interacting Hardware
Electronic Mail, Newsgroups, Internet Chat	Newsgroups

- **Demonstrating**, combined with Writing, represents the portion of a portfolio rich in the application and transfer of learning. Demonstrations include the text of classroom presentations, speeches, oral interpretations, audiovisual materials, and completed projects using multisensory exhibits. Demonstrating software and hardware are among the most popular packages of the Intelligent Portfolio:

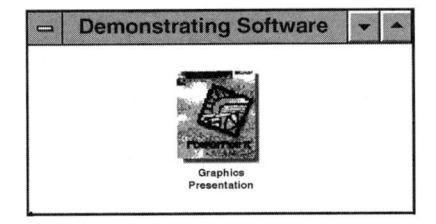

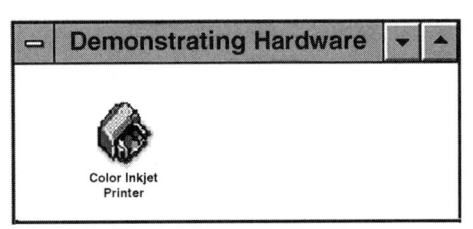

Demonstrating Software	Demonstrating Hardware
Graphics Presentation	Color Inkjet Printer

Organizing the Artifacts of the Intelligent Portfolio

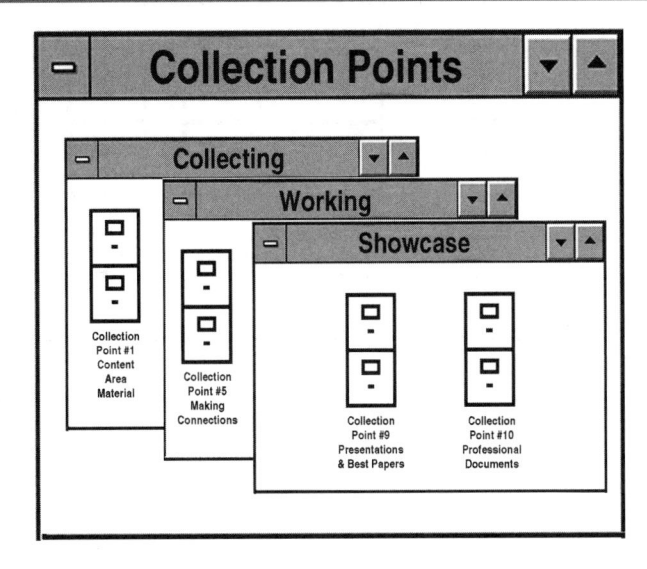

Collection Points

- Collecting
  - Collection Point #1 Content Area Material
- Working
  - Collection Point #5 Making Connections
- Showcase
  - Collection Point #9 Presentations & Best Papers
  - Collection Point #10 Professional Documents

216 *Professional Portfolios for Teachers*

As with the Smart Portfolio, Collecting, Working, and Showcase represent the artifact folders of the Intelligent Portfolio. By considering these repositories, a pattern emerges for easy storage and retrieval of artifacts.

- The **Collecting Folder** focuses on acquiring knowledge and skills. Most of the evidence of learning will be housed in the Collecting folders of the Intelligent Portfolio.
- The **Working Folder** holds artifacts created as knowledge is applied and new skills are acquired.
- The **Showcase Folder** contains artifacts that are moved into this folder when they are ready to be published and shared with your colleagues. Published artifacts are maintained in the Showcase folder.

The Collection Points of the Intelligent Portfolio

The Intelligent Portfolio provides up to 12 Collection Points to hold your electronic artifacts. We will create these areas as directories or file folders on the computer. They are divided among the Collecting, Working, and Showcase folders. However, each has a specific purpose and not all the Collection Points are used in every implementation of the Intelligent Portfolio. Still, let's examine each one before we proceed further.

Collecting Folders. Four Collection Points are offered for the task of Collecting artifacts. Each of the following graphics provides the specific types of artifacts that belong in each folder. Artifacts that you collect will be placed initially into one of these four folders: Content Area Materials, Classroom Resources, Library Resources, and World Wide Web Sites.

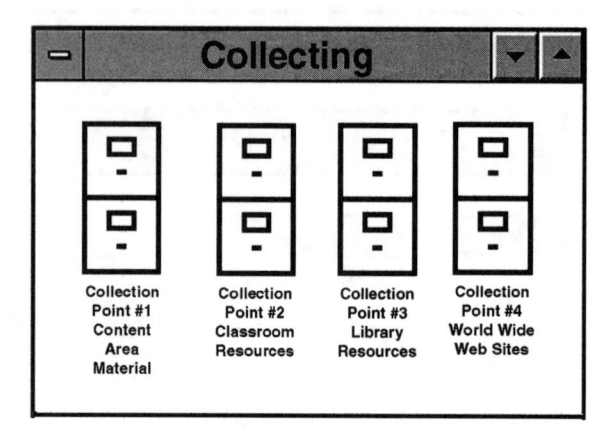

Collecting

Collection Point #1
Content Area Material

Collection Point #2
Classroom Resources

Collection Point #3
Library Resources

Collection Point #4
World Wide Web Sites

Working Folders consist of Making Connections, Reflection and Self-Assessment, Learning Projects, and Applications and Lessons. As knowledge is applied and new skills are acquired, artifacts are placed in Working folders. Again, four folders have been created for work in progress.

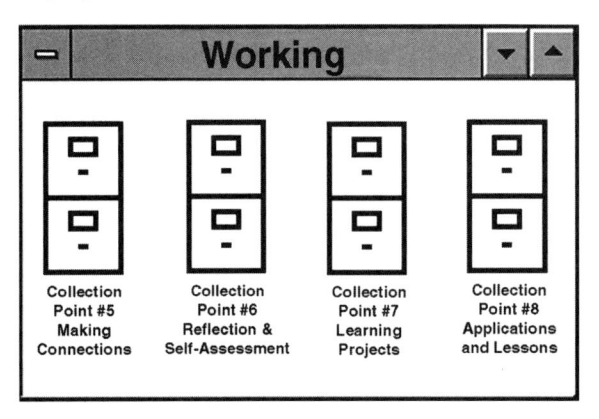

Showcase Folders. Artifacts assessed for their value might be moved to the Showcase folders of Service, Teaching, Scholarship, and Professional Documents and retained there permanently. For example, documents attesting to your professional development, such as teacher certification credentials, are captured in one of the Showcase Collection Points of the Intelligent Portfolio.

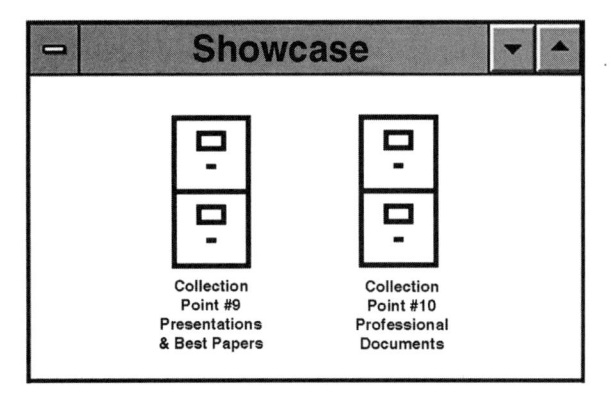

Assessing Your Portfolio. One of the benefits of the Intelligent Portfolio is the way learning is fostered through the assessment process. Assessment must be constant and continuous just as learning is constant and continuous. With a comprehensive portfolio, you are the most important evaluator of your own learning. You learn to determine its value and worth by analyzing your own portfolio using checklists, sometimes using questions to determine useful or appropriate artifacts. These exercises sharpen critical skills and aid in recognizing best practice and research. You set goals and decide whether they were met and what you learned in the attempt. Assessment gives you that insight into the process itself and how it connects to instruction.

Conclusion. That concludes our review of the Intelligent Portfolio. You now have two options.

Portfolio Exercise Main Menu. You can determine now whether the Intelligent Portfolio is the way to go for you. If so, click on the icon and we will return to the Portfolio Exercise Main Menu so you can move directly to the final section: **Build Your Portfolio.**

Smart Portfolio Review. Or, you can choose to take a look at the **Smart Portfolio.** This review will help you determine whether the Intelligent Portfolio is the best portfolio format for you at this time. If you would like to review the Smart Portfolio, click on this icon.

Stal_95.htm

Professional Portfolios for Teachers

The Smart Portfolio for the Teacher as Learner

Directions for Building Your Smart Portfolio

Here is what your Smart Portfolio will look like when you have the binder created for ease of use and assessment:

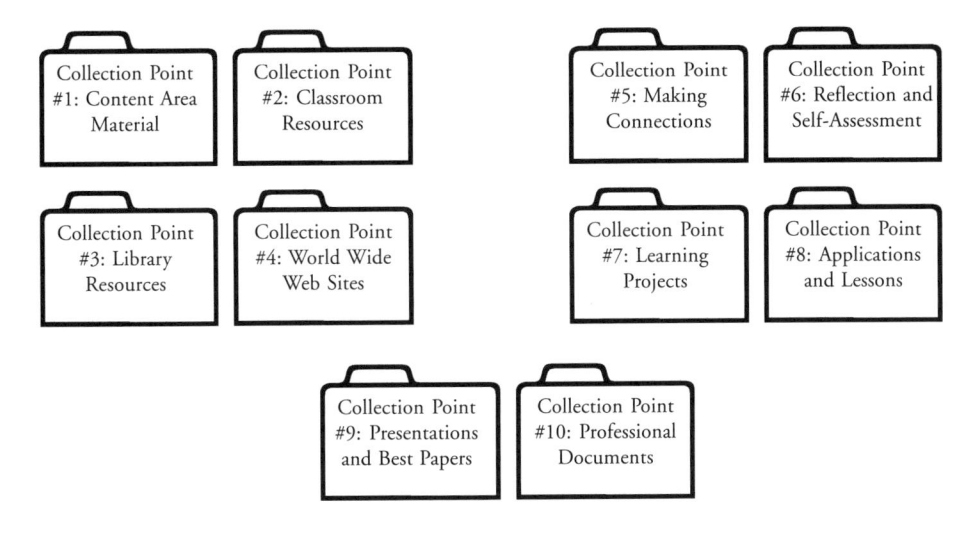

- Collection Point #1: Content Area Material
- Collection Point #2: Classroom Resources
- Collection Point #5: Making Connections
- Collection Point #6: Reflection and Self-Assessment
- Collection Point #3: Library Resources
- Collection Point #4: World Wide Web Sites
- Collection Point #7: Learning Projects
- Collection Point #8: Applications and Lessons
- Collection Point #9: Presentations and Best Papers
- Collection Point #10: Professional Documents

Step 1. Materials

Three-ring Binder (3-inch or 5-inch)
Index Tab Partitions (10 each)
Assorted Adhere Materials (such as glue, tape)

Step 2. Preparing the Binder

Using the Smart Portfolio diagram as a guide, prepare a three-ring binder and place three partitions (all the same color is recommended) — one each for the Collecting, Working, and Showcase sections.

Step 3. Indexing the Collection Points

Within the boundaries of the Collecting, Working, and Showcase sections of the portfolio, place one Index Tab Partition in the binder for each of the 10 Collection Points as shown in the Smart Portfolio diagram.

Collecting, Working, and Showcase Partitions

Collecting Artifacts. The foundations of the Smart Portfolio are supported by a number of Collection Points in which artifacts will be stored. Since the focus for the Teacher as Learner is on acquiring knowledge and skills, most of the evidence of learning will be housed in the *Collecting* partitions of the Smart Portfolio. Four Collection Points are offered for this task: Content Area Materials, Classroom Resources, Library Resources, and World Wide Web Sites. Artifacts that you collect will be placed initially into one of these four partitions.

Working Artifacts. As knowledge is applied and new skills are acquired, artifacts will be created and placed in *Working* partitions. Four partitions have been created for work in progress: Making Connections, Reflections and Self-Assessment, Learning Projects, and Applications and Lessons. Artifacts taken from the Collecting section of the Smart Portfolio are acted upon here in the Working section. As a result of these efforts, new artifacts are created. Some of these new artifacts are rejected and perhaps returned to the Collecting section.

Showcase Artifacts. Artifacts assessed for their value might be moved to the Presentations and Papers and retained there permanently. In addition, documents attesting to Professional Documents such as teacher certification credentials, will be captured in one of the *Showcase* Collection Points.

Remember that the emphasis for the Teacher as Learner will remain with Collecting. Users of the Smart Portfolio will be asked to concentrate on the accumulation of artifacts during the time when they are Teachers as Learners.

Step 4. Affixing Labels

Using the labels provided below, affix the Title and each of the Three Sections of the portfolio to the top of the partitions followed by labels for each of the 10 Collection Points.

To assist the first-time user of the Smart Portfolio, Foley will offer some specific examples of the artifacts that belong in each of the 10 Collection Points. Let's look at the Collection Points more carefully to see what specific teaching and learning artifacts we might gather.

Smart Portfolio for the Teacher as Learner

Collecting Artifacts

Collection Point #1

Place your Content Area Materials in this folder.

Content Area Materials
Units of Study
Model Lessons
Professional Journal Articles
Teaching Videos
Booknotes

Collection Point #2

Classroom Resources go in this folder.

Classroom Resources
Monographs on Classroom Discipline and Learning
Sample Teaching Lessons
Higher Order Thinking Strategies for Children
Multiple Intelligence Exercises

Collection Point #3

This point will be chock full of materials-- all from the library.

Library Resources
Pamphlet "How to Access the Card Catalog"
Personal Research Searches
Requests for Books, Articles, and Resources
Materials for Review

Collection Point #4

URLs from your most excieing Web sites go in this folder.

World Wide Web Sites
Search Engines
Quick Retrieval Instructions
Subject Matter Sites
Lesson Plan Sites
Collaborative Sites

Content Area Materials

Classroom Resources

Library Resources

World Wide Web Sites

Working Artifacts

Collection Point #5

Making Connections means sharing your artifacts with others.

Making Connections
Responses and Reactions to Readings
Journal Prompts
Recording Class Discussions
Lecture Interpretations

Collection Point #6

When it's time for "Taking Stock" place those artifacts in this folder.

Reflections & Self-Assessment
List of Personal Goals
Self-Assessing Questions and Answers
Reflections on Progress
Tracking Standards

Collection Point #7

Learnig Projects should be standard fare for the Teacher as Learner. They go in this folder.

Learning Projects
Plans for Instruction, Content and Assessments
Learning Center
Special Projects/Reports
Topics and Ideas for the Classroom

Collection Point #8

Put your efforst at devloping classroom-ready lessons here.

Applications and Lessons
Ready to Teach Units
Student Teaching Lessons
Exercises for the Classroom
Assessments (Tests, Quizzes, Rubrics)

Making Connections

Reflections & Self-Assessment

Learning Projects

Applications & Lessons

Showcase Artifacts

Collection Point #9

Remember, only finished artifacts, tested and reviewed are moved into this folder.

Presentations & Papers
Publication ready Reviews
 and Articles
Proposals
Formal Presentations
Your Philosophy of Teaching
 and Learning

Collection Point #10

The last folder will hod Teaching Credentials, Certrifications, etc.

Professional Documents
Transcripts
NTE Test Scores
Recommendations
Honors, Recognition, Awards
Experiences
Vitae

Presentations & Best Papers

Professional Documents

Step 5. Completing Your Smart Portfolio

Once the partitions are secured in the binder and labels have been affixed, the portfolio is ready to accept artifacts.

We strongly recommend that one of the first actions you take with your new portfolio is to create a Concept Paper, "My Philosophy of Teaching and Learning." This concept paper will help you think about how you conceive teaching and learning as issues in your own professional development. For the Teacher as Learner, this philosophy will, most likely, change over time. Any efforts you expend now to refine your understanding of these concepts will prove beneficial to you as you develop as an educator throughout your academic career.

Step 6. Exhibiting Your Smart Portfolio

Periodically, you will be asked to display the contents of your Smart Portfolio — or at least the most significant artifacts that you have accumulated. The following graphic depicts the use of a posterboard to assist with this exhibition. It is one way to demonstrate that you are using your Smart Portfolio for personal growth and professional development. Take advantage of this format if it proves useful.

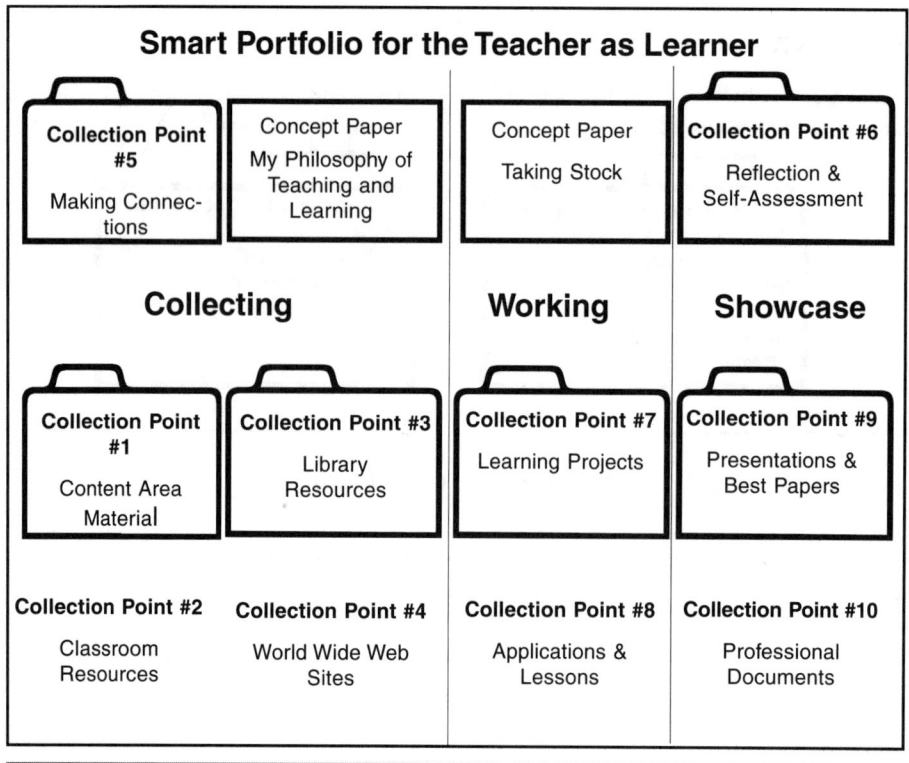

Smart Portfolio for the Teacher as Learner

Collecting	Working	Showcase
Collection Point #5 — Making Connections	**Concept Paper** — Taking Stock	**Collection Point #6** — Reflection & Self-Assessment
Concept Paper — My Philosophy of Teaching and Learning		
Collection Point #1 — Content Area Material	**Collection Point #7** — Learning Projects	**Collection Point #9** — Presentations & Best Papers
Collection Point #3 — Library Resources		
Collection Point #2 — Classroom Resources	**Collection Point #8** — Applications & Lessons	**Collection Point #10** — Professional Documents
Collection Point #4 — World Wide Web Sites		

Return to the Portfolio Exercise Main Menu

ital95.htm

Professional Portfolios for Teachers

The Intelligent Portfolio for the Teacher as Learner

Directions for Building Your Intelligent Portfolio for the Teacher as Learner

Building the Intelligent Portfolio is a combination of three simple electronic tasks:

(a) **Creating Folders** for Reading, Writing, Thinking, Interacting, and Demonstrating;
(b) **Populating Folders** with the most efficient and effective combination of software packages for the tasks at hand; and
(c) **Organizing Collection Points** to store the electronic information that will be accumulated in the Collecting, Working, and Showcase aspects of your portfolio.

Step 1. Create the Folders on Your Desktop

We will begin this exercise by creating a Windows desktop that resembles the graphic on the following page.

- From the Windows Desktop, OPEN *My Computer* by double-clicking on the icon.
- In the *File* Menu, click on your Hard Drive Icon to view the folders already created on your C: drive.
- Click on *File — New — Folder* from the Menu Bar to create a new folder which you will call *Intelligent Portfolio*. Once inside this new folder, create six more folders, one for each of the major components of the Intelligent Portfolio: Reading, Writing, Thinking, Interacting, and Demonstrating. Then one more for all your Collection Points.

Use the example above to guide you in creating the folders.

226 *Professional Portfolios for Teachers*

| Collection Points | Reading | Writing |
| Thinking | Interacting | Demonstrating |

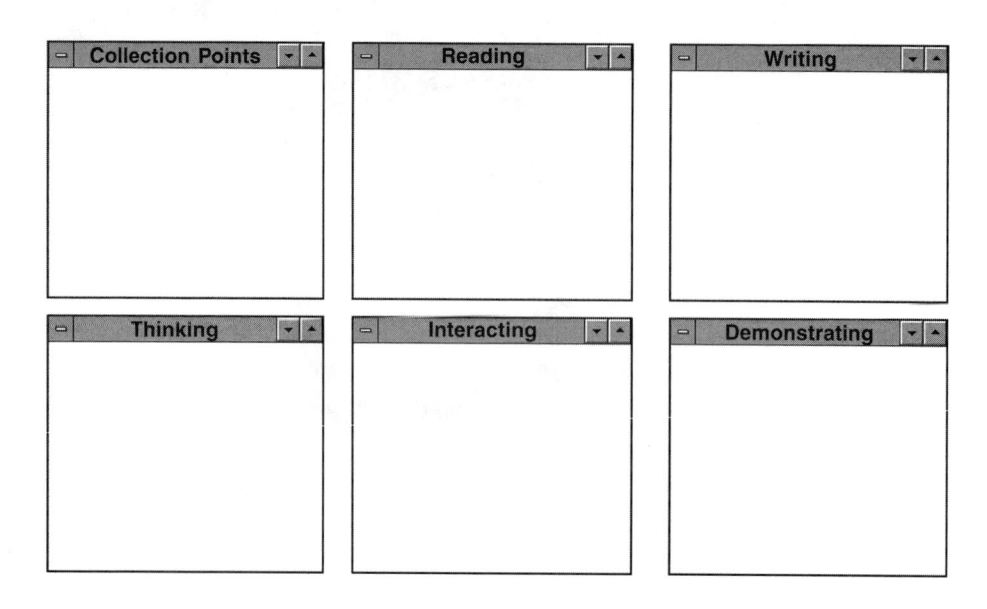

Step 2. Populate the Folders

The folders you just created on your hard drive must be populated with "shortcuts" that will reflect the most common applications in each of the portfolio components. The following graphics depict the specific software applications that should be included in the Intelligent Portfolio for the Teacher as Learner. Construct your portfolio to include as many of these packages as possible. If your computer does not come with these packages, we recommend that you find a source for these applications or substitute others of equal capability. It is acceptable to omit those you know you will not be using and add others that may not appear as options here.

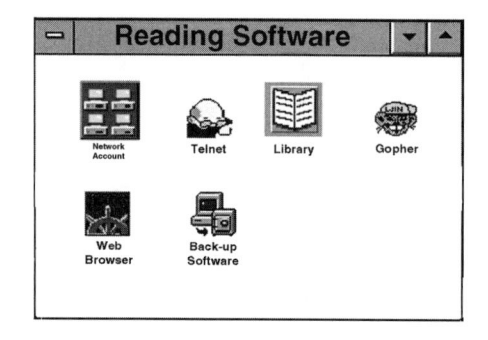

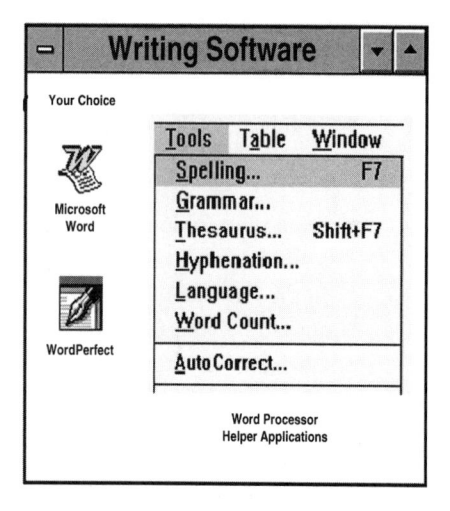

Reading Software

- Network Account
- Telnet
- Library
- Gopher
- Web Browser
- Back-up Software

Writing Software

Your Choice

Microsoft Word

WordPerfect

Tools	Table	Window
Spelling...		F7
Grammar...		
Thesaurus...		Shift+F7
Hyphenation...		
Language...		
Word Count...		
AutoCorrect...		

Word Processor
Helper Applications

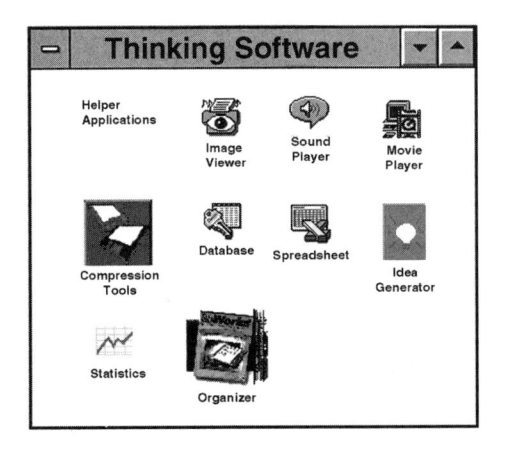

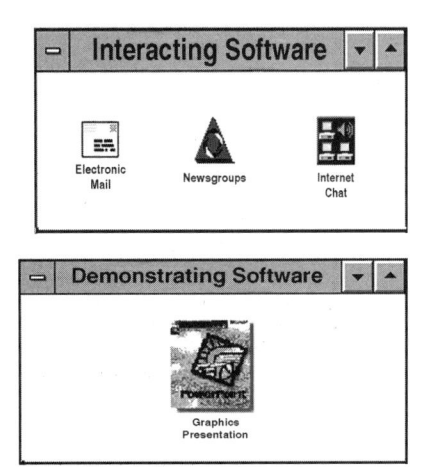

Step 3. Organize the Collection Points

You have already created the primary folder for your Collection Points. This initial folder will help you locate and retrieve artifacts throughout the lifetime of your portfolio. Next, we need to create 10 new folders within the Collection Point folder — one for each of the Teacher as Learner folders. From within the *Collection Point* Folder, Click on *File — New — Folder* from the Menu Bar and create 10 new folders. Name them as shown in the examples presented by Foley below. To assist the first-time user of the Intelligent Portfolio, Foley also offers some specific examples of artifacts that belong in each of the 10 Collection Points.

Collection Points are grouped into three major categories:

Collecting. Over 50 percent of the Intelligent Portfolio artifacts for the Teacher as Learner will be for the accumulation of resources. *Collecting* materials is paramount; retrieving that information at a later date will be similarly critical. By placing all your collecting artifacts in these four Collection Points, the task of locating resources at some subsequent date is made significantly easier. Four Collection Points are offered for this task: Content Area Materials, Classroom Resources, Library Resources, and World Wide Web Sites. Artifacts that you collect will be placed initially into one of these four folders.

Collection Point #1

Place your Content Area Materials in this folder.

Content Area Materials
Units of Study
Model Lessons
Professional Journal Articles
Teaching Videos
Booknotes

Collection Point #2

Classroom Resources go in this folder.

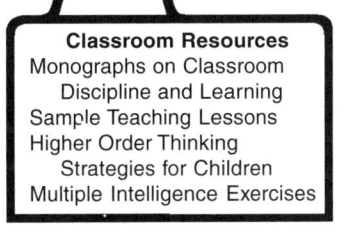

Classroom Resources
Monographs on Classroom Discipline and Learning
Sample Teaching Lessons
Higher Order Thinking Strategies for Children
Multiple Intelligence Exercises

228 *Professional Portfolios for Teachers*

Collection Point #3

This point will be chock full of materials-- all from the library.

> **Library Resources**
> Pamphlet "How to Access the Card Catalog"
> Personal Research Searches
> Requests for Books, Articles, and Resources
> Materials for Review

Collection Point #4

URLs from your most excieing Web sites go in this folder.

> **World Wide Web Sites**
> Search Engines
> Quick Retrieval
> Instructions
> Subject Matter Sites
> Lesson Plan Sites
> Collaborative Sites

Working. As knowledge is applied and new skills are acquired, artifacts will be created and placed in *Working* folders. Again, four collection points have been created for work in progress. They include: Making Connections, Reflections and Self-Assessment, Learning Projects, and Applications and Lessons. Artifacts taken from the Collecting section of the Intelligent Portfolio are acted upon here in the Working section. As a result of these efforts, new knowledge is created. Some of these new artifacts are rejected and perhaps returned to the Collecting section.

Collection Point #5

Making Connections means sharing your artifacts with others.

> **Making Connections**
> Responses and Reactions to Readings
> Journal Prompts
> Recording Class Discussions
> Lecture Interpretations

Collection Point #6

When it's time for "Taking Stock" place those artifacts in this folder.

> **Reflections & Self-Assessment**
> List of Personal Goals
> Self-Assessing Questions and Answers
> Reflections on Progress
> Tracking Standards

Collection Point #7

Learnig Projects should be standard fare for the Teacher as Learner. They go in this folder.

> **Learning Projects**
> Plans for Instruction, Content and Assessments
> Learning Center
> Special Projects/Reports
> Topics and Ideas for the Classroom

Collection Point #8

Put your efforst at devloping classroom-ready lessons here.

> **Applications and Lessons**
> Ready to Teach Units
> Student Teaching Lessons
> Exercises for the Classroom
> Assessments (Tests, Quizzes, Rubrics)

Showcase. Artifacts assessed for their value might be moved to the Presentations and Papers Collection Point and retained there permanently. Documents such as teacher certification credentials will be captured in the Professional Documents Collection Point.

Collection Point #9

Remember, only finished artifacts, tested and reviewed are moved into this folder.

> **Presentations & Papers**
> Publication ready Reviews
>   and Articles
> Proposals
> Formal Presentations
> Your Philosophy of Teaching
>   and Learning

Collection Point #10

The last folder will hod Teaching Credentials, Certifications, etc.

> **Professional Documents**
> Transcripts
> NTE Test Scores
> Recommendations
> Honors, Recognition, Awards
> Experiences
> Vitae

The emphasis for the Teacher as Learner will remain with Collecting. Users of the Intelligent Portfolio will be asked to concentrate on the accumulation of artifacts while they are Teachers as Learners.

Step 4. Completing Your Intelligent Portfolio

Now that you have created the folders and Collection Points for the Intelligent Portfolio for the Teacher as Learner, you can begin to use your computer to store and retrieve artifacts that will be used throughout your academic career. We will finish our directions with a few tips from Foley for using your portfolio.

Tips for Using the Intelligent Portfolio

1. Collecting is the focus of the Intelligent Portfolio for the Teacher as Learner.

Do not clutter your computer with software or hardware that will not contribute directly to the collection of artifacts. For example, desktop publishing, while an excellent tool for the preparation and final manuscript of papers and personal publications, is superfluous for the Teacher as Learner. One of the recommended word processors is more than capable for now; desktop publishing will appear in later versions of the Intelligent Portfolio.

2. Visit each Collection Point weekly.

As you progress through a pre-service program, revisit the artifacts collected, culling out the extraneous materials before becoming overwhelmed by data rather than information.

3. Continue to upgrade your Intelligent Portfolio.

Stay alert to the latest versions of operating systems, software, and hardware. Remember that the Intelligent Portfolio is a tool for a lifetime of professional development.

4. Don't limit the search for electronic artifacts.

Continue to explore all avenues of resources in pursuit of the best materials.

5. The future is on the Internet.

Devote time seeking artifacts on the Web. Artifacts captured on-line via the Web will be technically easier to store and incorporate into future works. You will not find it difficult to identify content area material on the Internet. The challenge, however, will be to gain the experience necessary to cull out pedagogically sound materials.

6. Take inventory of your Intelligent Portfolio usage.

The Intelligent Portfolio relies on the premise that professional development is a lifelong process which integrates reading, writing, interacting, thinking, and demonstrating in proper measure. Each element of the Intelligent Portfolio should be used periodically. Too much emphasis in any one area could indicate neglect of other key factors of your professional development. A look at the frequency of access will provide some indication.

Return to the Build Your Own Portfolio Menu

stae95.htm

Professional Portfolios for Teachers

The Smart Portfolio for the Teacher as Expert

Directions for Building Your Smart Portfolio

Here is what your Smart Portfolio will look like when you have the binder created for ease of use and assessment:

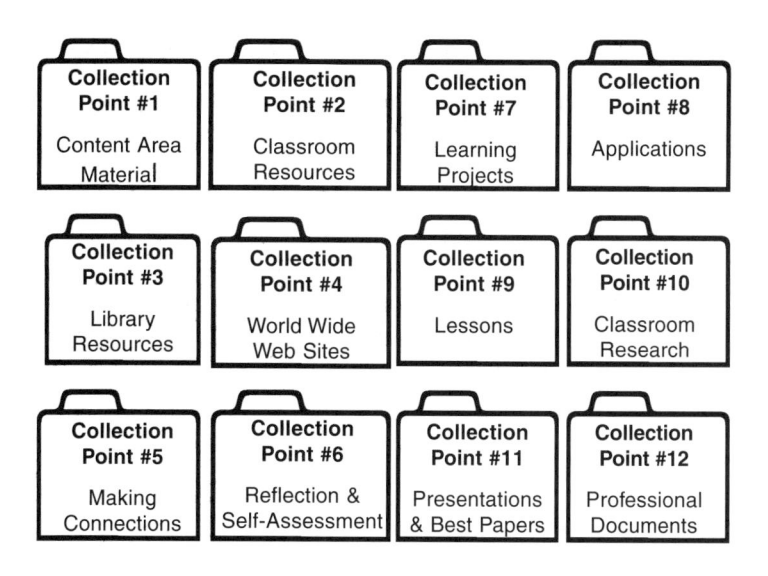

Collection Point #1 Content Area Material	Collection Point #2 Classroom Resources	Collection Point #7 Learning Projects	Collection Point #8 Applications
Collection Point #3 Library Resources	Collection Point #4 World Wide Web Sites	Collection Point #9 Lessons	Collection Point #10 Classroom Research
Collection Point #5 Making Connections	Collection Point #6 Reflection & Self-Assessment	Collection Point #11 Presentations & Best Papers	Collection Point #12 Professional Documents

Step 1. Materials

> Three-ring Binder (3-inch or 5-inch)
> Index Tab Partitions (12 each)
> Assorted Adhere Materials (such as glue, tape)

Step 2. Preparing the Binder

Using the Smart Portfolio diagram as a guide, prepare a three-ring binder and place three partitions (all the same color is recommended) — one each for the Collecting, Working, and Showcase sections.

Step 3. Indexing the Collection Points

Within the boundaries of the three Collecting, Working, and Showcase sections of the portfolio, place one index Tab Partition in the binder for each of the 12 Collection Points as shown in the Smart Portfolio diagram.

Collecting, Working, and Showcase Partitions

Collecting Artifacts. Content Area Materials, Classroom Resources, Library Resources, and World Wide Web Sites continue to hold artifacts acquired by reading, thinking, and interacting. If you are already using the Smart Portfolio, it should be overflowing with Collecting artifacts. Collecting remains critically important in all aspects of portfolio use to ensure the availability of up-to-date resources that will continue to generate new thinking.

Working Artifacts. As the Teacher as Expert begins to integrate and apply the knowledge of the Collecting artifacts, the resulting new materials are transferred to the Working Collection Points. One new folder and two revised folders are used in this version of the Smart Portfolio.

Showcase Artifacts. Showcase Collection Points have plenty of room for contributions from the Teacher as Expert. Presentations at national, regional, or local conferences and artifacts from parent-teacher meetings are placed in these Collection Points along with updated course transcripts, certificates of completion for in-service credits, letters of recommendation, and publication pieces.

The emphasis for the Teacher as Expert shifts to the Working Collection Points from the Collecting partitions, since the focus is now on the application of knowledge and skills and the discovery of useful and practical ways to put theories into practice.

Step 4. Affixing Labels

Using the labels provided below, affix the Title and each of the Three Sections of the portfolio to the top of the partitions followed by labels for each of the 12 Collection Points.

Foley will offer some specific examples of the artifacts that belong in each of the Collection Points. If you have already reviewed the previous Teacher-Learner implementation, you will note that one new partition and two revised containers make their appearance in this version of the Smart Portfolio. Also, there are also some other fundamental changes to the previous versions of the Smart Portfolio.

Smart Portfolio for the Teacher as Expert

Collecting Artifacts

Collection Point #1

This folder should already be filled with artifacts. Any new content material should be addded or replaced.

Content Area Materials
Journal Articles
Subject Matter Books
Textbooks
Raw Lesson Plans taken
　　from the Internet.

Collection Point #2

Classroom Resources go in this folder.

Classroom Resources
Monographs on Classroom
　　Discipline and Learning
Sample Teaching Lessons
Higher Order Thinking
　　Strategies for Teaching
Multiple Intelligence Exercises

Collection Point #3

Remember not to limit your library resources to only your own school library.

Library Resources
Requests for Books, Articles,
　　and Resources
Audiovisual Resources
Library Reference/Reserve
　　Materials

Collection Point #4

URLs for the Teacher as Expert consist of sites that promote teaching and learning for students as well as teachers.

World Wide Web Sites
Search Engines
Subject Matter Sites
Online Presentations
Student-oriented Research
Content Specialties
Education E-Zines

Content Area Materials

Classroom Resources

Library Resources

World Wide Web Sites

Working Artifacts

Collection Point #5

Interacting with your own artifacts and with colleagues and students.

Making Connections
Points of Contact
Mental Maps
Book notes
Insight into Classroom Issue/ Problems
Unresolved Questions

Collection Point #6

Self-assessment helps the educator improve teaching and better the profession.

Reflections & Self-Assessment
Self-Analysis of Lessons
Results of Student Surveys
Discipline Problems
Personal Philosophy of Teaching and Learning

Collection Point #7

If you use it in the classroom, store it in this Collection Point.

Learning Projects
Videos of Past Student Projects
Parents' Nite Program
Itinerary for Field Trips
Instruction for Senior Research Paper
Student Science Handouts

Collection Point #8   *NEW*

Here's one of the new Collection Points . . . sort of a 'parking lot' until you need the artifact in the classroom.

Applications
Next Semester's Units of Study
Enhancement Exercises
Thematic Units
Assessments Activities

Appendix   235

Collection Point #9

The second new Collection Point, your active Lessons, will all be placed in this folder with 5 subfolders.

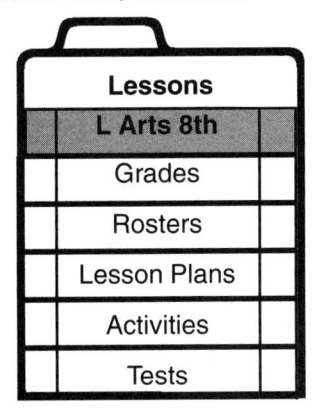

NEW

Lessons
L Arts 8th
Grades
Rosters
Lesson Plans
Activities
Tests

Collection Point #10

Here's the last new Collection Point. Any new ideas that deserve further investigation should go here.

NEW

Classroom Research
Experiential Teaching
Design for Study
Background Research
Student Survey of Teacher
    Effectiveness

Making Connections

Reflections & Self-Assessment

Learning Projects

Applications

Lessons

Classroom Research

Showcase Artifacts

Collection Point #11

Your Best Works go here. We moved this collection point up two notches to number 11.

Presentations and Best Papers
Submitted Reviews
Proposed Lesson Ideas
Teacher In-Service
  Workshops

Collection Point #12

The last folder for the Teacher as Expert continues to hold a growing number of professional artifacts.

Professional Documents
Graduate Transcripts
Teacher Evaluations
Test Scores
Honors, Recognitions, and Awards
Letters of Recommendations

Presentations & Best Papers

Professional Documents

Step 5. Completing Your Smart Portfolio

Once the partitions are secured to the binder and labels have been affixed, the portfolio is ready to accept artifacts.

We strongly recommend that you continue to work on your Concept Paper, "My Philosophy of Teaching and Learning." This concept paper will help you keep in the forefront your personal thinking about how you teach your students and how you yourself continue to learn. For the Teacher as Expert, this philosophy will necessarily change over time. Your grasp and application of sound teaching theories will continue to hone your understanding of these concepts as lifelong learning becomes something you not only preach but practice.

Step 6. Exhibiting Your Smart Portfolio

Periodically, you will be asked to display the contents of your Smart Portfolio — or at least the most significant artifacts that you have accumulated. The following graphic depicts the use of a posterboard to assist with this exhibition. This is one way to demonstrate that you are using your Smart Portfolio for personal growth and professional development. Take advantage of this format if it proves useful.

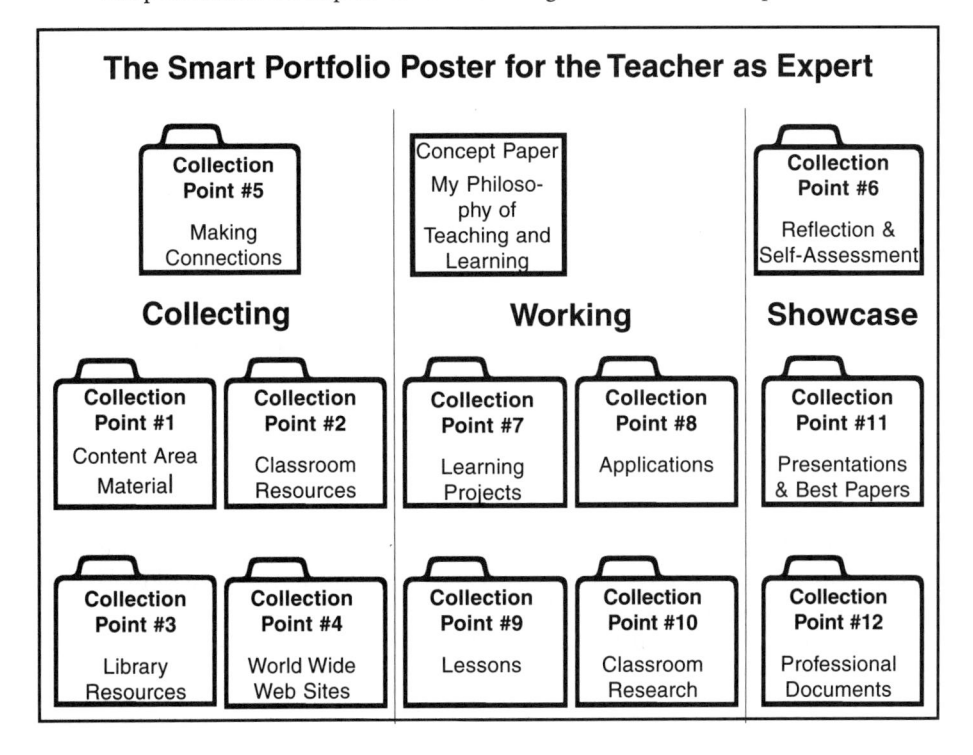

The Smart Portfolio Poster for the Teacher as Expert

Collecting	Working	Showcase
Collection Point #5 — Making Connections	**Concept Paper** — My Philosophy of Teaching and Learning	**Collection Point #6** — Reflection & Self-Assessment
Collection Point #1 — Content Area Material	**Collection Point #7** — Learning Projects	**Collection Point #11** — Presentations & Best Papers
Collection Point #2 — Classroom Resources	**Collection Point #8** — Applications	
Collection Point #3 — Library Resources	**Collection Point #9** — Lessons	**Collection Point #12** — Professional Documents
Collection Point #4 — World Wide Web Sites	**Collection Point #10** — Classroom Research	

Return to the Portfolio Exercise Main Menu

The Intelligent Portfolio for the Teacher as Expert

Directions for Building Your Intelligent Portfolio for the Teacher as Expert

Building the Intelligent Portfolio is a combination of three simple electronic tasks:

(a) **Creating Folders** for Reading, Writing, Thinking, Interacting, and Demonstrating;
(b) **Populating Folders** with the most efficient and effective combination of software packages for the tasks at hand; and
(c) **Organizing Collection Points** to store the electronic information that will be accumulated in the Collecting, Working, and Showcase aspects of your portfolio.

This version of the portfolio contains software that supports the hands-on design, development, and application of demonstrating, interacting, thinking, writing, and reading artifacts so important for the practicing teacher.

Step 1. Create the Folders on Your Desktop

We will begin this exercise by creating a Windows desktop that resembles the graphic on the following page.

- From the Windows Desktop, OPEN *My Computer* by double-clicking on the icon.
- In the *File* Menu, click on your Hard Drive Icon to view the folders already created on your C: drive.
- Click on *File — New — Folder* from the Menu Bar to create a new folder which you will call *Intelligent Portfolio*. Once inside this new folder, create six more folders, one for each of the major components of the Intelligent Portfolio: Demonstrating, Interacting, Thinking, Writing, and Reading. Then one more for all your Collection Points.

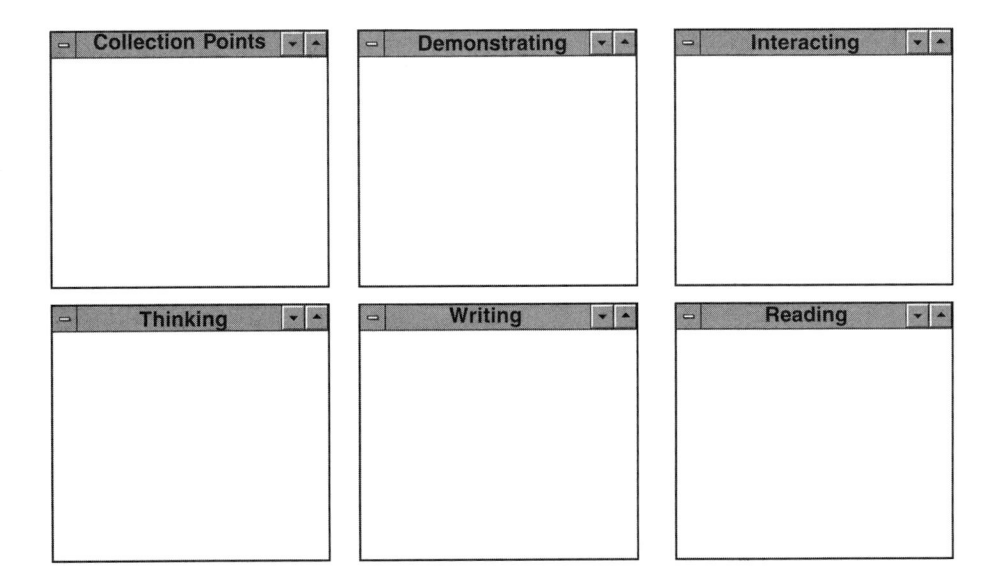

[Collection Points] [Demonstrating] [Interacting]

[Thinking] [Writing] [Reading]

Use the example above to guide you in creating the folders.

Step 2. Populate the Folders

The folders you just created on your hard drive must be populated with "shortcuts" that will reflect the most common applications in each of the portfolio components. The following graphics depict the specific software applications that should be included in the Intelligent Portfolio for the Teacher as Expert. Construct your portfolio to include as many of these packages as possible. If your computer does not come with these packages, we recommend that you find a source for these applications or substitute others of equal capability. It is acceptable to omit those you know you will not be using and add others that may not appear as options here.

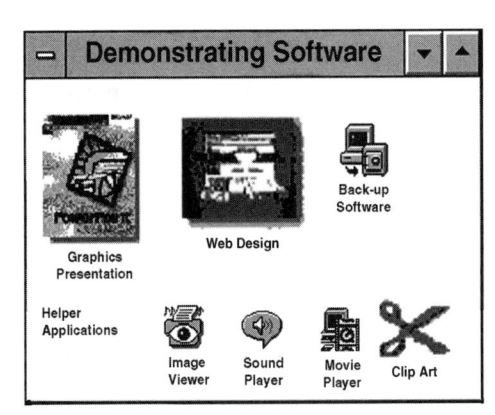

Demonstrating Software
- Graphics Presentation
- Web Design
- Back-up Software
- Helper Applications
- Image Viewer
- Sound Player
- Movie Player
- Clip Art

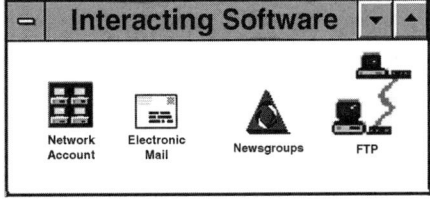

Interacting Software
- Network Account
- Electronic Mail
- Newsgroups
- FTP

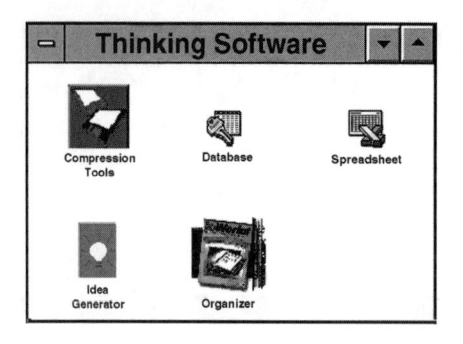

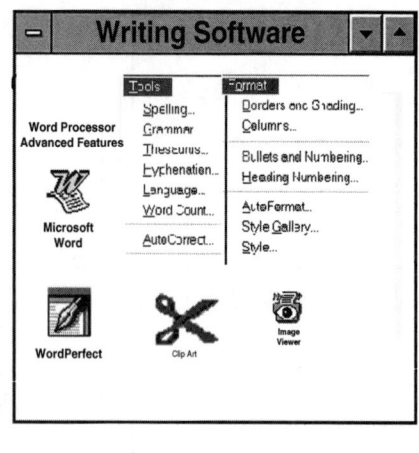

Step 3. Organize the Collection Points

You have already created the primary folder for your Collection Points. This initial folder will help you locate and retrieve artifacts throughout the lifetime of your portfolio. Next, we need to create 12 new folders within the Collection Point folder — one for each of the Teacher as Expert folders. From within the *Collection Point* Folder, Click on *File — New — Folder* from the Menu Bar and create 12 new folders. Name them as shown in the examples presented by Foley below. He will offer some specific examples of the artifacts that belong in each of the Collection Points. If you have already reviewed the previous Teacher-Learner implementation, you will note that one new folder and two revised folders make their appearance in this version of the Intelligent Portfolio.

Collection Points are grouped into three major categories:

Collecting. Although reduced in terms of its impact, collecting artifacts will continue to further the professional development of the teacher. For the Teacher as Expert, the *Collecting folder* is primarily a repository to aid in the development of working artifacts.

Appendix 241

Collection Point #1

This folder should already be filled with artifacts. Any new content material should be addded or replaced.

Content Area Materials
Journal Articles
Subject Matter Books
Textbooks
Raw Lesson Plans taken
  from the Internet.

Collection Point #2

Classroom Resources go in this folder.

Classroom Resources
Monographs on Classroom
  Discipline and Learning
Sample Teaching Lessons
Higher Order Thinking
  Strategies for Teaching
Multiple Intelligence Exercises

Collection Point #3

Remember not to limit your library resources to only your own school library.

Library Resources
Requests for Books, Articles,
  and Resources
Audiovisual Resources
Library Reference/Reserve
  Materials

Collection Point #4

URLs for the Teacher as Expert consist of sites that promote teaching and learning for students as well as teachers.

World Wide Web Sites
Search Engines
Subject Matter Sites
Online Presentations
Student-oriented Research
Content Specialties
Education E-Zines

Working. The *Working folders* take on the Collection Points of importance for this version of the portfolio. Over half of the artifacts contained here will be the result of new thinking that supports the hands-on design, development, and application of demonstrating, interacting, thinking, writing, and reading so important for the practicing teacher.

Collection Point #5

Interacting with your own artifacts and with colleagues and students.

Making Connections
Points of Contact
Mental Maps
Book notes
Insight into Classroom Issue/ Problems
Unresolved Questions

Collection Point #6

Self-assessment helps the educator improve teaching and better the profession.

Reflections & Self-Assessment
Self-Analysis of Lessons
Results of Student Surveys
Discipline Problems
Personal Philosophy of Teaching and Learning

Collection Point #7

If you use it in the classroom, store it in this Collection Point.

Learning Projects
Videos of Past Student Projects
Parents' Nite Program
Itinerary for Field Trips
Instruction for Senior Research Paper
Student Science Handouts

Collection Point #8 NEW

Here's one of the new Collection Points . . . sort of a 'parking lot' until you need the artifact in the classroom.

Applications
Next Semester's Units of Study
Enhancement Exercises
Thematic Units
Assessments Activities

Collection Point #9 NEW

The second new Collection Point, your active Lessons, will all be placed in this folder with 5 subfolders.

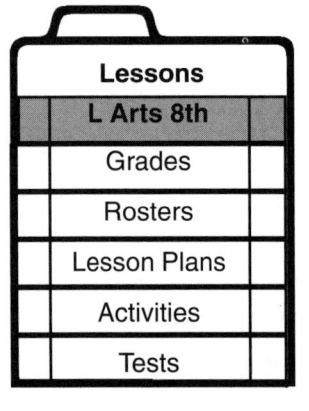

Lessons
L Arts 8th
Grades
Rosters
Lesson Plans
Activities
Tests

Collection Point #10 NEW

Here's the last new Collection Point. Any new ideas that deserve further investigation should go here.

Classroom Research
Experiential Teaching
Design for Study
Background Research
Student Survey of Teacher Effectiveness

Showcase. For the Teacher as Expert, *Showcase artifacts* will account for approximately 25 percent of the contents of the Intelligent Portfolio. The teacher in the classroom will have more opportunity to display the results of new thinking than did the teacher as learner; however, this folder does not take on its final prominence until the implementation of the later Teacher as Scholar Intelligent Portfolio.

Collection Point #11

Your Best Works go here. We moved this collection point up two notches to number 11.

Presentations and Best Papers
Submitted Reviews
Proposed Lesson Ideas
Teacher In-Service
　Workshops

Collection Point #12

The last folder for the Teacher as Expert continues to hold a growing number of professional artifacts.

Professional Documents
Graduate Transcripts
Teacher Evaluations
Test Scores
Honors, Recognitions, and Awards
Letters of Recommendations

The emphasis of the Intelligent Portfolio for the Teacher as Expert will shift to the Working aspects of the teacher in the classroom. This folder will become predominant throughout the classroom career of the educator.

Step 4. Completing Your Intelligent Portfolio

Now that you have the folders and Collection Points for the Intelligent Portfolio for the Teacher as Expert, you can begin to use your computer to store and retrieve artifacts that will be used throughout your time in the classroom. We will finish our directions with a few tips from Foley for using your portfolio.

Tips for Using the Intelligent Portfolio

1. Working is the focus of the Intelligent Portfolio for the Teacher as Expert.

Do not clutter your computer with software (or hardware for that matter) that will not contribute directly to the development of new artifacts. Desktop publishing, while an excellent tool for the preparation and submission of papers and personal publications, remains an unnecessarily complex package. While it produces outstanding copy-ready manuscripts, for the Teacher as Expert, a full-featured word processor is more than satisfactory.

2. Visit each Collection Point periodically.

As you progress through your academic semesters, revisit the artifacts you have developed and used in the classroom. Unsuccessful items should be returned to their original collection points while tested and validated artifacts remain in Collection Point #5 or moved to a Showcase location.

3. Continue to upgrade your Intelligent Portfolio.

Stay alert to the latest versions of operating systems, software, and hardware. Remember that the Intelligent Portfolio is a tool for your lifetime of professional development.

4. Continue to collect artifacts.

Whereas the Teacher as Learner found a resource-intensive environment in the classroom from which to gather new materials, the Teacher as Expert depends on interacting and thinking skills to locate new artifacts. It will be incumbent upon the teacher to seek out artifacts that reflect new thinking and make informed decisions on whether to augment or replace previously collected artifacts.

5. The future is on the Internet.

The Teacher as Expert requires access to the Internet. If your school does not support this requirement, the teacher should make sure to get access at home. It's that important. Capturing artifacts on-line via the Web will nearly always be technically easier than any other form of data capture. Exploration of the vast resources of the Web will be time well spent if that information can be converted to educational instruction either via on-line access or material incorporated into student handouts.

6. Take inventory of your Intelligent Portfolio use.

The Intelligent Portfolio is based on professional development as a lifelong process involving demonstrating, interacting, thinking, writing, and reading. The hardware and software packages recommended in this chapter work together to make a successful Intelligent Portfolio. A shared use of each folder should be an indicator that you are satisfactorily addressing the key areas of your professional development.

7. Enroll in technical classes that support your Intelligent Portfolio.

Each hardware and software package has features far exceeding the basics that lend themselves to the Intelligent Portfolio. Most colleges and universities have a wealth of computer courses for the beginner and the expert. Take advantage of these mini-courses.

Return to the Build Your Own Portfolio Menu

Professional Portfolios for Teachers

The Smart Portfolio for the Teacher as Scholar

Directions for Building Your Smart Portfolio

Here is what your Smart Portfolio will look like when you have the binder created for ease of use and assessment:

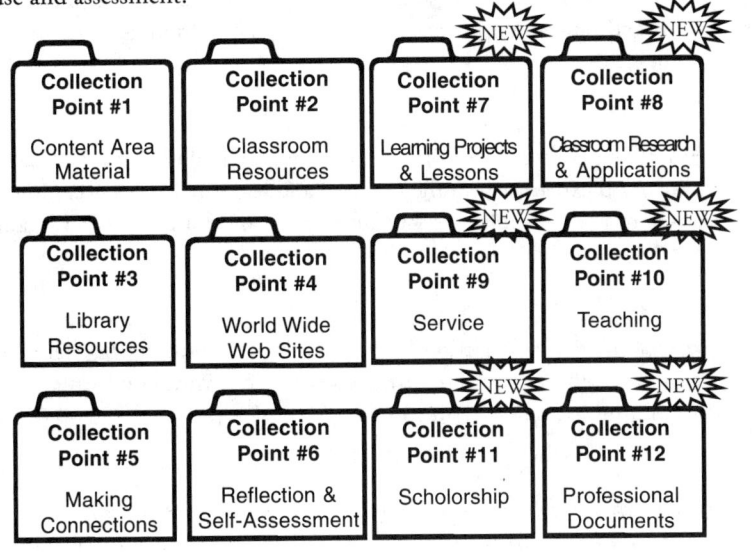

Collection Point #1 Content Area Material	Collection Point #2 Classroom Resources	Collection Point #7 (NEW) Learning Projects & Lessons	Collection Point #8 (NEW) Classroom Research & Applications
Collection Point #3 Library Resources	Collection Point #4 World Wide Web Sites	Collection Point #9 (NEW) Service	Collection Point #10 (NEW) Teaching
Collection Point #5 Making Connections	Collection Point #6 Reflection & Self-Assessment	Collection Point #11 (NEW) Scholarship	Collection Point #12 (NEW) Professional Documents

Step 1. Materials

> Three-ring Binder (3-inch or 5-inch)
> Index Tab Partitions (12 each)
> Assorted Adhere Materials (such as glue, tape)

Step 2. Preparing the Binder

> Using the Smart Portfolio diagram as a guide, prepare a three-ring binder and place three partitions (all the same color is recommended) — one each for the Collecting, Working, and Showcase sections.

Step 3. Indexing the Collection Points

> Within the boundaries of the three Collecting, Working, and Showcase sections of the portfolio, place one index Tab Partition in the binder for each of the 12 Collection Points as shown in the Smart Portfolio diagram.

Collecting, Working, and Showcase Partitions

Collecting Artifacts. Just as the Teacher-Learner is a collector, so is the Teacher as Scholar, but for a markedly different reason. The Teacher as Learner builds a knowledge base and makes connections in order to understand and apply the literature in the field. The Teacher as Scholar collects artifacts to add to a personal knowledge base. It is a prerequisite to be aware of current thinking before attempting to extend or generate new knowledge in the field.

Working Artifacts. The Teacher as Scholar demonstrates an ability to integrate and apply knowledge, skills, and experiences in the teaching and learning experience. Honing those skills and gaining expertise enables the scholar to showcase work and gain recognition for contributions to the field.

Showcase Artifacts. Showcase Collection Points are the domain of the Teacher as Scholar. The Showcase section of the portfolio provides new folders which are created to better serve this time of professional development.

The focus of new artifacts for this portfolio will be in the Showcase Partitions under Service, Teaching, and Scholarship. Collecting and Working support the portfolio and move the Teacher as Scholar from a participant to an authority in the field. Because of the nature of the Teacher as Scholar, the emphasis for the Smart portfolio is on expertise, honing skills, deepening understandings, and gaining recognition as a scholar.

Step 4. Affixing Labels

Using the labels provided below, affix the Title and each of the Three Sections of the portfolio to the top of the partition followed by labels for each of the 12 Collection Points.

Foley will provide examples of the artifacts that belong in each of the Collection Points. If you have already reviewed the previous Teacher-Learner or Teacher-Expert implementations, you will note two new folders in the dominant Showcase area and two revised folders in the Working partitions for this final version of the Smart Portfolio.

Smart Portfolio for the Teacher as Learner

Collecting Artifacts

Collection Point #1

This folder should already be filled with artifacts. But the Teacher as Scholar has sources for new artifacts beyond other educators.

Content Area Materials
Journal Articles
Subject Matter Books
Textbooks
Raw Lesson Plans taken from the Internet

Collection Point #2

Classroom Resources go in this folder.

Classroom Resources
Shared lessons from Colleagues
Classroom Handouts from Seminars/Sessions
Teaching Strategies Applied to New Situations

Collection Point #3

Library Resources are much more evident in this version of the Intelligent Portfolio.

Library Resources
Requests for Books, Articles, and Resources
Audiovisual Resources
Library Reference/Reserve Materials

Collection Point #4

URL's for the Teacher as Scholar consist of Sites that promote thinking about teaching and learning.

World Wide Web Sites
Search Engines
Subject Matter Sites
Educational Institutions
Commercial Software Sites
Content Specialties

Content Area Materials

Classroom Resources

Library Resources

World Wide Web Sites

Working Artifacts

Collection Point #5

Interacting can be the most versatile folder for the Teacher as Scholar.

Making Connections
Points of Contact
Mental Maps
Book notes
Insight into Classroom
Issues/Problems Unresolved
　Questions

Collection Point #6

Self-Assessment helps educators improve their manner of presentation and professional appearance

Reflections & Self-Assessment
Self-analysis of Presentation
　Skills
Personal Philosophy of
　Teaching and Learning
Session Feedbacks and
　Critiques

Collection Point #7 **NEW**

If you use it in the classroom, develop it here.

Learning Projects and Lessons
Completed Units of Instruction
In Progress Learning Projects
New Course Designs

Collection Point #8 **NEW**

Explore and take risks in this Collection Point. Try new strategies in the classroom. Evaluate your success.

Applications and Research
New Teaching Strategies
Findings from Journals
Research in the Discipline
Testing Results

| *Making Connections* |
| *Reflections & Self-Assessment* |
| *Learning Projects & Lessons* |
| *Classroom Research & Applications* |
| Showcase Artifacts |

Collection Point #9 *NEW*

Are you sharing your talents with the community and your discipline? Track those efforts here.

Service
Committee Meetings
Advisement
Task Force Member
Professional Organizations

Collection Point #10 *NEW*

Still teaching? Keep sharp by adding artifacts that improve your personal in-classroom skills.

Teaching
Teacher Effectiveness Forms
Assessment Tools
Rigorous Methodology Practice
Video

Collection Point #11 *NEW*

Display your published Best Work for all to see. Put any grants you received in this folder too.

Scholarship
Honors/Awards
Published Works
Successful Grants
Discipline-Specific Scholarly Work

Collection Point #12

The last folder is your most stable. Continue to amass professional career artifacts.

Professional Documents
Graduate Transcripts
Professional Awards
Professional Certifications
Teaching Certificates
Curriculum Vitae

Service

Teaching

Scholorship

Professional Documents

Step 5. Completing Your Smart Portfolio

Once the partitions are secured in the binder and labels have been affixed, the portfolio is ready to accept artifacts.

We strongly recommend that you continue to work on your Concept Paper, "My Philosophy of Teaching and Learning." This concept paper will help you think about how you conceive teaching and learning as issues in your own professional development. For the Teacher as Scholar, this philosophy has changed over time. Any efforts you expend now to refine your understanding of these concepts will prove beneficial to others as well as yourself as you continue to develop as a teacher-educator.

Step 6. Exhibiting Your Smart Portfolio

Periodically, you will be asked to display the contents of your Smart Portfolio — or at least the most significant artifacts that you have accumulated. The following graphic depicts the use of a posterboard to assist with this exhibition. This is one way to demonstrate that you are using your Smart Portfolio for personal growth and professional development. Take advantage of this format if it proves useful.

Smart Portfolio Poster for the Teacher as Scholar

Collection Point #5 — Making Connections

Concept Paper — My Philosophy of Teaching and Learning

Collection Point #6 — Reflection & Self-Assessment

Collecting

Collection Point #1 — Content Area Material

Collection Point #2 — Classroom Resources

Collection Point #3 — Library Resources

Collection Point #4 — World Wide Web Sites

Working

Collection Point #7 — Learning Projects & Lessons

Collection Point #8 — Classroom Research & Applications

Showcase

Collection Point #9 — Service

Collection Point #10 — Teaching

Collection Point #11 — Scholarship

Collection Point #12 — Professional Documents

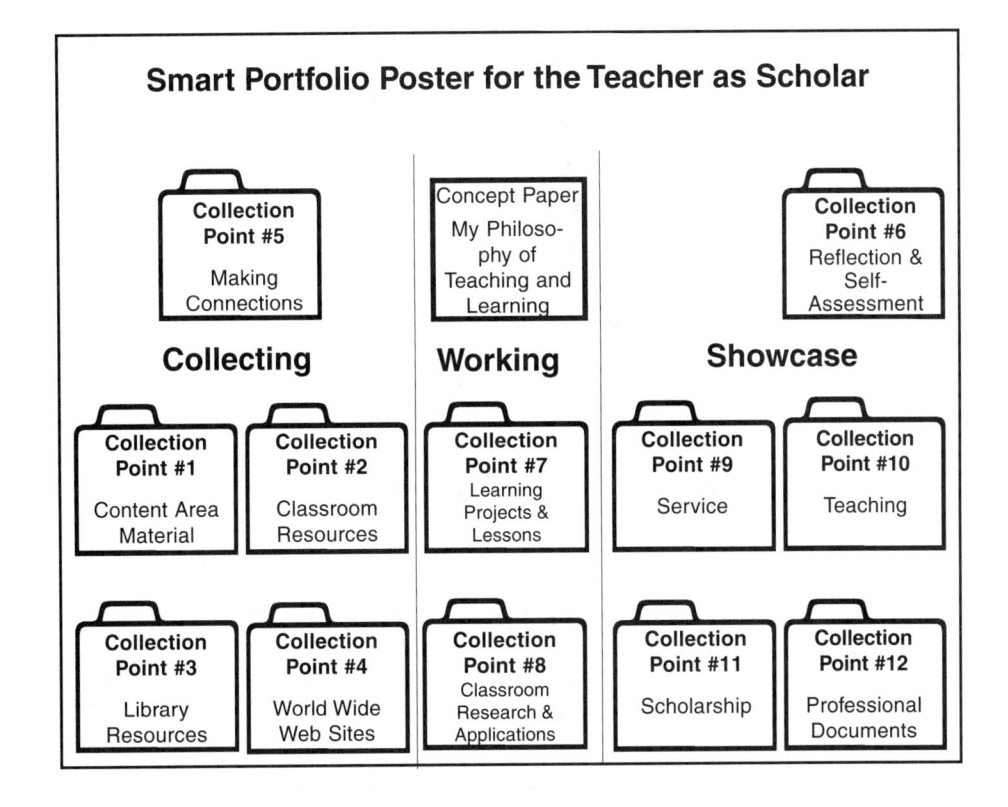

Return to the Portfolio Exercise Main Menu

itas95.htm

The Intelligent Portfolio for the Teacher as Scholar

Directions for Building Your Intelligent Portfolio for the Teacher as Scholar

Building the Intelligent Portfolio is a combination of three simple electronic tasks:

(a) **Creating Folders** for Reading, Writing, Thinking, Interacting, and Demonstrating;
(b) **Populating Folders** with the most efficient and effective combination of software packages for the tasks at hand; and
(c) **Organizing Collection Points** to store the electronic information that will be accumulated in the Collecting, Working, and Showcase aspects of your portfolio.

The emphasis of the Intelligent Portfolio for the Teacher as Scholar shifts to the contributory nature of the teacher. In this phase of one's career, the focus is on scholarship, publishing, presenting, and reporting new ideas. Interacting rises to the forefront as the portfolio supports the design, development, and presentation of new thinking.

Step 1. Create the Folders on Your Desktop

We will begin this exercise by creating a Windows desktop that resembles the graphic on the following page.

- From the Windows Desktop, OPEN *My Computer* by double-clicking on the icon.
- In the *File* Menu, click on your Hard Drive Icon to view the folders already created on your C: drive.

Collection Points	Interacting	Reading

Thinking	Demonstrating	Writing

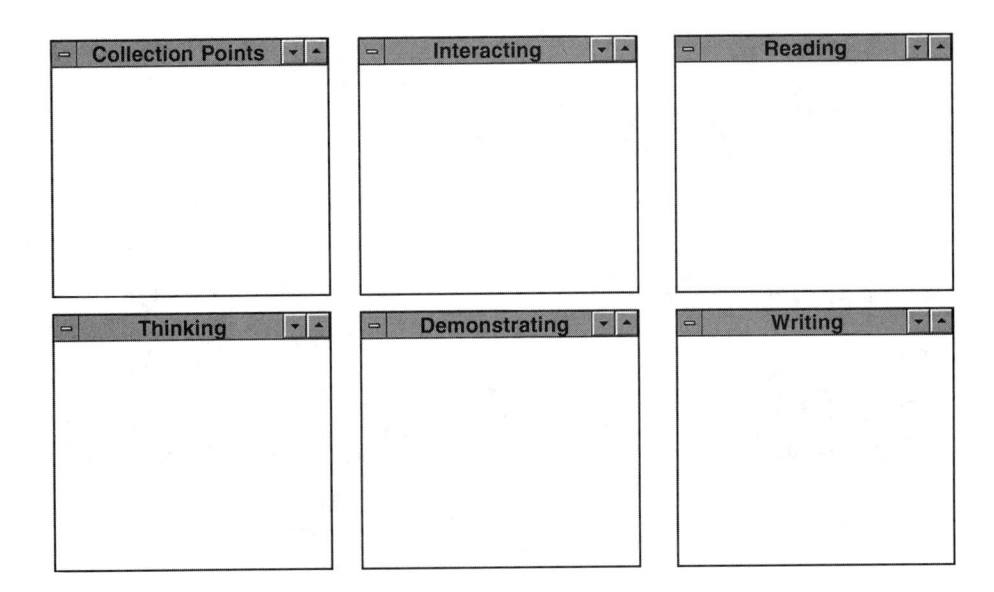

- Click on *File — New — Folder* from the Menu Bar to create a new folder which you will call *Intelligent Portfolio*. Once inside this new folder, create six more folders, one for each of the major components of the Intelligent Portfolio: Reading, Writing, Thinking, Interacting, and Demonstrating. Then one more for all your Collection Points.

Use the example above to guide you in creating the folders.

Step 2. Populate the Folders

The folders you just created on your hard drive must be populated with "shortcuts" that will reflect the most common applications in each of the portfolio components. The following graphics depict the specific Software applications that should be included in the Intelligent Portfolio for the Teacher as Scholar. Construct your portfolio to include as many of these packages as possible. If your computer does not come with these packages, we recommend that you find a source for these applications or substitute others of equal capability. It is acceptable to omit those you will not be using and add others that may not appear as options here.

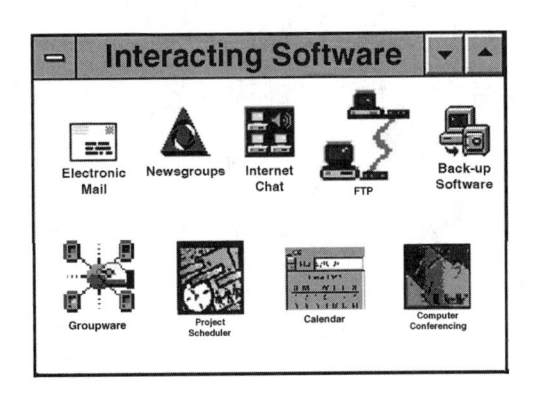

Interacting Software

Electronic Mail, Newsgroups, Internet Chat, FTP, Back-up Software

Groupware, Project Scheduler, Calendar, Computer Conferencing

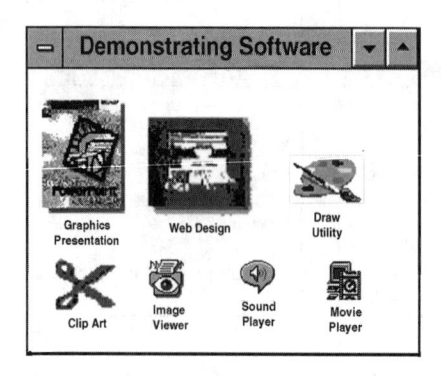

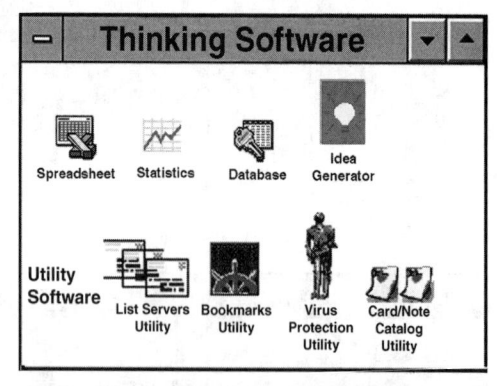

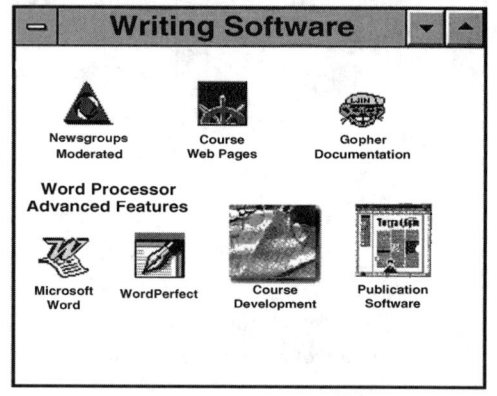

Step 3. Organize the Collection Points

You have already created the primary folder for your Collection Points. This initial folder will help you locate and retrieve artifacts throughout the lifetime of your portfolio. Next, we need to create 12 new folders within the Collection Point folder — one for each of the Teacher as Scholar folders.

From within the *Collection Point* Folder, Click on *File — New — Folder* from the Menu Bar and create 12 new folders. Name them as shown in the examples presented by Foley below. He will offer some specific examples of the artifacts that belong in each of the Collection Points. If you have already reviewed the previous Teacher-Learner or Teacher-Expert implementations, you will note two new folders in the dominant Showcase area and two revised containers in the Working folders for this final version of the Intelligent Portfolio.

Collection Points are grouped into three major categories:

Collecting. The *Collecting Folder* serves as a temporary repository for artifacts. Artifacts move from the Collecting Folder to the Working Folder for implementation, then to the Showcase Folder as documented research, professional presentation, or proof of scholarship. Unlike other implementations of the portfolio, these materials are not expected to remain in the folders for an extended period of time. The Teacher as Scholar collects materials important enough to make timely contributions to the profession and discards those which do not.

Collection Point #1

This folder should already be filled with artifacts. But the Teacher as Scholar has sources for new artifacts beyond other educators.

Content Area Materials
Journal Articles
Subject Matter Books
Textbooks
Raw Lesson Plans taken from the Internet

Collection Point #2

Classroom Resources go in this folder.

Classroom Resources
Shared lessons from Colleagues
Classroom Handouts from Seminars/Sessions
Teaching Strategies Applied to New Situations

Collection Point #3

Library Resources are much more evident in this version of the Intelligent Portfolio.

Library Resources
Requests for Books, Articles, and Resources
Audiovisual Resources
Library Reference/Reserve Materials

Collection Point #4

URL's for the Teacher as Scholar consist of Sites that promote thinking about teaching and learning.

World Wide Web Sites
Search Engines
Subject Matter Sites
Educational Institutions
Commercial Software Sites
Content Specialties

Working. For the Teacher as Scholar, the *Working Folder* takes on a somewhat different purpose than the previous Teacher-Expert implementation. Although the Working Folder remains a "temporary storage" location for work in progress as material passes from collection to completion, for the Teacher as Scholar it also serves as a place to hone your skills and try new things. In this version of the Intelligent Portfolio, reflections, goals, milestones, and projects are maintained to support the evolution to showcase artifacts. Some 25 percent of your efforts in this stage of professional development will consist of work-in-progress under various stages of development.

Collection Point #5

Interacting can be the most versatile folder for the Teacher as Scholar.

Making Connections
Points of Contact
Mental Maps
Book notes
Insight into Classroom
Issues/Problems Unresolved
  Questions

Collection Point #6

Self-Assessment helps educators improve their manner of presentation and professional appearance

Reflections & Self-Assessment
Self-analysis of Presentation
  Skills
Personal Philosophy of
  Teaching and Learning
Session Feedbacks and
  Critiques

Collection Point #7   *NEW*

If you use it in the classroom, develop it here.

Learning Projects and Lessons

Completed Units of Instruction
In Progress Learning Projects
New Course Designs

Collection Point #8   *NEW*

Explore and take risks in this Collection Point. Try new strategies in the classroom. Evaluate your success.

Applications and Research
New Teaching Strategies
Findings from Journals
Research in the Discipline
Testing Results

Showcase. The implementation of the Intelligent Portfolio has shifted focus as it attempts to stay abreast of the maturing educator. The contents of the *Showcase* portion of the portfolio will grow as presentations, publications, and course materials swell these folders with electronic files representing your best research, writing, and professional development efforts.

Collection Point #9 *NEW*

Are you sharing your talents with the community and your discipline? Track those efforts here.

Service
Committee Meetings
Advisement
Task Force Member
Professional Organizations

Collection Point #10 *NEW*

Still teaching? Keep sharp by adding artifacts that improve your personal in-classroom skills.

Teaching
Teacher Effectiveness
   Forms
Assessment Tools
Rigorous Methodology
   Practice
Video

Collection Point #11 *NEW*

Display your published Best Work for all to see. Put any grants you received in this folder too.

Scholarship
Honors/Awards
Published Works
Successful Grants
Discipline-Specific
   Scholarly Work

Collection Point #12

The last folder is your most stable. Continue to amass professional career artifacts.

Professional Documents
Graduate Transcripts
Professional Awards
Professional Certifications
Teaching Certificates
Curriculum Vitae

The emphasis of the Intelligent Portfolio for the Teacher as Scholar will be on the Showcase folder of the portfolio. This folder will become the most used component of your portfolio as you share your thinking with colleagues and peers.

Step 4. Completing Your Intelligent Portfolio

Now that you have the Folders and Collection Points for the Intelligent Portfolio for the Teacher as Scholar, you can begin to use your computer to store and retrieve artifacts that will be used throughout your time as an educator. We will finish our directions with a few tips from Foley for using your portfolio.

Tips for Using the Intelligent Portfolio

1. Showcasing your best work is the focus of the Intelligent Portfolio.

Unlike previous applications, this version of the Intelligent Portfolio will contain several additional items of both hardware and software to support the development efforts that make the Teacher as Scholar unique. The primary suggestion is to depend on previous artifacts stored in the Intelligent Portfolio to target the various presentations, publications, and course materials to be developed. Do not spend an inordinate amount of time being awed by the collections of the past but rather in determining the best areas for the future of education.

2. Visit Collection Points following the completion of any artifact added to the portfolio.

Unlike previous versions which suggested weekly or semester visits with your artifacts, the Teacher as Scholar Intelligent Portfolio requires less frequent reviews. New additions (and perhaps deletions as well) should trigger a review of a particular Collection Point to ensure that added material is worthy of remaining in your portfolio and material you are considering for deletion is justified.

3. Continue to upgrade your Intelligent Portfolio.

Perhaps the only consistent tip throughout all implementations of the Intelligent Portfolio is to continually upgrade hardware and software. Such attention will ensure compatibility with state-of-the-art technology and new approaches to using that technology in the classroom. New operating systems, software versions, and hardware peripherals should be evaluated in light of how each can benefit the Intelligent Portfolio for the tasks at hand. Do not upgrade just for the sake of having the latest and greatest technology; few can afford that luxury. Rather, make changes that will enhance the ability of your Intelligent Portfolio to serve as a lifelong tool for learning and development.

4. Remain current on instructional technology.

Previous implementations cautioned against changing software unless there were mitigating circumstances such as local support or better pricing. For the Teacher as Scholar, upgrades should be more methodical. As a proponent of technology in the classroom, you must stay abreast of the latest developments in instructional media. Your reading artifacts should include technology-oriented periodicals specifically addressing computers in the classroom.

5. The future is on the Internet.

Many of the folders and Collection Points identified in this chapter involve (or depend upon) the Internet either as a source of information or as a host on which the information will reside. Devote a significant proportion of your time and effort interacting with your Intelligent Portfolio in these areas. The future scholar will be expected to use the Internet not only as a source of research, but also as a warehouse for your own best works — offered in electronic context to share with fellow educators.

Return to the Build Your Own Portfolio Menu

INDEX

A

Accountability, 5
Apple-compatible system, 45, 84, 128
Applications
    Intelligent Portfolio
        expert, 72, 75
        scholar, 118
    Smart Portfolio
        expert, 95
        scholar, 140
Applications and Lessons
    Intelligent Portfolio, 23
        learner, 55
    Smart Portfolio, 13
        learner, 36
Artifacts
    defined, 13
    Intelligent Portfolio, 19–24
        Collecting folder, 19–21
        Showcase folder, 23–24
        Working folder, 21–23
    Smart Portfolio, 13–14
        Collecting, 13
        Organizing artifacts, 14
        Showcase, 13,14
        Working, 13
Assessing Portfolio, 62, 65
    Smart Portfolio, 37, 77, 119–120
Assessing professional portfolio, 151–184
    Portfolio Assessment Tool (PAT), 152–160
        I. Formative Assessment, 152–153
        II. Summative Assessment, 153–154
        III. Final Comments, 154
        for teacher as expert, 168–174
        for teacher as learner, 161–167
        for teacher as scholar, 175–181
    portfolio exhibition, 182–184
    rubric, 183
Authoring tools, 18
Automatic corrections, 47

B

Back-up software, 44, 83, 126
Best Papers. *See* Presentations and Best Papers
Best Practices, 4
"Bookmark," 21, 131
Browser. *See* Web browser software

C

Calendar, 127
Campbell, D., et al., 4
Card Catalog, 131–132
    automated, 17
CD-ROM, 17, 19, 21
    burner, 137
    drive, 84
    player, 45, 128
    portfolio exercise, 25–28
Classroom Activities
    Intelligent Portfolio
        expert, 95
    Smart Portfolio
        expert, 73
Classroom Applications, 13
Classroom Research
    Intelligent Portfolio
        expert, 96
        scholar, 140
    Smart Portfolio
        expert, 73, 76
Classroom Research
    Intelligent Portfolio, 21
        expert, 92
        learner, 53
        scholar, 139
    Smart Portfolio, 13
        expert, 72, 74
        leaner, 34, 35
        scholar, 117
Classroom teacher, and portfolio evolution, 4
Clip Art software, 133
Collecting Artifacts, 13

260 Professional Portfolios for Teachers

Collecting Folder, 19–21
    Intelligent Portfolio
        expert, 92–93
        learner, 52, 53–54
        scholar, 138–139
    Smart Portfolio
        expert, 72
        learner, 33–34
        scholar, 115–116
Collection Points, 19
    Intelligent Portfolio
        expert, 91–97
        learner, 52–56
        scholar, 138–142
    Smart Portfolio
        expert, 72–76
        learner, 33–34, 35–36
        scholar, 115, 117–119
Color inkjet printer, 51, 84, 89, 134
Compression and decompression tools, 47, 87
Computer, *See* laptop computer; Personal computer
Computer conferencing, 127
Concept paper, 37
Content Area Material
    Intelligent Portfolio, 20
        expert, 92
        learner, 53
        scholar, 138–139
    Smart Portfolio, 13
        expert, 72, 74
        learner, 33–34, 35
        scholar, 117

D

Danielson, K., 5
Database management, 48
    software, 130–131
Database software package, 18, 87
Decompression tools. *See* compression and decompression tools
Demonstrating
    Intelligent Portfolio, 19
        expert, 81
        learner, 42
        scholar, 124
    Smart Portfolio, 13
        expert, 69–70
        learner, 32
        scholar, 114
Demonstrating Hardware
    teacher as expert, 83–84
        CD-ROM drive, 84
        color inkjet printer, 84
        flat panel projector, 84
        hard drive (2-gigabyte), 84
        laptop computer, 84
        zip drive, 84
    teacher as learner, 51
        color inkjet printer, 51
    teacher as scholar, 134–135
        color printer, 134
        digital camera, 135
        expanded memory, 134
        high-speed modem, 135
        large-capacity hard drive, 134
        one-gun projector, 134–135
Demonstrating software
    teacher as expert, 83
        back-up software, 83
        graphics software, 83
        Web design software, 83
    teacher as learner, 51
        Graphics presentation software, 51
    teacher as scholar, 132–134
        drawing package, 133
        Graphics Presentation software, 132–133
        image viewer and clip art software, 133
        sound and movie player software, 133–134
        Web Design software, 133
Desktop publishing, 18
Desktop scanner, 91, 130
Digital camera, 135
Digital library files, 17
Distance learning media, 19
Doctoral candidates, introduced to professional portfolios, 143–147
Drawing package, 133

E

Electronic books, 17
Electronic Mail (email), 17, 49, 85, 125
Electronic mailing lists, 17, 18
Email, 17, 49, 85, 125
Expanded Memory, 132, 134

F

File Transfer Protocol (FTP), 86, 126
Five Foundations
    Intelligent Portfolio, 17–19
        demonstrating, 19
        interacting, 18–19
        reading, 17–18
        thinking, 18
        writing, 18
    Smart Portfolio, 11–13
        demonstrating, 13
        interacting, 12
        reading, 12
        thinking, 12
        writing, 12
Flat panel projector, 84
Formal assessment, 37–77
Formative assessment, 151, 152–153
Frequently asked questions, 27–28

G

Glatthorn, A., 5
Gopher documentation management, 44, 90, 129
Grades/Grade Sheets
    Intelligent Portfolio
        expert, 95
    Smart Portfolio
        expert, 72
Grammar checker, 18
Graphics Presentation software, 19, 51, 83, 132–133
Groupware, 126

H

Hard drive, 17, 49, 84, 132, 134
Helper applications, 19
High-speed modem, 17, 45, 86, 128, 135
Horace's Hope (Sizer), 182
How to Develop a Professional Portfolio: A Manual for Teachers (Campbell, et, al.), 4
Hypertext markup language (HTML), 136
Hyphenator, 18, 47

I

Idea Generator software, 48, 131
Image Viewer, 18, 47
    software, 133
Informal assessment, 37, 77
Inkjet printer, color, 51, 84, 89, 134
Intelligent Portfolio
    prototype studies
        teacher as expert, 99, 104–108
        teacher as learner, 59, 61–62, 64–65
    for teacher, 17–24
        artifacts of, 19–24
        foundations of, 17–19
        platform for, 17
    for teacher as expert, 81–98
        step one: creating portfolio folders, 81–82
        step two: populating portfolio folders, 82–91
        step three: organizing folders and collection points, 91–97
        Foley tips, 97–98
    for teacher as learner, 41–57
        step one: creating portfolio folders, 41–42
        step two: populating portfolio folders, 42–51
        step three: organizing folders and collection points, 52–56
        Foley tips, 56–57
    for teacher as scholar, 123–142
        step one: creating portfolio folders, 123–124
        step two: populating portfolio folders, 125–137
        step three: organizing folders and collection points, 138–141
        Foley tips, 142
Interacting
    Intelligent Portfolio, 18–19
        expert, 81
        learner, 42
        scholar, 123
    Smart Portfolio
        expert, 70
        learner, 32
        scholar, 113
Interacting hardware
    teacher as expert, 86
        high-speed modem, 86
    teacher as learner, 50
    teacher as scholar, 127–128
        CD-ROM player, 128

high-speed modem, 128
microphone, 128
multimedia sound card, 128
multimedia speakers, 128
personal computer, 127–128
video camera, 128
Interacting software
   teacher as expert, 85–86
      electronic mail, 85
      File Transfer Protocol (FTP), 86
      Network Account, 85
      Newsgroups, 85
   teacher as learner, 49–50
      electronic mail, 49
      Internet Relay Chat, 50
      Newsgroups software, 49–50
   teacher as scholar, 125–127
      back-up software, 126
      calendar, 127
      computer conferencing, 127
      electronic mail, 125
      File Transfer Protocol, 126
      Groupware, 126
      Internet Relay Chat, 126
      Newsgroups, 125–126
      project scheduling software, 126–127
Internet Relay Chat (IRC), 50, 126
Internet Service Provider (ISP), 43, 85
Interstate New Teacher Assessment and Support Consortium (INTASC), 4

L

Laptop computers, 17, 44, 84, 127
Laser printer, 47, 89, 134
   color, 134, 137
Learning projects
   Intelligent Portfolio, 22
      expert, 94
      learner, 55
      scholar, 140
   Smart Portfolio, 13
      expert, 72, 75
      learner, 36
      scholar, 118
Lesson Plans
   Intelligent Portfolio
      expert, 95
   Smart Portfolio
      expert, 73

Lessons
   Intelligent Portfolio
      expert, 95–96
      scholar, 140
   Smart Portfolio
      expert, 72, 76
      scholar, 118
   See also Application and Lessons
Library account, 43–44, 90
Library Resources
   Intelligent Portfolio, 21
      expert, 92
      learner, 53
      scholar, 129, 139
   Smart Portfolio, 13
      expert, 72, 74
      learner, 34, 35
      scholar, 117
List server, 131

M

Macintosh operating system, 17
   accessing CD-ROM exercises, 27
   recommended system, 45, 84
Making Connections
   Intelligent Portfolio, 22
      expert, 94
      learner, 54
      scholar, 139
   Smart Portfolio, 13
      expert, 72, 75
      learner, 36
      scholar, 118
McLaughlin, M., 4
Microphone, 128
Modem, high-speed, 17, 45, 86, 128, 135
Moderated newsgroups, 135–136
Movie Player, 47
   software, 133
Multimedia players, 18
Multimedia sound card, 128
Multimedia speakers, 128
Murray, J., 4

N

National Board of Professional Teaching Standards (NBPTS), 3
National Council of Accreditation of Teacher Education (NCATE), 3

National education organizations, and portfolios, 3
National Teacher Examination, 151
National Writing Project, 3
Netscape, 44
Network Account, 43, 85
New Professional Teacher Standards Development Project (NCATE), 3
Newsgroups, 19, 49–50, 85, 125–126
    moderated, 135–136

O

One-gun projector, 134–135
Organizer software, 48, 87
Organizing artifacts of Smart Portfolio, 14
Outsmarting IQ, The Emerging Science of Learnable Intelligence (Perkins), 11

P

Perkins, D., 11, 14
Personal Computer, 44–45, 59, 127–128
    Apple-compatible system, 45, 84, 128
    Windows-compatible system, 45, 84, 128
Philosophy of teaching and learning, teacher's, 22, 37, 77, 120
Portfolio Assessment Tool (PAT), 152–160
    I. Formative Assessment, 152–153
    II. Summative Assessment, 153–154
    III. Final Comments, 154
    for teacher as expert, 168–174
    for teacher as learner, 161–167
    for teacher as scholar, 175–181
Portfolio exercise, 25–28
    accessing CD-ROM exercises, 26–27
    frequently asked questions, 27–28
    step one: artifacts exercise, 25
    step two: learner, expert, or scholar?, 25–26
    step three: Smart or Intelligent portfolio, 26
    step four: build portfolio, 26
Portfolio exhibition, 182–184
    rubric, 183
Portfolio poster, 37–38
    Smart Portfolio
        expert, 77–78
        learner, 37–38
        scholar, 120

Portfolios in education, 3–8, 11
    as assessment tool, 3, 11
    classroom teacher, influence of, 4
    national education organizations, influence of, 3
    professional portfolios
        in teacher development, 4–5
        in teacher education, 5
    teacher-education, influence of, 3–4
Portfolios in Teacher Education (McLaughlin & Vogt), 4
Presentations and Best Papers
    Intelligent Portfolio, 23
        expert, 96
        learner, 55
    Smart Portfolio, 14
        expert, 76
        learner, 36
Professional Documents
    Intelligent Portfolio, 23–24
        expert, 96
        learner, 55
        scholar, 141
    Smart Portfolio, 14
        expert, 76
        learner, 36
        scholar, 117, 119
Professional Portfolios
    assessing, 151–184
    introduced to doctoral candidates, 143–147
    in teacher development, 4–5
    in teacher education, 5
Project management software, 18
Project scheduling software, 126–127
Prototype studies
    Intelligent Portfolio, 59, 61–62, 64–65
    Smart Portfolio, 59, 60–61, 63–64

R

Random access memory (RAM), 17
Reading
    Intelligent Portfolio, 17–18, 41
        expert, 82
        learner, 41
        scholar, 123–124
    Smart Portfolio, 12
        expert, 70
        learner, 31

scholar, 114
Reading hardware
    teacher as expert, 90–91
        desktop scanner, 91
    teacher as learner, 44–46
        CD-ROM player, 45
        high-speed modem, 45
        personal computer, 44–45
        zip drive storage, 45
    teacher as scholar, 129–130
        desktop scanner, 130
Reading level gauge, 18
Reading Software
    teacher as expert, 89–90
        Gopher, 90
        Library account, 90
        Telnet communications software, 90
        Web Browser software, 90
    teacher as learner, 43–44
        back-up software, 44
        Gopher documentation management, 44
        Library, 43–44
        Network Account, 43
        Telnet communications software, 43
        Web Browser software, 44
    teacher as Scholar, 128–129
        Gopher documentation management, 129
        Library resources, 129
        Telnet software, 128–129
        Web Browser software, 129
Reflection and Self-Assessment
    Intelligent Portfolio, 22
        expert, 94
        learner, 54
        scholar, 140
    Smart Portfolio, 13
        expert, 72, 75
        learner, 36
        scholar, 118
Reflective self-assessment, 5
Reflective thinking, 11
Reliability, 151
Research
    Smart Portfolio
        scholar, 118

Retrieving information, 61
Rogers, S., 5
Rosters
    Intelligent Portfolio
        expert, 95
    Smart Portfolio
        expert, 72–73

S

Scanner, 91, 130
Scholarship (collection point), 116, 119, 141
Self-assessment, 37. *See also* Reflection and Self-Assessment
Service (collection point), 116, 118, 141
Showcase artifacts, 13, 14
Showcase folder, 23–24
    Intelligent Portfolio
        expert, 96
        scholar, 140–141
    Smart Portfolio
        expert, 73
        scholar, 116–117
Sizer, Ted, 182, 184
Smart Portfolio
    prototype studies
        teacher as expert, 99–104
        teacher as learner, 59, 60–61, 63–64
    for teacher, 11–15
        artifacts of, 13–14
        building, 14
        five foundations of, 11–13
        organizing artifacts of, 14
    for teacher as expert, 69–80
        beginning point, 69–70
        Foley tips, 80
        organizing portfolio, 71–73
        portfolio poster, 77–78
        what to collect, 73–77
        who will assess portfolio, 77
    for teacher as learner, 31–40
        beginning point, 31–32
        Foley tips, 40
        organizing portfolio, 32–35
        portfolio poster, 37–38
        what to collect, 35–37
        who will assess portfolio, 37
    for teacher as scholar, 113–121

beginning point, 113–115
Foley tips, 121
organizing portfolio, 115–117
portfolio poster, 120
what to collect, 117–119
who will assess portfolio, 119–120
Sound player, 18 47
    software, 133
Spell checker, 18, 46
Spreadsheets, 18
    software, 48, 87, 130
Statistics package, 48–130
Storing information, 61
Student assessment, and portfolios, 3, 4, 5
Subject matter specialists, 93
Summative assessment, 151, 153–154

T

Table of contents writer, 46
Teacher
    as expert, 26
        assessment tool for, 168–174
        Intelligent Portfolios for, 81–98
        portfolios in transition, 99–109
        Smart Portfolio for, 69–80
    as learner, 25–26
        assessment tool for, 161–167
        Intelligent Portfolio for, 41–57
        portfolios in transition, 59–66
        Smart Portfolio for, 31–40
    as lifelong learners, xi, 5, 11
    as scholar, 26
        assessment tool for, 175–181
        Intelligent Portfolio for, 123–142
        portfolios in transition, 143–147
        Smart Portfolio for, 113–121
Teacher education, and portfolio evolution, 3–4
Teacher Portfolios: Literacy Artifacts and Themes (Rogers & Danielson), 5
Teacher's Portfolios: Fostering and Documenting Professional Development (Glatthorn), 5
Teaching (collection point), 116, 119, 141
Telnet communications software, 43, 90, 128–129
Templates, 46–47
Tests and Quizzes

Intelligent Portfolio
    expert, 95
Smart Portfolio
    expert, 73
Thesaurus, 18, 46
Thinking
    Intelligent Portfolio, 18
        expert, 81–82
        learner, 42
        scholar, 124
    Smart Portfolio, 12
        expert, 70
        learner, 32
        scholar, 114
Thinking hardware
    teacher as expert, 87
        hard drive, 87
    teacher as learner, 49
        hard drive, 49
    teacher as scholar, 132
        expanded memory, 132
        hard drive (2-gigabyte), 132
        zip drive, 132
Thinking journal, 12
Thinking software
    teacher as expert, 86–87
        compression and decompression tools, 87
        database software, 87
        electronic spreadsheets, 87
        organizer software, 87
        thinking software, 87
    teacher as learner, 47–48
        compression and decompression tools, 47
        database management, 48
        Idea Generator software, 48
        image viewers, 47
        movie players, 47
        organize software, 48
        sound players, 47
        spreadsheet software, 48
        statistics packages, 48
        World Wide Web Helper Applications, 47
    teacher as scholar, 130–132
        bookmarks, 131
        card catalog, 131–132
        database management software, 130–131

Idea Generator software, 131
list server, 131
spreadsheets, 130
statistical software, 130
utility software, 131
virus protection, 131

U

Uniform Resource Locator (URLs), 21, 54
Utilities, 19
Utility software, 131

V

Validity, 151
Video camera, 128
Video clip player, 18
Virus protection, 131
Visuals software package, 88
Vogt, M., 4

W

Web Browser software, 44, 90, 129
Web Design software, 19, 83, 133
Web Helper Applications, 18, 47
Web pages, 136
Widows operating system, 17
    accessing CD-ROM exercises, 27
    compatible systems, 84, 128
    recommended system, 45
Word counter, 18, 46
Word processing, 18
Word processors, 46, 88
    automatic corrections, 47
    hyphenations, 47
    spell checker, 46
    Table of Contents writer, 46
    templates, 46–47
    thesaurus, 46
    word-count feature, 46
Working artifacts, 13
Working folder, 21–23
    Intelligent Portfolio
        expert, 94–96
        learner, 52, 54–55
        scholar, 139–140
    Smart Portfolio
        expert, 72–73
        learner, 34
        scholar, 116

World Wide Web (WWW) sites
    Helper Applications, 18, 47
    Intelligent Portfolio, 17, 21
        expert, 92–93
        learner, 53–54
        scholar, 139
    Smart Portfolio, 13
        expert, 72, 75
        learner, 34, 36
        scholar, 118
Writing
    Intelligent Portfolio, 18
        expert, 82
        learner, 41
        scholar, 124
    Smart Portfolio, 12
        expert, 70
        leaner, 31
        scholar, 114
Writing hardware, 47
    teacher as expert, 89
        color inkjet printer, 89
        laser printer, 89
    teacher as learner, 47
        inkjet printer, 47
        laser printer, 47
    teacher as scholar, 137
        CD-ROM burner, 137
        Color laser printer, 137
Writing software
    teacher as expert, 88
        visuals software package, 88
        word processors, 88
    teacher as learner, 46–47
        word processors, 46
    teacher as scholar, 135–137
        course development software, 136–137
        desktop publishing software, 136
        full-featured word processor, 136
        Gopher documentation, 136
        Moderated newsgroups, 135–136
        Web pages, 136

Z

Zip drive, 17, 19, 44, 45, 83, 84, 132

About the Authors

Bonita L. Wilcox, Ph.D., taught secondary school English for seventeen years. At the university, she teaches courses in English Education, writing for publication, and institutional strategies. She advises students in the graduate School of Education in the Department of Instruction and Leadership. Dr. Wilcox is a member of the NCATE Board of Examiners, and she edits the Professional Books column for *The Reading Teacher*. Her publications include pieces in the *Journal of Adolescent and Adult Literacy, English Journal,* and the *American Journal of Occupational Therapy*. Her research focus is on the professional development of teachers. Dr. Wilcox has shared her ideas on portfolios at national and international conferences. She received her Ph.D. from the University of Pittsburgh in 1990, and she lives with her husband in rural Pennsylvania.

Lawrence A. Tomei, Ed.D., is the Special Assistant to the Dean for Teaching and Technology. His responsibilities include developing and teaching workshops, seminars, and in-service programs; providing student advisement and supervisory services; and actively participating in the School of Education's preparation for regional and national accreditation. His expertise includes educational psychology, teaching and learning strategies, and the use of technology in the classroom. He directs the M.Ed. program in Instructional Technology at Duquesne University.

He holds a B.S.B.A. from the University of Akron; M.P.A. and M.Ed. from the University of Oklahoma; and an Ed.D. from the University of Southern California.

Dr. Tomei has been a featured guest speaker at the National Catholic Education Association national conferences and the Association of Teacher Educators. His topics have included Small Computers in the Classroom; Selecting Hardware and Locating Educational Software; and Educational Strategies for Computers in the Classroom. His most recent publications include *Time for Action: Classroom Teachers and the Information Super Highway* (*Momentum Magazine*, April–May 1996); *Preparing an Instructional Lesson Using Resources Off the Internet* (*T.H.E. Journal*, September 1996); and *Instructional Technology: Choosing a Pedagogy for the Future* (*T.H.E. Journal*, December 1997).